WITHDRAWN

WITHDRAWN

PUBLIC RELATIONS
AND AMERICAN DEMOCRACY

STUDIES IN PUBLIC OPINION

A series under the editorial sponsorship
of the *Public Opinion Quarterly*
and directed by a committee consisting of Gordon W. Allport,
Hadley Cantril, W. Phillips Davison

PUBLIC RELATIONS
AND
AMERICAN DEMOCRACY

By J. A. R. Pimlott

WITHDRAWN

PRINCETON, NEW JERSEY

PRINCETON UNIVERSITY PRESS

1951

Copyright, 1951, by Princeton University Press
London: Geoffrey Cumberlege, Oxford University Press

Printed in the United States of America
by Vail-Ballou Press, Inc., at Binghamton, N.Y.

301.154
P644p

To

Anne and Benjy

30274

30274

◇◇

PREFACE

◇◇

THIS book is the result of researches made during and since a stay of almost a year in the United States in 1947–1948 under a British Home Civil Service Fellowship awarded by the Commonwealth Fund of New York. My primary debt is, therefore, to the Trustees of the Fund thanks to whose generosity it was made possible. As one of the many beneficiaries of the Fund it will perhaps not be out of place for me to acknowledge the remarkable contribution which it has made to Anglo-American understanding and to the furtherance of postgraduate studies and scholarship.

A work like this is a partnership in which the chief contribution of the author is the synthesis and interpretation of material collected from others. In addition to reading as widely as possible, I have talked or corresponded with some three hundred people about public relations in its various aspects—public relations practitioners; newspapermen, broadcasters, advertising men, and others connected with the media of mass communication; legislators, administrators, businessmen, and others whose contribution derived from their experience as employers and clients of public relations practitioners; social scientists, and students and teachers of political science, government, and related subjects as well as of public relations and publicity. Considerably the largest single category were men and women on the information staffs of federal government agencies. I was able to travel, and, in addition to the experts, I also talked with many people in different parts of the country whose help was not less valuable because their only claim to speak was that like the rest of us they belong to the "publics" whom it is the object of the "new profession" of public relations to influence. But "public relations" and all that it implies

vii

are so much a part of American life that it is hardly possible to pick up a newspaper or take a journey without getting new insight into its significance. It may not be literally true that, as was said in 1946, "almost everything we read in our newspapers today has been submitted or passed upon by a public relations man." [1] That such a statement can be made without being patently incredible illustrates the pervasiveness of public relations activities in the American society.

I do not propose to mention all of those to whom I am indebted, even where I can identify them. They are too numerous. I hope that they will accept this expression of my thanks to them collectively. If I needed proof that Americans deserve their reputation for generosity, helpfulness, and frankness to visitors from overseas, they certainly provided it. At the risk of being invidious, I must, however, make a few exceptions, where the help I have had has been in various ways quite exceptional.

I shared to the full in the genius for helpfulness of Mr. E. K. Wickman and Mr. Lansing V. Hammond of the Education Division of the Commonwealth Fund. Others to whom I am particularly indebted for help of differing kinds—ranging from the supply of information and criticism of the draft manuscript in part or as a whole to general advice and encouragement—include the following: Mr. Waldo M. Abbot; Mr. W. Howard Chase; Mr. Drew Dudley; Dr. Rex F. Harlow; Mr. Robert E. Harper; Mr. and Mrs. T. S. Thyne Henderson; Mr. Francis A. Henson; my mother in law, Mrs. Ethel Puffer Howes; Professor Harold D. Lasswell; Professor Alfred McLung Lee; Dr. Rensis A. Likert; Mr. Walter Lippmann; Mr. Anthony Netboy; Professor J. K. Pollock; Mr. Don K. Price; Mr. Theodore S. Repplier; Mr. Benjamin Sonnenberg; and Mr. James W. Young. I have assumed that the many federal information officers who helped me would prefer to be anonymous. It should not of course be thought that any of the people I have mentioned share the responsi-

---

[1] Shepard Henkin, *Opportunities in Public Relations*, New York, Vocational Guidance Manuals, 1946, 5.

bility for any of the views I have expressed; I know that some of them differ from me on important points.

The Hoover Commission, mentioning in 1949 the areas of the federal government requiring further study, stated that there might be "much needed work to be done in such fields as public relations." "Bibliography is still meager," said two leading public relations exponents, Glenn and Denny Griswold, of public relations generally in 1948.[2] It is certainly strange that, though so much has been written, mostly of little enduring value, on different aspects of "public relations," no systematic study of the American public relations group as a whole has been published; and Professor J. L. McCamy's *Government Publicity*, which was published in 1939, still stands alone as an authority on the public relations activities of Federal agencies. I hope that this book will help to fill what are indeed conspicuous gaps in the literature alike of public relations, mass communication, and government: and that the disadvantages of writing about another country will be offset by the greater detachment which this makes possible.

J.A.R.P.

Wimbledon, England
June 1950

[2] *Your Public Relations*, ed. Glenn and Denny Griswold, New York, Funk and Wagnalls, 1948, 18.

CONTENTS

PART I

THE PUBLIC RELATIONS SCENE

CHAPTER 1

◇◇

TOWARD A "NEW PROFESSION"?

◇◇

"PUBLIC RELATIONS" is not a peculiarly American phenomenon, but it has nowhere flourished as in the United States. Nowhere else is it so widely practiced, so lucrative, so pretentious, so respectable and disreputable, so widely suspected and so extravagantly extolled.

Those who are engaged in this colorful craft form one of the professional and semi-professional groups which have come into being or increased in importance as society has become more complex and the national income has multiplied:—accountants, real estate men, brokers, architects, dentists, chiropodists, almost ad infinitum. They belong to the still growing section of the population which makes its living out of the system of mass communications. Like teachers, ministers of religion, labor leaders, newspapermen, novelists, they are people who—as some social psychologists would say—"manipulate symbols." More simply, their chief tools are words. They are concerned with men's opinions, and with the opinions of men in the mass. Hence their special importance for democracy. It is no accident that they are to be found near all the foci of power.

"Everybody is talking about public relations," Rex F. Harlow, president of the American Council on Public Relations, wrote in 1945, "but nobody seems to know too much about the meaning of the term." "Today public relations is a crazy patchwork of ideas and activities." [1] Putting the same thought

[1] Rex F. Harlow, "Public Relations at the Crossroads," *Public Opinion Quarterly*, 8 (4), Winter 1944–45, 551.

differently, (a) "public relations" is used in a variety of ill-defined senses; and (b) public relations practitioners are only partially differentiated as a distinct specialist category. Much that public relations leaders would acknowledge as "public relations" is done under other names—such as "information," "publicity," and even "education": they would disown much that is called "public relations."

The term is used in at least three main senses—for relations with the public: for the state of an institution's or an individual's relations with the public: and for the activities of public relations practitioners. "One of the most interesting instances of bad public relations," according to Professor N. S. B. Gras, "comes from the history of the Church, especially about 1350–1550." "The public relations of any institution, i.e. the measure of its prestige," said W. Emerson Reck, "is the sum of all the impressions people have regarding the institution." "My business," ran an advertisement in the *Editor and Publisher* in 1948, "is Public Relations. All inclusive, with gift of ideas from publicity to organization and employee relations. With dignity or with a flare. Permanent." [2]

This multiple usage has caused much confusion. So has the failure to recognize that in the third sense "public relations" is a term of art. It is a portmanteau description of the activities of those who describe what they do as public relations. It does not necessarily follow that these activities are connected with "public relations" in the other senses, or that they are exclusively concerned with it in those senses.

Professor Eric F. Goldman has discovered an example of "public relations" being used for relations with the public as long ago as 1882. This was in an address by Dorman Eaton to the Yale Law School on "The Public Relations and Duties of the Legal Profession." [3] There was a touch of genius about its appropriation to describe the flourishing press agents and pub-

---

[2] N. S. B. Gras, *Shifts in Public Relations* (reprinted from the *Bulletin* of the Business Historical Society, Boston, Mass., October 1945), 4; W. Emerson Reck, "Public Relations; A Team Job," *College Public Relations*, 2 (12), December 1946; *Editor and Publisher*, 81 (20), May 8, 1948, 79.

[3] Eric F. Goldman, *Two-Way Street* (Boston, Bellman Publishing Co., 1948), 2.

licity men of the first decade of the present century. When this happened and who was responsible remain to be discovered. In 1911 the annual report of American Telephone and Telegraph had a heading "public relations," [4] and the usage was evidently common by 1913. Talking in that year of "The Railroads and Public Relations," J. H. Baumgartner, publicity representative of the Baltimore & Ohio Railroad, said that in response to the agitation which some years before had crystallized into antagonism to business, the railroads "moved to get in closer touch with the public. Departments of public relations were established by some of the roads, as well as by many of the industrial and manufacturing concerns and public service corporations. Many of the railroads and other interests I have mentioned established departments of publicity, which handle largely matters of public relations, and with the cooperation of the press, endeavor to effect a fair understanding between the business interests on one side, the editor and the public on the other. . . . A railroad regards its publicity department as the mouthpiece of the management." [5]

Public relations exponents are naturally inclined to overemphasize the novelty of specialist public relations. By reiteration a legend has won general acceptance, and it recurs in the literature. According to the legend the main phases were these. Nineteenth century press agentry was chiefly circus and stage ballyhoo. Early in the new century Ivy L. Lee discovered that sound policies were the key to successful publicity; a former newspaperman turned press agent, he looked upon himself as a "Physician to Corporate Bodies," and he started the process in the course of which "publicity" matured into "public relations." The Creel Committee of the first World War dramatized the possibilities of publicity and trained some of the leading practitioners of the next generation. In the 1920's Edward L. Bernays and others harnessed modern psychology to the older techniques. The depression of the 1930's taught American business by the hard way that good relations with the

[4] Norton E. Long, "Public Relations Policies of the Bell System," *Public Opinion Quarterly*, 1 (4), October 1937, 6n.

[5] *Editor and Publisher*, 13 (5), July 19, 1913, 97.

public were essential to its survival, and provided the climate for the efflorescence of what by this time could properly be called a "new profession."

The legend telescopes and oversimplifies a story which is much more complex. It began when men started to get into the newspapers information favorable to their employers or to others for whom they were acting as paid or unpaid agents. Alfred McLung Lee has shown that there have been press agents almost as long as there have been newspapers. They existed in the United States during the eighteenth century, and probably earlier in England. They helped to bring about the American Revolution; Samuel Adams wrote "artful" and "carefully biased" reports of events like the Boston Tea Party, and "energetically arranged their dissemination." [6]

It is true that the nineteenth century press agents were chiefly associated with the stage and the circus, but they were also to be found in other spheres—notably politics—where dependence upon the favor of the general public was direct and obvious, and toward the end were being increasingly employed by hotels, railroads, and shipping companies. The development was a corollary of the rise of modern advertising, and it is likely that the remarkable upsurge of press agentry and publicity in the early years of the new century was due more to trends which were already operating than to any deliberate reaction from the attitude exemplified in the famous phrase: "The public be damned!" Certainly it extended far beyond the realms of the industrial barons—to the universities, the churches, government, even, we are told, to judges and spring poets.[7] The *Denver* (Colo.) *Republican* in 1909 gave a vivid picture of this extraordinary phase. "New press agents are being born every minute. You can hear forty of them howling or laughing in every city block." A writer in the *Saturday Evening Post* said in the same year that there were ten thousand press agents in New York City, "divided, roughly, into two sections, the literary and the physical, and subdivided into

[6] Alfred McLung Lee, *The Daily Newspaper in America* (New York, Macmillan, 1937), 40.
[7] *ibid.*, 444: and *Editor and Publisher, passim.*

the honest and the dishonest." [8] It is a measure of the prosperity attained by the more successful that J. I. C. Clarke was said to have received $20,000 a year as press agent of Standard Oil.[9]

According to the legend, this was the period during which Ivy L. Lee and fellow pioneers gained the ear of John D. Rockefeller, Jr., and other business leaders, and press agentry and publicity began the transformation into "public relations" which was not fully effective until the 1920's. An authoritative history of the public relations group remains to be written—it offers an enviable opportunity to some enterprising historian—, and there is little secondary material against which the legend can be checked. This is unfortunate not least because writers on public relations are more than ordinarily prone to attach a spurious novelty to the things of the moment simply because they pretend to be new. Enough information is, however, available to show how often the appearance of novelty is deceptive.

The modern public relations counsel is needlessly coy about his descent from the press agents of the stage and circus. Their techniques were not always as crude as is sometimes supposed. To take an outstanding example of the contrary, Barnum's circus had a comprehensive public relations program. Without the aid of Freud, Barnum probed deep into the mass mind. He cultivated opinion makers in the shape of Kings and Presidents, Governors and other notabilities. He took special pains to influence the younger generation through their teachers and directly, even to the extent of publishing under his own name juvenile books which were written by his press agent: he appeared as "a good-natured, benevolent-looking, middle-aged gentleman" in one of them, *Lion Jack: A Story of Perilous Adventures among Wild Men and the Capturing of Wild Beasts*. For the sake of his reputation he patronized animal welfare societies and gave lectures for charity. The serious public relations problem presented by the hostility of the churches was successfully countered by publicity which stressed the Christian character of Barnum's shows, and by more practical

---

[8] *Editor and Publisher*, 9 (7), August 14, 1909, 6; and 8 (40), April 3, 1909, 6.
[9] *ibid.*, 13 (7), August 2, 1913, 133.

measures such as admitting clergymen and their wives without payment.[10]

So, too, with the publicity men of the new century. Not only did they make use of a wide range of techniques and media—including movies, competitions, "weeks and days" (Coffee Week, Oyster Week, Textile Week, Salmon Day, Vinal Day, Child Labor Day, were a few of many in 1913), "educational" methods, and what would now be called public relations advertising. It is almost uncanny to find how often they anticipated the major public relations themes of the present time. The American way of life, the free enterprise system, better race relations, the importance of the small man in the ownership of big business, were all developed on lines which are still familiar. And what could strike a more contemporary note than this statement by Douglas N. Graves on behalf of the Associated Advertising Clubs of America in 1913? "Men are learning that the first justification for commerce must be service. . . . Righteousness in business is but another expression for efficiency and success in business." [11]

New methods have come into use since 1913. Old ones have been refined. Lessons have been learned from the social sciences. But, contrary to the legend, no sudden leaps forward have been made. Change has been gradual rather than catastrophic. Good evidence of this is provided by the slowness with which the new nomenclature has taken root. "Public relations" had obvious attractions as a title for the publicity men who were striving to throw off the bad associations of propaganda and ballyhoo. It conveyed the sense of public service. Its want of precision was an asset; it did not pin its users to an unduly restricted view of their functions. Yet even in the more rarefied circles it did not obtain a conclusive ascendancy over other descriptions until the Second World War, and its ascendancy is still far from absolute elsewhere.

As we have seen, there were public relations departments

---

[10] See, e.g., M. R. Werner, *Barnum* (New York, Harcourt, Brace, 1923), *Barnum's Own Story*, ed. Waldo R. Browne (New York, Viking Press, 1927), and Lee, *op. cit.*

[11] *Editor and Publisher*, 13 (10), August 23, 1913, 204.

before 1913. "Director of Public Relations" is said to have been first used in 1919. "Public relations counsel" was coined by Edward L. Bernays and came into use in the early '20's. But when leading public relations practitioners got together to form a national association in 1936 they chose to call it the National Association of Accredited Publicity Directors, and it was not until 1944 that they changed its name to National Association of Public Relations Counsel. It was not until 1946 that the American College Publicity Association, which had started in 1917 as the American Association of College News Bureaus, became the American College Public Relations Association. In 1935 there were still only ten public relations counselors in the New York telephone directory as compared with 76 "publicity service bureaus." By 1939 there were 74 as compared with 120, but the publicity category continued to be the more numerous until the war. In 1948 there were 336 entries under public relations and 232 under publicity. Both groups had grown in spectacular fashion, but public relations firms were increasing in number more rapidly than publicity bureaus. Neither category was self-contained, and it was symptomatic of the continued fluidity of usage that some important public relations counsel appeared under both headings. "Press agent" survived as a separate category, but only as a lingering vestige from the past with a cross-reference to "publicity service bureaus" and without any entries.

In the light of history the most important change in American public relations since the First World War may prove to have been the growing self-consciousness and cohesion of its practitioners—not any change in the character of the activities pursued. Bernays claimed in *Crystallizing Public Opinion* (1923) that public relations was a "new profession." Stated with varying degrees of confidence, the claim is now common form. One of the objects of the National Association of Accredited Publicity Directors in 1936 was "to promote and maintain the highest standards of service and of conduct by all members of the publicity profession."

There are many possible criteria of a profession, and the term is loosely used—sometimes for not much more than a white-collar occupation involving a fairly high degree of specialized skill. Much depends on the circumstances. It is possible to speak of both teaching and the law as professions, but the usage is not exactly the same. There are senses in which public relations can be called a profession, but to talk of its practitioners becoming a recognized profession can mean very little unless it means that they will form an organized professional group more or less comparable to the lawyers. The following tests at any rate should be satisfied:

(1) The members of the group should pursue essentially similar activities, based upon a body of knowledge or techniques which can be identified as their own specialty. (2) They should themselves be identifiable: it should be possible to say who does and who does not belong to the profession. (3) They should be organized, if only to set common standards for recognition and ethical practice, and to give some guarantee that they will provide the public with service of high quality, performed out of a sense of social responsibility as well as for private gain. "A profession," said the Commission on Freedom of the Press, "is a group organized to perform a public service." [12] (4) They should feel that they are a profession—as doctors, dentists, lawyers, naval officers, certainly do.

Judged by these criteria, public relations practitioners are still a long way from constituting a profession. But they are beginning to feel that they are one, and some important consequences flow from the awareness of common interests and purposes which this feeling reflects. A pattern is forming. There is a natural tendency toward synthesis and rationalization among men and women who share the same aspirations. Common problems are focused and discussed. Points of view develop. More attention is paid to ethical and technical standards. Leaders and organizers appear. All these processes can be seen in American public relations.

The literature of public relations provides one measure of the process of integration. That books should be written on the theory and practice of public relations presupposes that there

[12] Commission on Freedom of the Press, *A Free and Responsible Press* (University of Chicago Press, 1947), 76.

will be a market for what is written and that there is a more or less common body of knowledge. The books in their turn strengthen the sense of sharing a distinct specialty, and help to promote uniformity of thought and practice.

In 1948 the Library of Congress contained roughly 130 books dealing with public relations or publicity generally—all were cataloged under "publicity"—apart from the many volumes which referred incidentally to the subject. The figure is rough because the selection was necessarily arbitrary, but it is sufficient for the present purpose that the literature was considerable. Two points stand out when it is examined. First, the output was slight in the 1920's and for most of the 1930's: it rose steeply during and after the war. "Bibliography is still meager," wrote Glenn and Denny Griswold in *Your Public Relations* (1948), "but books serving the field are appearing more frequently." Secondly, the content of most of the published material was unimpressive or worse, though the Griswolds may have been right in claiming that the editorial merit had improved substantially in the last few years.[13] The publications in the Library of Congress ranged from reports of speeches and conferences to full length volumes. A good many were promotional, either for publicity and public relations in general or for the authors or their employers in particular. Even when more ambitious claims were made, almost all dealt principally with techniques of publicity, and became confused and vague when the author ventured from the practical to the more speculative. The literary standard was low for a group one of whose chief skills is with words, and originality of either treatment or content was unusual.

Bernays' pioneer volume, *Crystallizing Public Opinion*, though published as long ago as 1923, stood alone among works dealing specifically with public relations in having exerted any influence outside the narrow public relations world or much influence within it. Not that the manuals and com-

---

[13] Glenn and Denny Griswold, "Responsibilities and Potentialities," in *Your Public Relations, The Standard Public Relations Handbook*, edited by them (New York, Funk and Wagnalls, 1948), 18. Quoted subsequently as Griswolds, *Your Public Relations*.

pendia addressed to lay as well as to professional practitioners
—on public relations for churches or "How to Interview" or
"Getting Results from Suggestion Systems" or the now fairly
numerous general handbooks—are without value or to be despised. Far from it. They have done much to disseminate technical information and practical experience, to raise standards
of performance, to foster the sense of belonging to a profession, to interest prospective clients, and even to focus thought
on the purposes which public relations serves in society. But
they are expository rather than creative, empirical rather than
scientific; only disappointment awaits those who look for evidence that public relations is the "science and art" mentioned
in the by-laws of the Public Relations Society of America.

In these circumstances greater importance attaches to the
few studies of more scientific pretensions such as Robert K.
Merton's *Mass Persuasion* (1945), James L. McCamy's *Government Publicity* (1939), and Harold P. Levy's two Russell Sage Foundation studies—*A Study of Public Relations*
(1943), which deals with the public relations of a state public
assistance department, and *Building a Popular Movement*
(1944), which is about the Boy Scouts of America. They are
so illuminating for their special fields that they draw attention to the need for many more studies of the same kind. They
provide some of the case material which is essential if public
relations is to be systematically taught or studied either as a
craft or a sociological phenomenon. So, over a wider area than
public relations in the specialized sense, do books like Zechariah Chafee, Jr.'s *Government and Mass Communications*
and the succession of important volumes dealing with American foreign policy and public opinion which have appeared
since the war—such as Thomas A. Bailey's *The Man in the
Street* (1948), Leonard S. Cottrell, Jr.'s and Sylvia Eberhart's
American Opinion on World Affairs in the Atomic Age (1948),
and *Public Opinion and Foreign Policy*, edited by Lester
Markel (1949).

It cannot be said that the treatment of public relations in
general works on sociology, social psychology, communication, and for that matter public and business administration is

much more satisfactory: it is almost always fragmentary and ill-informed. It is a pity that there is no history of the public relations group. It would help greatly in getting the contemporary scene into perspective. N. S. B. Gras's *Shifts in Public Relations* (1945) is a stimulating interpretation of changes in the relations between business and the public from medieval to modern times, but it is only an essay, and it touches only cursorily on the evolution of public relations specialists. Eric F. Goldman's *Two-Way Street* (1948) is a lively history of public relations counselors. It contained new and illuminating material, but it is very short, its scope is narrow, and its focus is distorted by the author's preoccupation with the exploits of two men—Lee and Bernays.

As unifying influences, the periodicals which deal with public relations are in some ways more important than the books. They reach a bigger readership and their impact is more continuous. They are better adapted for the discussion of current problems and the interchange of technical information. They also serve as media for news of the public relations world—personal and other items which help their readers to keep in touch with what is happening to fellow practitioners; few bonds are stronger than participation in the same gossip.

There is no commercially published journal on general sale devoted exclusively to public relations matters. They receive fairly full treatment, however, in the business columns of newspapers like the *New York Times*, and in advertising, publishing and business magazines like the *Editor and Publisher*, *Printer's Ink*, *Advertising and Selling*, and *Tide*; *Tide* introduced a special public relations section in 1945, and began to describe itself as "the news magazine of advertising, marketing, and public relations."

A news letter, *Public Relations News*, available only to subscribers, was founded in 1944 by Glenn and Denny Griswold and claimed to be "the first and only national weekly publication entirely devoted to reporting and interpreting developments in the public relations field." It has had an influential circulation mainly among business public relations executives, but it could not take the place of a full length technical and professional magazine on general sale. At the academic level *Public Opinion Quarterly* has been an important medium for discussion of the theoretical background of practice in mass communications, including public relations.

There remain the periodicals of the public relations associations. Only two have been of serious pretensions. *College Public Relations* has been mainly devoted to news about the American College Public Relations Association and to elementary articles on practical publicity: it was converted from a monthly to a quarterly publication in 1949, when a news letter was introduced to serve the former purpose. *Public Relations Journal*, the monthly organ which the Public Relations Society of America inherited from the American Council on Public Relations, has been more ambitious. It has set out to be a medium for the exchange of experience and ideas. It would be unfair to judge it by academic standards. The task has proved difficult, and it would be surprising if many of the articles had not exhibited the want of objectivity which has characterized the literature of public relations in general.

The associations themselves are the chief outward expression of the increased self-consciousness of the public relations group. They are also one of the chief factors in heightening it. They could not exist unless their members had a sense of common interests and distinctive characteristics; once in being they strengthen *esprit de corps*. They are forums in which different points of view can be reconciled, leaders can influence the rank and file, and the rank and file can influence the leaders. They can provide authoritative spokesmen to express collective views. They offer machinery through which ethical and technical standards can be raised and discipline introduced, and a means by which moral pressure and public condemnation can be directed against those who by charlatanry and sharp practice are bringing the whole group into disrepute. They can help to promote good corporate public relations.

It is significant that associations of public relations practitioners have also been formed since the war in Britain, France, Holland, and Norway. They differ in various ways from the American associations, as they do from one another—the Dutch organization is, for example, confined to a small group from state enterprises, public utilities, and large corporations—but they meet essentially the same needs and face much the same problems. Their sense of common purpose was expressed by the declaration in favor of an international association which was signed by public relations men from Belgium, Britain, France, Holland, Norway, the United States, and the Western Union Organization, who attended the Utrecht Fair in 1950. The objects of the association, it was suggested, might be to raise standards of ethics and skills, to improve the conditions under which public relations operates throughout the world, and to work for better international understanding in the widest sense.

Of the two national associations in the United States the more important is the Public Relations Society of America, which was formed in 1948 by the merger of the National Association of Public Relations Counsel and the American Council on Public Relations. The former was strongest in New York and the East: the latter, which had been started in 1939 primarily for research and training, had grown into a professional association mainly for the West Coast. At the end of 1949, the new society had about 800 members drawn for the most part from the upper strata of the practitioners employed by the bigger business undertakings and to a lesser extent independent counselors in successful practice on their own account. It has had close affiliations with the National Association of Manufacturers. The American Public Relations Association, though according to itself "conceived" in 1937, was established in 1944. It has been strongest in Washington, D.C., but its 400 members in 1947 came from 43 states as well as Australia, England, Argentina, South Africa, Hawaii, and Canada. Its membership has been more diversified than the Public Relations Society's, and a notable feature has been the large part which has been taken by the public relations executives of trade associations.

The other associations are either local or specialized. Those like the San Francisco Public Relations Roundtable and the Chicago Publicity Club that are local, including branches of the national associations, do much the same in their own areas as the national associations on a larger scale. Of the specialist associations the most important has been the American College Public Relations Association. Though it goes back to 1917 it did not grow rapidly until the Second World War: it had over 800 members in 1949. The School Public Relations Association was formed with 14 members in 1935: it had 109 members in 1945–1946, 250 at the end of 1947, and over 600 in 1949. Newcomers in 1949 were the Financial Public Relations Association and the Association of Municipal Public Relations Officers, one of whose objects was to encourage recognition of the "municipal public relations profession."

The Library Public Relations Council and the National Publicity Council for Health and Welfare Services cover some of the same ground as the public relations associations. The former was set up in 1939 "to investigate and promote every phase of library public relations, and to serve as a clearing house for materials, techniques and methods." The National Publicity Council for Health and Welfare Services started in 1922 as the Committee on Publicity Methods of the National Conference of Social Work: in 1947 it had 1861 members, many of them institutions, and operated as "a clearing house for publicity ideas and techniques and for information on mass education in the fields of health and public welfare."

The Public Relations Society of America has been inclined to regard high-level public relations as its special possession, but all the associations are linked by a feeling of kinship and by similar preoccupations. They are much concerned with status. They are anxious to improve technical and ethical standards. They see a great future for the "new profession." They are on eager watch for new fields to conquer and for opportunities to advertise public relations achievements.

Appointments like Joseph L. Egan's as president of Western Union and even those of Eric Johnston, Charles Luckman, and Paul Hoffman have been acclaimed almost *ad nauseam* as evidence in support of the attractive thesis that "this next period in American business history will be that of the public relations man." [14] Egan's appointment was mentioned by three separate writers in the Griswolds' handbook, *Your Public Relations*. Just as in the past business has turned for its top posts now to engineers, now to lawyers, now to experts in finance, so it is argued, it will turn in the future to experts in the management of relations with the public. As was said in 1949 by a writer in *Fortune* magazine: "The day is surely coming when American business, so long run by its production men and super-salesmen, must be run by men who put public relations ahead of everything else." [15]

This is a vision. It may give encouragement and inspiration, but the immediate objectives of the group are more prosaic. There are still many organizations which need to be persuaded of the basic doctrine that the employment of public relations specialists is essential to efficient management; many more have still to learn the elementary lesson that they will not enjoy the full benefits of doing so unless they give the public relations department a proper status.

Broadly there are three levels at which the public relations expert can be employed: (a) he may be a mere technician whose job is to publicize measures in the formulation of which he has had no share; (b) in order that he may do his publicity job better, he may be kept in touch with policy discussions and invited to contribute to them so far as publicity questions arise; (c) he may share in general policy making.

The aim of the associations is to lift the majority of their members to the second and third categories. It was moderately stated in a leaflet, *Your Public Relations Executive*, which the American Public Relations Association published in 1948 for the guidance of businessmen: "Since top management must be mindful of the public, the public relations executive in the most successful organization usually reports to the President, and Executive Vice President, or even the Chairman of the Board. It is part of his responsibility to ascertain public atti-

[14] Shepard Henkin, *Opportunities in Public Relations* (New York, Vocational Guidance Manuals, 1946), 11.

[15] *Fortune*, 39 (5), May 1949, 68.

tudes and probable public reactions; then see that they are brought to management attention before policy decisions are made. With good policies so established, the task of merchandizing involves consideration of the public groups which must be reached."

According to one of their leading spokesmen, W. Emerson Reck, college public relations directors should be in the president's cabinet.[16] A familiar complaint in *Channels*, the organ of the National Publicity Council for Health and Welfare, has been the failure of the managing boards of social welfare agencies to take their public relations advisers into proper consultation before deciding questions of policy.

These are ideals. Even in business many big corporations have not seen the light, and continue to place their public relations activities under advertising, sales and other executives. Clark Belden gave the Boston University School of Public Relations in 1947 the following examples of executives acting in public relations capacities: "the publicity manager, the advertising manager, the personnel manager, the labor relations manager, the customer relations manager, the sales promotion manager, the sales manager, the educational director, the assistant to a president, the assistant to a vice-president, the auditor, the assistant treasurer, or the assistant secretary." [17]

In spheres other than business the differentiation of the public relations function has been even less complete. This is partly but not wholly a question of scale: the smaller the organization the less likely, other things being equal, that it will be able to support a separate public relations department. In the larger federal agencies differentiation is fairly advanced; in state and municipal governments it is the exception rather than the rule. In the smaller colleges the president himself often looks after public relations or the responsibility is assigned to another administrative officer or to a member of the

[16] Advocated in W. Emerson Reck, *Public Relations, A Program for Colleges and Universities* (New York, Harper, 1947), and in other writings.

[17] Clark Belden, *Opportunities Facing Boston University's New School of Public Relations* (Boston University School of Public Relations, 1947), 4.

faculty. *The Public Relations Directory and Yearbook* [18] listed 53 labor organizations in 1945: the officers responsible for public relations included president, secretary, financial secretary, research director, business agent, manager, educational and welfare director, as well as director of publicity and director of public relations. Harold P. Levy complained in 1949 that only about 100 community chests employed public relations practitioners, and only about 100 out of 235 family agencies had full-time public relations people.[19]

In one sense there can be no fuller recognition of the importance of a management function than that the chairman or president should take personal charge. For him to do so is, however, a tacit denial of the need to employ a specialist. And that is damaging to the specialist's own aspirations. A lay university president would not think of acting as his university's legal adviser. The interests of the specialist lie in the acceptance of the claim that it is dangerous for management to dispense with his expert knowledge and judgment. As things are, the large number of cases in which unspecialized executives handle public relations is evidence of the prevalent assumption that it does not call for expert qualifications.

Because it involves recognition by independent bodies of high standing, the growth of university and college courses in public relations—leading in a few cases to bachelor's and higher degrees—is a development of special significance for the future of the public relations group. Important public relations counsel and executives have shown that they realize this by closely associating themselves with the most ambitious and widely publicized of these ventures—the School of Public Relations at Boston University, which was set up in 1947. It is not only that in American conditions academic recognition is part of the full equipment of a self-respecting profession. University courses and research will also help to provide a firmer founda-

---

[18] *The Public Relations Directory and Yearbook*, Vol. I, ed. Karl E. Ettinger (New York, Public Relations Directory and Yearbook Inc., 1945).
[19] Harold P. Levy, "Are Social Workers Public Relations' 'Poor Relations'?" *Public Relations Journal*, 5 (6), June 1949, 28.

tion on which to base the claims of public relations practitioners to possess expert qualifications, and to sort out the different views about the boundaries of public relations practice.

But the evolution of public relations training cannot be explained primarily as a response to the needs of the group itself. Many of the courses are ancillary to training in other subjects and provide instruction in the elements of public relations for prospective entrants into occupations where there is a large measure of contact with the public, such as education, the ministry, public administration, business, and hotel management. Others are incidental to courses in communication techniques, notably journalism. Only a few aspire to give a comprehensive introduction to a career in public relations or publicity.

Alfred McLung Lee found in 1947 that at least thirty universities and colleges listed courses labeled "public relations" —there were 47 such courses altogether—, in contrast with 21 institutions offering such courses in 1945.[20] In 1948 Stewart Harral made a survey of 62 universities and colleges which offered "public relations" courses, and of 20 with courses in publicity. Relatively to the university system as a whole, the number was small, and only five of the institutions mentioned by Harral had five or more courses in public relations and publicity.[21]

But the quantity of the training was not the most interesting feature. The provision for university training was increasing fast. There were opportunities for majoring in public relations which had not existed before the war. In so far as it is possible to generalize, the tendency was for public relations courses of the ambitious variety to spring up in schools and departments dealing with communication, journalism, and publicity; no clear line divided "public relations" and "publicity," but "public relations" was tending to be taught in addition to "publicity" and to supplant it as a description.

[20] A. M. Lee, "Trends in Public Relations Training," *Public Opinion Quarterly*, 11 (1), Spring 1947, 83–91.

[21] Kindly supplied by the author, Stewart Harral, Director of Public Relations, University of Oklahoma.

As is illustrated by the literature, the growth of the associations, and the state of university training, the public relations group has made dramatic progress during and since the war, but its evolution is still in a fluid phase. It is cohering but still inchoate. It is uncertain of itself. It is immature. Its place in management is ill-defined. Hence the preoccupation with status. Hence the confusion of nomenclature. Hence also the vitality, sometimes naïve enthusiasm, even missionary spirit, which are among the most agreeable expressions of its youthfulness. In an important study of the personnel and ideology of public relations in 1949, Leila A. Sussmann found that public relations practitioners showed several signs of belonging to a relatively new and unorganized occupation: in the sample she examined there was a high proportion of young men in top positions, social mobility was above the average, and the proportion of Republicans was atypically low.[22]

"Public relations is not yet a profession," said one of the younger leaders, Earl Newsom, in 1945. "But it is far more exhilarating to enter a field when it is new, when all the inevitable discoveries have not been made, when there is pioneering to be done." [23]

[22] Leila A. Sussmann, "The Personnel and Ideology of Public Relations," *Public Opinion Quarterly*, 12 (4), Winter 1948–49, 697–708.

[23] Earl Newsom, *Approaches to Public Relations*. Address to a public relations conference of Standard Oil Co. (N.J.) and affiliated companies, November 1945 (privately printed, n.d.), 21.

CHAPTER 2

PUBLIC RELATIONS IN PRACTICE

No INTERPRETATION of the role of public relations practitioners in American society will be valid unless it is firmly based on what they actually do rather than on what they think they ought to be doing or would like other people to think they are doing. This chapter will, therefore, be given up to a bird's-eye view of public relations in practice—by way of preface to the examination in the next chapter of the attempts which have been made to formulate a "philosophy" of public relations and to the case study of federal government public relations which will occupy Part II.

There is much which is hidden from the outside observer. The advice given to clients and employers is confidential: only the action taken, and by no means always that, is visible. The published material tends to emphasize the spectacular and the sensational, and to concentrate on successes to the exclusion of failures. Enough information is, however, obtainable to enable a sufficiently reliable impression to be formed. Short of giving away confidences, leading practitioners have described the ways in which they have tackled particular problems. There is no need for reticence about the publicity campaigns which on any view are normal end-products of public relations practice. The papers and memoirs of the leading actors are shedding new light on the inside story of government public relations during the New Deal and war periods, and Congress and the press have kept the current activities of departmental information divisions under close scrutiny. Private gossip, public inquiries, Court proceedings, magazine articles, works of fiction like

22

Charles Yale Harrison's lurid but circumstantial *Nobody's Fool* (1948), help to pierce the darker corners.

First for a few vignettes.

From business:

(a) "The Greatest Story Ever Told," a radio program based on the life of Christ, won for Paul W. Litchfield, chairman of the Goodyear Company, an award from the National Association of Public Relations Counsel in 1948 for the greatest contribution to the national welfare through public relations during the past year.

(b) In a successful prewar campaign the cedar chest manufacturers set out to restore their product to popularity by associating it with romance in the minds of those about to marry. It was presented as the "hope chest," and the campaign culminated with a "Fall in Love Week." [1]

(c) "Such is the influence of motion pictures on public opinion," said Harry McHose, president of the Cigar Institute of America and president of the American Public Relations Association, in 1948, "that the cigar industry was almost ruined in the 1920's and 1930's by unintentional acts of the film producers. Cigar smoking was once so highly regarded that it was reserved for peers. But, in the '20's and '30's the public saw on the silver screen only gangsters and roughnecks smoking cigars. The result was that cigar sales dropped. When *public relations men* pointed out to the film producers that they were unintentionally ruining an industry by presenting only unpleasant characters with cigars, they immediately stopped." [2]

(d) Quaker Oats Company public relations in 1949 included a traveling show; literature on background scientific information and product facts; school study programs; local press relations; annual local press dinners; and among other things "a quiet grassroots build-up for 'Pancake Day.' Quaker discovered this old European pre-Lenten festival being observed in several U.S. communities, and by lending a hand,

[1] Described in Theodore R. Sills and Philip Lesly, *Public Relations, Principles and Procedures* (Chicago, Richard D. Irwin, 1945), 73–4.

[2] *Washington P.R. News-Letter* (American Public Relations Association), No. 12, February 1948.

hopes to build the colorful custom into something pretty potent saleswise." [3]

From education:

The Public Relations Department of the College of the City of New York claimed in 1947 to have increased enrollments in adult education from 3,000 to 4,500. News releases and feature stories resulted in over a hundred items in New York newspapers. When twice as many women as men joined the folk-dancing course, a short feature was issued. It told how eighteen ladies "would be unable to dance the polka, mazurka, and schottische unless an equal number of gentlemen came to the rescue by signing up." They did. [4]

From the labor unions:

(a) In 1947 Local B 1031 of the International Brotherhood of Electrical Workers (AFL) in Chicago spent $20,000 on a safety film for which it received only a brief title credit. "Actually," said *Tide* magazine, "the film does a first-rate job promoting the idea that a union is a useful outfit that invests members' hard-earned dues in something besides strike funds, business managers' salaries, and clambakes to keep members happy." [5]

(b) "Must we strike to get a decent, living wage?" was the heading of a Department Store Employees Union (AFL) leaflet issued during a dispute with San Francisco stores in 1948. "The boss got a raise. We helped our employers make the biggest profits in their history. . . . We got both high prices and low wages. . . . We are willing to negotiate. If that fails, we are willing to submit our dispute to arbitration. If these peaceful means fail to bring about a satisfactory settlement, we have no choice except to strike." [6]

From the churches:

Literature issued by the Joint Committee on Public Relations for Methodist Educational Institutions included blotters, sermonic materials on Christian Higher Education,

[3] *Tide*, 23 (41), October 14, 1949, 27 seq.
[4] *College Public Relations*, 30 (3), December 1947, 5.
[5] *Tide*, 21 (27), July 4, 1947, 49.
[6] Leaflet handed to me in San Francisco, 1948.

posters, guidance for lawyers and trust officers on the subject of wills, and promotional leaflets under a score of titles.[7]

From the armed forces:

Accordingly to an editorial in the *Infantry Journal* (September 1948), which General Bradley described as "splendid," " 'Army public relations' have greatly expanded in the past ten years—grown in breadth and amount of activity. They consist far less today of seeking publicity for commanders and attempting to keep unfavorable news from the public than they do of honest effort to tell the public what the Army is doing and why it is doing it."

From the newspapers:

The *Minneapolis Star-Tribune* won the award for the best public relations or community service program in the 1947 Newspaper Promotion Contest of the *Editor and Publisher*. Its entry included a program of information on world affairs, intended primarily for high schools and directed by a university professor with the aid of an advisory committee of editors.[8]

From literature:

"In recent years," said Louis Bromfield in 1947, "writers and sometimes publishing houses have engaged the services of public relations or advertising firms to promote new writers and their works or rehabilitate old and tired ones." [9]

With Congress:

"Modern public relations counsel," said George B. Galloway, "appear openly as witnesses at committee hearings, lay down a barrage of letters and telegrams on congressional offices, and use all the techniques of high-pressure publicity—press, radio, movies, advertising, pamphlets, books, magazines, exhibits—in an attempt to arouse legislative and public support for their programs." Lou Fisher, public relations manager, National Association of Independent Tire Dealers, reported in 1948: "Congress evidently appreciates the thinking of public relations men and their value. A greater number of public

[7] *College Public Relations*, 30 (5), February 1948.
[8] *Editor and Publisher*, 81 (15), March 11, 1948, 63.
[9] *Saturday Review of Literature*, 30 (52), December 27, 1947, 7.

relations men serve as advisors to Committees and Members of Congress, help in preparing speeches and guide them on policy." [10]

From the federal government:

In their final report the Citizens Food Committee under Charles Luckman described their origin: "Our government had no statutory powers to oblige anyone to give up food so that Europe might live. . . . President Truman acted. He launched a new experiment in public conservation. This was to be a unique test of a new technique in emergency voluntary action in peacetime. . . . It was clear from the outset that inasmuch as grain was to be obtained through purely voluntary measures, an intensive campaign of mass information as to the issues involved, and the benefits to be realized, had to be undertaken at once." [11]

From city government:

The city of San Diego was widely congratulated on a new style of annual report, in which civic solemnity was sacrificed to popular writing and racy humor:

"Health . . . Pull up that tin of hard tack and we'll tell you how we know and also about the doings of the M.D.'s, D.V.M.'s, and the B.V.D.'s. (You thought that last was underwear, didn't you. It stands for Bureau of Venereal Diseases.)

"Streets . . . Didya know that if we took all the trash gathered by the power street sweepers and the white wings during the year, packed it neatly into 3-foot square, cellophane containers stacked one on top of the other, we would have a column reaching 37,470 feet into the clouds?

"Police . . . Eight hundred and seventy-one fools were arrested for drunk driving. Our sense of humor can find nothing funny in driving an automobile while under the influence of evil spirits. The judges could put these criminals away for life and we'd never shed a tear." [12]

[10] George B. Galloway, *Congress at the Crossroads* (New York, Thomas Y. Crowell Co., 1946), 298; and *Washington P.R. News-Letter, op. cit.*
[11] Citizens Food Committee, *Final Report,* 1947.
[12] *City of San Diego Year Book* 1946–47 (processed, 1947), 40, 58, 16.

From the courts:

A leaflet, *Their Future Goes Hand in Hand with Yours,* issued by the Denver (Colo.) Juvenile and Family Court, gave good advice to parents in the form of thirteen rules for their guidance:

"How to Make Delinquents. If these instructions are carefully followed, we guarantee that your child will become delinquent and subsequently tried in the Juvenile Court. . . .

"Don't give your son any religious or spiritual training. Just take care of his bodily needs. . . .

"Never give a child a reason for the commands laid upon him; let him guess. . . . It's much easier. . . ." [13]

From private life:

"Seldom does a wedding attract national attention as did that of Franklin D. Roosevelt, Jr. to Miss Ethel du Pont. The appetite of the public for news was not easily satisfied. . . . A month before the wedding was scheduled to take place . . . [public relations] counsel was retained." [14]

Impossible to categorize:

When Major F. Benjamin Carlin and his wife, starting in 1948 on the first jeep trip round the world, politely declined help from a U.S. destroyer off Atlantic City, they asked the destroyer to telephone a New York public relations man and tell him the jeep was all right. Ware Lynch, president of Russell Birdwell and Associates, then told the full story of the adventure. [15]

The humorous touch:

"Take the doughnut," wrote Bert Nevins in 1949. "First, we organized the National Dunking Association, a non-political, non-dues-paying organization that exists solely for good fellowship. . . . We elaborated on the art of dunking. We sponsored public debates on dunking methods. We persuaded radio comedians to tell dunking jokes. . . . We ran

[13] Leaflet given to me at Denver, Colo., 1948.
[14] Edward C. Kienle, "Press Relations and a Wedding," *Public Opinion Quarterly*, 1 (4), October 1937, 136–8.
[15] *New York Herald Tribune*, August 12, 1948.

dunking contests and selected dunking queens." [16]

And here also is a glimpse behind the scenes by Constance Hope, a public relations counsel with an unusual capacity to laugh at herself:

"The Public Relations Counsel is rich like anything . . . Unlike his lowlier brethren, the P.R.C. claims he spends more time keeping his client's name out of the paper than he does getting it in. He prepares impressive campaigns, studded with surveys, graphs and excerpts from Freud, to show how he will mold the mass mind, psycho-analytically. (The P.R.C. scorns anything less than eight-cylinder words.) . . . The symbol of the Public Relations Counsel should be the whitewash brush, rather than the typewriter. As his name implies, his function is keeping the vested interests on a friendly footing with their public. His worst nightmare is a headline beginning 'SOULLESS CORPORATION'; his sure out, to have the president of same build a wing for Harvard. And when a scandal or an awkward lawsuit is about to break, there you will find the P.R.C. with kid gloves and pail of whitewash.

"So reach for a grain of salt the next time you read that a library has been endowed to the tune of three million dollars. Maybe a senatorial investigation is scheduled to begin next week.

"Or maybe there's a woman in the case." [17]

Now for some more detailed examples—most of them campaigns which have been commended by public relations exponents.

1. First, a business campaign with a fairly simple object which received an award from the American Public Relations Association in 1946. National Ice Public Relations, the public relations organization of the ice manufacturers, set out to revive an industry which was endangered by the competition of the mechanical refrigerator. A central feature was a series of radio programs, "This Is the Ice Age." These "voiced the

---

[16] Bert Nevins, "Public Relations on the Lighter Side," *Public Relations Journal*, 5 (9), September 1949, 1–2.

[17] Constance Hope, *Publicity Is Broccoli* (Indianapolis and New York, Bobbs-Merrill, 1941), 18–19.

values of Iceman's Ice to modern America in *authoritative words* by prominent guest speakers," who included three federal government officials. Ice industry spokesmen also took part in popular programs on each of the major networks. *Liberty, McCall's, True Confessions*, the *New York Times*, the *Christian Science Monitor* were a few of "the hundreds of *big-name, big-circulation* magazines and newspapers which carried articles, news stories and pictures about Ice and its many uses, all arranged by NPIR." The theme was rammed home by other methods—in trade magazines; in exhibits at annual conventions of trade organizations like the National Association of Retail Grocers and the Vegetable Growers Association of America; through cooperation with food manufacturers, distributors, wholesalers, and retailers; by personal contacts with key people; by large scale advertising with "31 full page, dynamic messages, all in *full natural colors*"; by the distribution of over 60,000 pieces of "ice-educational material" a month for use by hundreds of schools and colleges.[18]

2. Ice is preeminently clean, respectable, and acceptable to the American public. Another trade association which was honored by the American Public Relations Association in 1946 had a tougher task. The American Association of Small Loan Companies—later, for obvious public relations reasons, renamed the National Consumer Finance Association—had to "create a more favorable public opinion regarding the small loan business." As the association recognized, it was not only a question of overcoming age-old prejudices; it was impossible to defend the practices which some firms still followed.

The campaign used an indirect approach. It was designed to sustain the morale of small loan company employees, and to use them as agents of public information and as exemplars of the services which the companies were rendering to the community. A series of pamphlets briefed them to answer questions on which there was popular misunderstanding. Why were

[18] *What goes on here?* (Washington, D.C., National Ice Public Relations brochure, n.d.). This campaign is also described in *Public Relations in Action*, ed. Philip Lesly (Chicago, Ziff Davis, 1947), which is a compendium of cases which received awards from the American Public Relations Association in 1946.

interest rates seemingly so high? What were the actual profits? Why was the small loan business essential? They were given some sound advice on "customer relations": "1. Be sincere. Sincerity is the yeast that mellows the whole loaf of human relations. . . . 3. Be interested in the other fellow's affairs. 4. Call him by name." The employee could take a justifiable pride in his job:

"Yes, you can be proud of this vital business in which you are engaged. . . . For this business deals directly with great masses of American citizens and deals with them in a most constructive and intimate manner, helping them over financial hurdles, guiding them through budgetary difficulties, counseling them on many important human problems. The breadth and scope of its opportunity for service challenges the imagination and enterprise of everyone engaged in it." [19]

3. The popularization of bowling showed how public relations could be used to introduce new habits in the interests of a commercial group:

"The promotional activities which led to its outstanding success were merely the outward manifestations of a deep-seated analysis and approach to the entire field of public recreation, social problems of leisure time, and the trends of sport preferences. . . .

"The goal was to popularize the sport, thereby raising its status as a profitable business and making possible higher standards."

The campaign was planned with full regard to mass psychology. "The first step was to associate bowling with the proper people"—by building up bowling stars as sports heroes, by getting the right sponsors for tournaments, by spreading stories of heroes of other sports who bowled for fun. "Gradually the men of America took up bowling. Respectability and example of others brought the first dividends."

The next move was to bring the women in. For them the appeal had to be different. Soon the country was reading of the advantages of bowling as an aid to health and beauty, and

[19] *Public Relations in Action* (Washington, D.C., National Consumer Finance Association, 1947). This campaign is also described in Lesly, *op. cit.*

30

learning how the stars of Hollywood were turning the pastime to good account. Then "came style stories and pictures, with expert designers providing neat outfits for the woman bowler." But women would be slow to take up a sport at which their unskilled efforts might make them seem ridiculous. Experts were, therefore, sent on tour to give free lessons; "How to Bowl" articles were run in newspapers and magazines; and publicity was given to female champions. And so on. Bowling must not be a mere passing craze. Leagues were organized; employers were persuaded that company teams would be good for morale; to interest the coming generation and to fill in slack periods during the day, high school leagues were set up.

Then, "with bowling established as the principal extracurricular interest of thousands, a campaign was undertaken to point out the importance of proper equipment in bowling." [20]

4. Paul Garrett, public relations vice-president of General Motors, has been one of the leading exponents of the view that the public relations function must be closely integrated with policy making and is inextricably interwoven with other management functions.

Special interest, therefore, attaches to the account of General Motors public relations which he gave to a conference organized by the National Association of Manufacturers in 1945. He explained that basic public relations policy was formulated at monthly meetings of the Public Relations Policy Group: he took the chair, and under him there sat the chairman, vice-chairman, and president, the executive vice-presidents, the vice-presidents in charge of personnel, research, distribution, employee cooperation, and legal counseling, and the director of customer research. Beneath the Policy Group was the Public Relations Planning Committee, which comprised the heads of the twelve sections in the Public Relations Department, namely, editorial policy, press relations, institutional advertising, plant city relations, institutional radio, General Motors clubs, motion pictures, rural communities, Washington contact, labor liaison, stockholder relations, educational service.

[20] Sills and Lesly, *passim*.

Garrett quoted from an actual statement submitted to the management group of the corporation, which gave the following "notable examples in which the corporation and its divisions have been successful in 'sensing' the public relationship 'aspect' of situations, and in applying remedial measures at the source"; whether the words "public relationships" were mentioned in the discussions was not important.

(a) General Motors "headed off the 'business as usual' criticism following Pearl Harbor as applied to hoarding machine tools: by offering to others machines we could not use in war production."

(b) It avoided "any important charge" of war profiteering by voluntarily limiting war profits at the beginning of the war.

(c) It "made a conscious effort not to create 'war boom' or 'ghost' towns."

(d) Early in the war it "anticipated a potential state of chaos in handling the immediate postwar market for cars," and, to ensure the loyalty of dealers, established "a system of priorities in postwar car allotments for dealers who 'stuck through.'"

(e) "Early in 1943 the development of a bad manpower, housing and transportation situation in Trenton, N.J., as a result of Eastern Aircraft expansion was headed off: by community action initiated through the division."

(f) "In Dayton a hostile attitude toward General Motors and its divisions was thawed: by a public relations program put into operation locally through the Dayton Plant City Committee." [21]

5. The last example came from a leading public relations executive; this comes from a leading firm of public relations counsel, Hill & Knowlton. It was not intended for publication, but was selected from the firm's files by the La Follette Committee to illustrate the services it rendered. It provides an unusual opportunity of peeping behind the scenes—not indeed to discover the sensational, but for a view of the general run of public relations business. Don Knowlton is writing to tell prospective clients what Hill and Knowlton could do for them.

[21] Paul Garrett, *A Case Example in Public Relations* (privately printed, n.d.).

This was in 1937, but a letter written in similar circumstances today would sound very much the same.

Bender Body Company,   April 22nd, 1937
W. 62nd & Barberton Ave., Cleveland, Ohio.

Gentlemen:

At the suggestion of Mr. Parsons of Wm. J. Mericka & Co., we are making you the following proposal for developing and handling a program of publicity and public relations for your company:

PURPOSES

The purposes of a publicity and public relations program are:

(a) To make a company more widely known and its name more familiar to the general public throughout the country.

(b) To assist in the sales promotion of specific products.

(c) To see to it that facts and news about the company are correctly reported in the newspapers and magazines.

(d) Your company should, we believe, be interested in all of these objectives.

It would be to your advantage to have more people throughout the United States familiar with the name of your company and with its products. This would be beneficial both from the sales standpoint and from the standpoint of the standing and reputation of the company. It would be especially important when and as the stock of the company is listed on the exchange.

On the product promotion side, publicity in newspapers and magazines, particularly on trailers, would be a substantial aid in sales promotion.

From time to time there is news arising in your company in which newspapers are interested as a matter of course, and which you want to be sure is correctly presented. Included in such material would be news concerning earnings, personnel changes or promotions, announcements regarding new products, or anything that might develop in the labor situation. News materials of this sort should be properly prepared and given to the newspapers so that it will be correctly reported.

FUNCTION OF OUR ORGANIZATION

The firm of Hill and Knowlton is set up for the purpose of handling publicity and public relations for corporations and business organizations.

33

We act as a clearing house for all of the news arising in a company which we serve, and in addition create for our clients a large amount of material appearing in newspapers and magazines, which otherwise would not appear.

Our experience covers a rather broad field of industrial activity. We have offices in both Cleveland and New York. In the Cleveland territory we have among our clients, Republic Steel Corporation, The Warner & Swasey Company, The Austin Company, The Standard Oil Co. of Ohio, and a number of other concerns of comparable size. In our New York office we handle public relations for the American Iron & Steel Institute.

Particularly for The Austin Company and for Warner & Swasey we have consistently developed a great deal of publicity in trade and business magazines of the type which we believe your company would want in connection with buses and bus transportation.

For The Standard Oil Co. of Ohio we have developed a great deal of newspaper publicity on the subject of automobile travel and have developed a technique which we believe could successfully be applied to obtaining newspaper publicity for Bender trailers.

Examples of various types of publicity which we have obtained for some of our clients are attached so you may see the nature and scope of work which we do.

SPECIFIC PUBLICITY FIELDS TO BE DEVELOPED FOR BENDER BODY COMPANY

In the main, types of publicity which we believe might be developed for Bender Body Company are as follows:

1. *Institutional.*—Under this classification would fall general news about the company, dealing with its financial affairs, plant expansions, sales, personnel changes, etc.

2. *Special trade paper articles and trade paper material.*—We would undertake to secure publication of articles of a semi-technical or trade nature on the subject of bus transportation and allied subjects in transportation and other trade magazines—these articles dealing, of course, with Bender Body products.

3. *General articles.*—From time to time we would undertake to secure publication of articles in general business magazines which would be of a non-technical nature but would be designed to bring the name of the Bender Body Company before a larger number of business men. By way of illustration, one such article might be an article signed by someone in your company, discussing the problems

34

of school transportation, for publication in a magazine dealing with school problems. Another might be an article on trends in bus transportation, designed for publication in a magazine such as American Business, signed of course by someone in your company.

4. *Trailer publicity.*—This would be out-and-out product promotion publicity. It would be our aim to get as much publicity as we could on Bender trailers in newspapers, particularly in automobile sections. In addition, of course, considerable publicity on this subject could also be obtained in magazines. If possible, we would attempt to localize some of the trailer publicity so as to bring into the stories the names of local dealers.

COST AND METHOD OF HANDLING

It has been our experience that developing publicity for a company is a proposition which takes a considerable amount of time and continuity of effort. First of all, we must become familiar with the affairs and products of the company. It then takes some time before we can actually develop publicity material and get it into print. Over a period of months, efforts along this line are cumulative. For the first two or three months the amount of publicity obtained might be comparatively small—then, however, it begins to build up and by the end of six to nine months a steady volume of publicity might be maintained. Full results are often not apparent until more than a year has elapsed—for the simple reason that developing publicity for a company is a matter, to a large extent, of building up a company's reputation—and after such a reputation has been built up it then becomes easier to secure for the company a larger volume of publicity.

Owing to these facts, our business is set up upon a basis of a continuing arrangement on a flat monthly fee, plus out-of-pocket expenses.

Our fee for handling publicity and public relations for the Bender Body Company would be $500.00 a month. Out-of-pocket expenses would include such items as postage, mimeographing, traveling, if any, etc., incurred on behalf of the company.

In addition to the above, a substantial allowance would have to be made for expenses incurred in the securing and preparation of publicity material. Most of this would be in connection with trailer publicity. This would involve the taking of a great many photographs—possibly getting people to pose for some photographs. Prints or mats of photographs would have to be made for newspaper purposes and these would have to be mailed to various papers in different parts of the country. We would suggest that a minimum of $2,500.00 a year be allowed for preparation of publicity material.

Summing up, the outside expense of a publicity program of the type above described might involve setting aside a yearly budget of $10,000.00, of which $6,000.00 would represent the fee of Hill and Knowlton—with the other $4,000.00 allowed as a budget for the other items above mentioned, and with the understanding, of course, that only such portion of the $4,000.00 would be spent as was found necessary in the preparation and handling of publicity material.

We are sending a copy of this letter to Mr. Parsons.

Yours very truly,
DON KNOWLTON [22]

6. The New York smallpox epidemic of 1947 provides an excellent example of public relations as a tool of public administration.

It was the first smallpox epidemic since 1912, and the city was unprepared. Mayor O'Dwyer approved a proposal of the health authorities that there should be a voluntary campaign to vaccinate the whole population—nearly eight million people. The only possible method was public information and persuasion.

Speed was essential. To avoid panic was only less important than to get the people vaccinated. For both purposes the cooperation of the press was indispensable, and the newspapers were taken into complete confidence. They were told of the danger of panic and assured that all their questions would be answered frankly. To show that vaccination was painless and quick, the Commissioner of Health, Dr. Israel Weinstein, vaccinated every reporter who interviewed him, and squads of doctors were sent to vaccinate newspaper staffs at their work. The newspapers responded admirably. They exercised proper restraint; they checked rumors with the health authorities;

[22] Senate Committee on Education and Labor, *Subcommittee on Violations of Free Speech and Rights of Labor*, Hearings, Part 40, Exhibit 6301 (1939). This is part of the voluminous material collected for the famous La Follette Report. It is an important source for the study of public relations in practice.

they kept the story alive in their columns. All the publicity was directed to the single theme that vaccination is the only sure protection against smallpox. A public information center was set up. The help of labor unions and other groups was enlisted. The Commissioner spoke on the radio; radio spot announcements constantly reminded listeners of the campaign. Movie news and television companies at their own request were allowed to "shoot" an actual vaccination.

The campaign was a success. More than six million people were vaccinated, and the epidemic was checked.[23]

7. None but a few anti-vaccinationists would question the legitimacy of the last campaign. Few questioned the legitimacy of the great savings bond drives of the war. Robert K. Merton has made a fascinating case study of one episode in the wartime savings program which is interesting for several reasons. It illustrates the effectiveness of modern methods of mass persuasion in favorable conditions; it examines some of the resistances which had to be overcome, including the suspicion with which the ordinary man views the attentions of professional manipulators of opinion; it throws light on the psychology of the techniques which were employed; and it casts doubt upon the propriety of some of them.

Dr. Merton told the haunting story of a day in September 1943, when, as a marathon war bond drive, the radio star Kate Smith broadcast more than sixty times at quarter-hour intervals from 8:00 one morning until 2:00 the following morning. Many listeners were so exhilarated that they could not drag themselves from the loudspeaker; and the drive realized $39 million, in contrast with $1 million and $2 million in her previous all-day performances.

How did Kate Smith secure these remarkable results? The theme on which she chiefly relied was sacrifice: others included what Merton called participation (the sense of sharing in a common enterprise), competition (doing better than other places and helping Kate Smith to surpass previous drives), the "familial theme" ("get the boys back"), and facilitation (ease

---

[23] Karl Pretshold and Caroline C. Sulzer, "Speed, Action and Candor," *Channels*, 25 (1), September 1947.

of telephoning a promise to buy bonds). She appealed to patriotism, to sentiment, to guilt feelings, but not directly to self-interest—the advantages, for example, of saving for a rainy day.

"Linking herself with the cardinal American values," she addressed herself to her listeners' emotions rather than to their reason, and the personal rapport which she established with some of them was such that, though they realized that it was irrational, they fully expected that when they called she would answer the telephone in person. In so far as she argued her case, her chief point was that unless the public bought bonds the military would go short of supplies; she said nothing of the importance of savings as an anti-inflationary measure. Few listeners detected the fallacy in the first argument and the omission of the second.[24]

8. The Congress of Industrial Organizations won an award from the American Public Relations Association in 1946 for its success in winning support for a minority opinion.

In 1945 the CIO wanted to secure the support of the workers for its postwar program and to show that this was in the interests of the community as a whole. It was handicapped by lack of funds and by the control which hostile groups exercised over the mass media. It had the advantage of possessing an extensive local organization through its constituent unions and their six million members. One of the primary objects was to educate the members so that they could educate non-members.

News releases (an average of ten a week), press conferences and other familiar devices were used to make news and information readily and speedily available through the general press and radio. The Publicity Department "explored all possibilities for applying modern journalistic techniques"—among them comic strips, picture stories, women's and children's features—in order to increase the circulation of the *CIO News* and other publications.

A special campaign was necessary to get adequate radio facilities, in the face particularly of the refusal of time on the

[24] Robert K. Merton, *Mass Persuasion. The Social Psychology of a War Bond Drive* (New York, Harper, 1946).

ground that labor programs were controversial. The matter was taken to the Federal Communications Commission, and in the end the broadcasters' code "was revised to allow greater opportunity for labor to obtain paid or free time, and the National, Columbia, and American networks agreed to grant sustaining time to the major labor organizations for regular weekly programs." In these the CIO emphasized "simple popular presentation and an individualized approach, using the most modern and professional techniques of dramatization, music and entertainment, to attract and hold listeners of all shades of opinion." It obtained time for speeches by its leaders, arranged for them to take part in forum programs, and encouraged CIO unions to set up FM stations. Pamphleteering, "with a warmly human and concrete personal approach and with profuse illustrations," reinforced the more generalized impact of the other media.

Special attention was devoted to service men and veterans; publicity was supplemented by practical measures such as the provision of canteens and the establishment of servicemen's committees. Publications were regularly sent to "some 75,000 influencers of public opinion." Cooperation was maintained with church, business, farm and other organizations; unions with their own public relations machinery supported the main effort; special CIO committees on all kinds of national problems played an important part in the program as a whole.

Finally, said the CIO in describing the program, "attention must be called to the following two basic factors, which largely determine the success or failure of all CIO's public relations activities:

"1. The major policies of the CIO, as democratically determined at its conventions, and the actions of President Murray and other leaders in implementing these policies, are the basic determinant in all CIO public relations.

"2. The direct impact of CIO's 6,000,000 members on the communities in which they live—the human relationships established—is equally decisive. The personal contacts of CIO members, and the standing they and their local unions achieve through their community work, determine the opinion most citizens will have of the CIO even more than the most skillful work of public relations experts."

The campaign succeeded. More precisely, its chief purposes were achieved, though not necessarily entirely owing to the campaign. Most servicemen returned with marked labor sympathies; anti-labor hysteria was conspicuously absent, and most of the postwar strikes enjoyed wide community support; the standing of the CIO in national and international affairs was enhanced.[25]

9. Lastly, the delightful story of how, at a cost of $1,050, public relations was used to promote the reputation of a man who had been dead for more than a century.

The man was Tom Paine. Largely owing to his religious views, he had on several occasions failed to be elected to the Hall of Fame of New York University. The Thomas Paine Memorial Committee wanted to make sure that he would succeed in the elections of 1945. They hired a New York public relations counsel; the publisher of a new biography of Paine contributed part of the cost.

The counsel began by arranging a press release reporting that a statue of Paine which had been given to France by the memorial committee had been saved from the Germans, and was going to be restored by the French government. Editorial memoranda to the daily newspapers and the Negro press pointed out that America had failed to do Paine a similar honor, and suggested that it would be an appropriate time to remedy the neglect by adding this great champion of liberty to the Hall of Fame. The Negroes were reminded of his interest in emancipation. Paine's biographer, W. E. Woodward, went on the air, and script material was supplied to radio commentators.

It was discovered that when Paine returned from France in 1809 the city of New Rochelle had denied him the right to vote on the ground that by accepting honorary French nationality he had lost his American citizenship. It was suggested to the Mayor of New Rochelle that he should restore Paine's citizenship posthumously. The Mayor agreed, and the ceremony was

[25] Described by Lesly, *op. cit.*

the most publicized community event of Independence Day, 1945. All the major news broadcasts reported it. Senator James Mead read the Mayor's proclamation into the *Congressional Record*. Editorial comment began to appear. The columnists were interested.

The climate of opinion was sympathetic when the electors met, and this time Tom Paine got his niche in the Hall of Fame.[26]

Then, by way of contrast with methods which succeed best if they are not obtruded, there is "public relations advertising," in which public relations practice makes its most obvious impact on the general public. It has enjoyed a considerable vogue since the war, and has attracted to it an aura of novelty which is only partly justified. It flourished before the first World War, and had a wave of popularity immediately after 1918. *Editor and Publisher* commented in 1919 that:

"The drift seems to be strongly set toward advertising designed to sell POINTS OF VIEW, economic creeds, opinions, states of mind, to the people. The advertiser, with selfish purposes, with profit-motives, attempts to create a barrage of public opinion behind which he may operate in security. Should the newspaper make this possible for him?" [27]

"Public relations advertising" is advertising which, as the *Editor and Publisher* said, is "designed to sell POINTS OF VIEW, economic creeds, opinions, states of mind, to the people." The state of mind may be simply an impression that the advertiser is a worthy citizen—as with advertisements contributed to charitable causes and to government publicity. This is "public service" advertising. It finds organized expression in the Advertising Council, which will be described in a later chapter.

Or the advertisement columns may be used as a public platform for the ventilation of views on current issues which affect the advertiser's interests. It has long been a weapon in the settlement of strikes. In the Bell telephone strike of 1947 the union complained that the company had an unfair advantage because its greater resources enabled it to make more use of ad-

[26] Described by Lesly, *op. cit.*
[27] February 15, 1919, quoted by Lee, *The Daily Newspaper*, 456.

vertising. The same platform is used to tell the public about longer term policies and how they serve the public interest.

Many business corporations have gone further; large sums have been spent on publicity to promote the reputation and policies of American business in general. In 1947 and 1948 corporations advertised widely on such themes as the efficiency of American business, the importance of productivity in raising standards of life, the equitable distribution of the proceeds of business enterprise, the widespread ownership of American industry, the dependence of the employee upon capital for his job and the highest earnings in the world.

In the *Saturday Evening Post* of May 22, 1948, "America's *business*-managed, tax-paying, electric light and power companies" published photographs illustrating "the neighborly doings of electric company people"—how one taught a blind woman to cook, others helped to organize cattle shows for young farmers, and another saved the lives of two little girls. The Bell Telephone System asked: "Who pays for telephone expansion?" and answered: "Investors do." And the National Association of Manufacturers showed that when everything was added up, "just about every family in America today is a part 'owner' of business," and explained one of the miracles of the American profit system:

"For, while most Americans think 10 to 15 cents out of each dollar of sales would be a *fair* profit for business to make—government figures show that industry averages less than half that much! And that half of what industry does make goes right back into business to pay for the development that brings more Americans more good things than are enjoyed by any other people on earth!"

That was public relations advertising. So were American Heritage advertising by business undertakings in connection with the Freedom Train, the advertisements of United States Steel explaining the rise in steel prices early in 1948, the General Electric series of the same year opposing wage increases on the ground that "if there were a 3rd round the referee might get knocked out," and AFL advertisements attacking the Taft-Hartley Bill in 1947.

So far this chapter has been largely concerned with the high-lights. For the most part, however, public relations in practice means the handling of disconnected and usually trivial incidents arising from the day-to-day impact upon their environment of many thousands of organizations, large and small, important and unimportant. The president of a university is going to make a speech. He may need the help of his public relations director in preparing it: he will certainly need help in distributing it to the press and radio. There are changes in the faculty: a news release is necessary, and inquiries have to be answered. The local community is in uproar because a Left-wing speaker is to address a student group: should a public statement be made? A professor is arrested or elected to Congress: how is the incident to be presented? Press photographers must be given facilities for a dramatic performance. A benefaction is received: it must be fittingly acknowledged in a way which will encourage others to be equally generous. The alumni bulletin must meet its deadline.

The majority of public relations practitioners have few opportunities for ambitious adventures in mass persuasion, and modern practice stresses the importance of pinpointing the target as far as possible. Hence the compartments into which it is common to divide public relations—"customer relations," "dealer relations," "stockholder relations," "government relations," "employee relations," "community relations," "alumni relations," "faculty relations," "student relations," "parent relations," and so on indefinitely. Each compartment requires more or less specialized handling, and each involves a continuous operation which needs skillful attention to detail rather than a flair for the spectacular. Some of the most interesting technical developments have occurred in these specialized areas.

Concentration upon "employee" and "stockholder" relations has emphasized the inadequacy of old-fashioned methods of conveying information to the man in the street. There has been a remarkable proliferation of publications for employees—the technique itself goes back at least to the middle of the last century—and the content and presentation of reports to stockholders have been improved: corresponding improvements have taken place in the reporting of governmental bodies, universities and social welfare agencies. Along with it all has gone quickened experiment with alternatives to the printed word, such as the comic strip, the movie, and the "open house," and with methods such as readability formulae by which written material may be made easier to understand. And there has been growing interest in scientific methods of gauging opinions and attitudes; they would be used more but for the relatively high cost and the limitations on their practical usefulness in matters of day to day management.

For most of these purposes the public relations man must make use of other specialists—radio writers, film producers, advertising agents, opinion researchers, readability experts, specialists in employee magazines or plant tours or exhibits, and so forth. By comparison with these his talents are generalized. His is the broad view. He is the coordinator, and the liaison officer between his firm and other communication experts. He must decide when outside help is required and from whom it can be best obtained. It is his duty to translate the requirements of management to the outside specialist, and he will often have to interpret the latter's advice to management and follow through action upon it.

Nobody knows how many people are engaged in public relations in the United States. It would indeed be a difficult calculation to make, in view of the variety in the descriptions under which they operate and—the other way round—the heterogeneity of the activities which are combined with public relations. A prospective client who referred to the *Public Relations Yearbook and Directory* in 1945 would have found at the one extreme of specialization a "funeral service public relations counsel" (in California, if this need be said), and at the extreme of catholicity a firm which ranged over "public relations planning, publicity, wage and salary administration, incentive programs, research and organization surveys, personnel procedures, labor relations," and the versatile "orator, advertising stylist, and executor of several historic publicity and promotion

44

projects," who offered "Industrial Design, Public Relations, Product Design, Product Development, and . . . the design technique in advertising, merchandising, and all the processes of marketing." It might be thought that precise figures would be obtainable for the federal government if nowhere else, but, as we shall see, the calculation is not only clouded by political controversy, but would present insoluble problems of definition even to an entirely disinterested statistician.

If account is taken of all who are directly and indirectly employed in public relations on a wide interpretation of the term —including those engaged on routine duties and on the actual production of publicity material—the total may well run into six figures. If the calculation is confined to those whose responsibilities or qualifications are up to the standards laid down for membership of the public relations associations, it may not exceed 10,000. The associations had about 3,000 members in 1948, but their coverage was far from complete. In the same year, as we have seen, the Manhattan telephone directory listed 336 "public relations counselors" and 232 "publicity service bureaus." Usage varied from place to place, but there were 115 "counselors" and 57 "publicity service bureaus" in Chicago, 101 "public relations advisors" and 17 under "publicity" in Washington, D.C.—note the significant difference in the proportions—, 51 entries under "public relations service" in San Francisco and 23 under publicity (1947), 8 "consultants" and 8 publicity firms in St. Paul and Minneapolis, 28 "counselors" and 4 publicity firms in Detroit, 20 "counselors" and 10 under publicity in Cleveland (1947), 9 "counselors" and 5 under publicity in Greater Houston (1947), and 5 "counselors" and one under publicity in New Orleans.

It would be interesting to study the density of public relations and publicity services in different cities, but that is not the immediate point. Some of the publicity firms have no place in a calculation which deals with public relations—often they are merely production agencies for publicity material. The same may be true of some which appear in the public relations category. But many of the publicity firms are indistinguishable from most of the public relations counselors, others have public relations departments, and some appear under both headings, as was the case, for example, with all the Greater Houston "publicity agents."

It cannot be far wrong to say that the number of firms engaged in public relations activities in the great cities in 1948—whether they used the term or not—was of the rough order of about a thousand, and the number of individuals holding responsible positions in them a good many more. This would account for the large majority of the practitioners in independent practice, though some addition would have to be made for the public relations departments of advertising agencies; but several times as many people must have been employed in responsible public relations positions in business undertakings, government, educational institutions, labor unions, welfare agencies, churches, political parties, and other organizations which offer openings to the "new profession." The American Public Relations Association quoted an estimate in *Pic* magazine in 1948 that 15,000 to 25,000 people were employed in public relations, including about 1,000 "qualified" as public relations counsel.[28] It left a wide margin for error, and in the absence of a precise definition of "public relations" its guess may be as good as any.

Some may complain that the account of public relations in practice in this chapter has done less than justice to the activities of the practitioners who operate in the higher regions of management, and that more should have been said about the contribution which they make in shaping the policies which they subsequently interpret and present. It is a sufficient answer that what has been attempted is to give a broad picture of public relations as it is actually practiced in the United States whether the milieu is Greater Houston, New Orleans, or the more sophisticated circles of Manhattan. The stratospheric practitioners are few in relation to the total even in New York City and in the bigger business corporations. It may be that they are the pioneers who are pointing the way which the generality will soon follow. That is a question which will be discussed in the

[28] *Washington P.R. News-Letter, op. cit.*

next chapter. Here we are concerned with the facts as they are. This minority have their place, and it is important beyond its quantity, but in an objective analysis of the whole scene it would be misleading to suggest that it was not quantitatively very small; they are numerically fewer than the artists in stunts and ballyhoo whom they regard as outmoded relics of the past.

CHAPTER 3

"PHILOSOPHY" OR "MUMBO JUMBO"?

IT IS a commonplace that what people say is often most revealing for the light which it throws upon themselves. This is certainly true of much that has been said about the "philosophy" of public relations. It would be a mistake to take the philosophizing very seriously. Strictly speaking there is no such thing as a "philosophy" of public relations. At its best the goal of the discussion is a rationale or *raison d'être* which will justify the participants' activities to themselves and to the world. At its worst it is sales talk calculated to create rather than dispel the mystery which is a valuable stock in trade of the spurious. Very often it is the confused expression of the hopes and aspirations of sincere men and women whose conviction of their importance to society outruns the facts and their capacity for orderly thought. There is more than a little substance in the charge that there is a "mumbo jumbo" of public relations.[1]

"In much that I hear and read about public relations," said Raymond Rubicam in 1948, "I am confused by the mystery with which the subject is surrounded, and I have to fight to cut through the high-flown language with which its simple nature is hidden from view."[2]

There are those of whom George A. Pettitt, assistant to the president of the University of California, complained that they

[1] e.g. Joseph G. Herzberg in *Late City Edition,* edited by him (New York, Holt, 1947), 227; and Roger William Riis, *New Leader,* May 17, 1947.

[2] Raymond Rubicam, *"Management's Use of Public Relations to Serve Freedom of Enterprise and Human Welfare"* (Boston University School of Public Relations, 1948), 1.

"tend to give the impression that their knowledge is a revelation from on high rather than something to be developed out of the facts of the activity to which it is applied." [3] A theme which often recurs is that the best results will be secured by following the teachings of Christ. Other public relations exponents rely overmuch on analogy and metaphor. Innumerable examples could be quoted. Public relations is a "philosophy and method of practice before the bar of public opinion." [4] It will lead to "the creation of a public conscience." [5] "While still adolescent it finds itself charged with the staggering task of protecting a whole nation's economic virtue." [6]

It is easy to get trapped in abstractions:

"Granting appropriate research and a receptive attitude towards its conclusions, the action will probably involve both a correction of the undesirable as well as an introduction of the desirable on a wider basis and perhaps also to a greater degree. The indicated action may be more or less extensive and costly and also restrictive as far as past practices are concerned. . . .

"Each of these three major considerations [research, receptivity, action] can and will be fulfilled best only when, as and if the persons concerned with a given public relations situation have placed themselves in a position to understand the broad requirements involved in each of the three steps.

"There is a final factor. It has multiple locations. It comes before Research and also after it. It comes before Receptivity and also after it. It comes before Action and also after it. . . . It is *objectives*." [7]

[3] *Public Relations Journal*, 3 (2), February 1947, 21.

[4] William H. Baldwin and Raymond C. Mayer, "On Buying Public Relations," *Public Opinion Quarterly*, 8 (2), Summer 1944, 231. The writers both held prominent positions in the National Association of Public Relations Counsel.

[5] Edward L. Bernays, *Crystallizing Public Opinion* (New York, Boni and Liveright, 1923), 218.

[6] Martin Dodge, *Public Relations Journal*, 2 (12), December 1946, 4.

[7] Clark Belden, Foreword to *Trade Association Executives and Public Relations* (Report of the Public Relations Committee of the American Trade Association Executives, Washington, D.C., 1945), v. The author, executive secretary of the New England Gas Association, was mentioned by the Griswolds in *Your Public Relations* as one of the leading pioneers in public relations.

Or, "the art of public relations is the facility with which a business deliberately and unselfishly lets the greater public interest mold and guide every phase of its activity—an operating philosophy which earns a right to serve the public and contribute to the social and economic welfare." [8]

Or, "Public relations . . . is the conscious reflection of a way of life toward a determined objective." [9]

Too much weight should not be given to verbal exuberances that are by no means a monopoly of the public relations world, but these examples could easily be multiplied and it would be wrong to pass them over as lacking in significance. They illustrate the widespread uncertainty which was exemplified by the replies when in 1947 *Public Relations News* invited definitions of public relations from its subscribers—"who, we felt, comprised the best cross-section of public relations brains in the country." Two thousand replies produced "a variety of concepts. They said that public relations is a science; a system; an art; a process; a function; a relationship; a humanizing genius; a term; a business; a profession; a method; an activity; a program; a policy; a pattern of behavior; a moral force." [10]

It was a remarkable demonstration of the desire to rationalize their activities which is so marked a characteristic of the public relations group. Defining public relations has been a favorite pastime at annual conferences and in the correspondence columns of the periodicals.

Amidst the confusion three main theories about the boundaries of public relations as a specialist activity can be discerned. The oldest and most firmly established is that it is primarily a matter of technical skill in influencing opinions and attitudes through the mass media. Those who subscribe to the other views think that this does not go far enough. The second school of thought argues that the sphere of the public relations specialist should embrace all the relations between an organization and the public because all contribute to its impact on public

[8] Francis W. Lovejoy, in *Lectures and Discussions on Public Relations* (San Francisco, American Council on Public Relations, 1941), 24.

[9] Baldwin and Mayer, 230.

[10] Denny Griswold, *Public Relations Comes of Age* (Boston University School of Public Relations, 1947), 3.

opinion. The third view is that the impact which is made depends above all else on the policies pursued and that the public relations specialist should share in the formulation of general policy on the ground that the probable effect on the public should be a primary factor in settling policy. The latter two views are often held together; they have much in common, and shade into one another.

Each of these alternatives is attractive to ambitious men and women who are anxious to extend their activities and to improve their status. Each is plausible. Each starts from a premise which is incontestable. It is undeniable that an institution's reputation will be affected by all its relations with the public and by the policies which it pursues. No amount of publicity by a transportation company will make up for wide-spread discourtesy by its employees or for failure on its own part to replace obsolete vehicles when it can manifestly afford to do so.

So far so good. These are truisms, though they need to be repeated. The issue is not, however, the importance of public relations in both senses. It is whether the special competence of the public relations practitioner—as he exists or is likely to exist—qualifies him either for a general supervisory or coordinating role over all relations with the public, or for participation in top level policy decisions. To go a step further, even if he is qualified, is he better qualified than specialists in other aspects of management?

The danger to the aspirations of the public relations group in both views is that they are so all-embracing as virtually to deny the need for employing specialists at all. It is particularly acute for the theory that all activities which impinge on the public should be within the province of the public relations specialist.

The difficulties are illustrated by a bird's-eye view of the field to be covered which Rex F. Harlow gave in 1945:

"Most competent public relations men would recognize that public relations includes all that is thought, said and done to create and maintain effective relations between an institution and its publics. Public relations is a broad term which covers an enormous range of activities. It includes personal relations, personnel relations, industrial relations, stockholder relations, board-of-director relations; customer relations, government relations and supplier-creditor relations; community relations and trade relations; opinion surveys, advertising, publicity, semantics, etc. Necessarily, public relations rests upon the social sciences; economics, sociology, psychology, political science, history and philosophy, to mention only a few of the more conspicuously related fields. In addition, public relations is generally taken to include such working tools as the press, the radio, motion pictures, printing, public speaking and professional writing." [11]

"But," Dr. Harlow went on, "it is absurd to think that we can build a workable profession within an organized body of principles, practices and tools, upon such a broad general base as the above. We have to set up limits. We must define scope. We are forced to make a selection of some of the more important specialized phases of the broad field, and build these into a profession."

That is the nub of the difficulty. If in fact public relations covers such an "enormous range of activities," where is the logic in basing the new profession only upon some of them? If it is absurd to base a "workable profession" upon them all, a necessarily arbitrary distinction must be drawn between those activities which the public relations group is to undertake, and those which are to be left to others.

It would not be unfair to say that this view of the sphere which public relations practitioners should occupy is partly due to a confusion of language. It assumes that there is a necessary connection between "public relations" as a term of art for a specialist activity and "public relations" in the literal sense of relations with the public. "Put the two words together in a different way," said Paul Garrett, "and you have 'relations with the public.'" [12] "Every meeting between 'the government' and the citizen," according to James L. McCamy, "is an episode in the

---

[11] Harlow, 554.

[12] Paul Garrett, *Public Relations—Industry's No. 1 Job*, Address to the Annual Convention of the American Association of Advertising Agencies, April 22, 1938 (privately printed, 1938).

complex flow of public relations." [13] According to W. Emerson Reck, it is bad college public relations for a professor to appear with dirty finger nails or untidy clothes.[14] As part of its public relations training, the New York Central Railroad System gave employees advice on letter writing and answering the telephone. Say "Dear Mr. Blank" instead of "Dear Sir," prefer "We are all genuinely sorry" to "We regret," and start a letter with "you" instead of "we" or "I." When the telephone rings, say "Sir" or "Madam," and not "Brother," "Sister," or "Lady." [15]

All this is valuable in its place. It is true in one sense that everybody who has dealings with the public is engaged in public relations. It is important to force home the point that publicity is no substitute for good administration, no easy way out for the lazy or the careless or the incompetent. What does not follow is that matters like these are or should be within the competence of the public relations specialist as he actually exists.

Indeed, to the extent that public relations is "just plain, ordinary, good common sense," "merely human decency which flows from a good heart," "a way of living, an attitude toward people, good habits and conduct reflecting in every contact with others," "applicable to all human relationships," or "endows a corporation with that which in an individual would be good manners and good morals," [16] it should be the affair of every executive, and it should not be necessary to employ a specialist.

To the extent that public relations depends on well-trained salesmen, clerks, or doorkeepers, on the location of buildings where they will be most convenient for the public, on their architecture or the color of their paint, or on the way in which

[13] James L. McCamy, *Government Publicity* (University of Chicago Press, 1939), vii.

[14] Reck, "Public Relations: A Team Job," *op. cit.*

[15] *Company Manners* (New York Central System pamphlet, n.d.).

[16] Lovejoy, 35; Charles T. Plackard, quoted in Dwight Hillis Plackard and Clifton Blackmon, *Blueprint for Public Relations* (New York, McGraw-Hill, 1947), 100; *Public Relations in Action*, 164; Lesly, v; James W. Irwin in *Public Relations Directory and Yearbook*, 75.

letters are drafted, it is the business of other specialists. It should not need a director of public relations to tell a college president—as was done in *How to Use Letters in College Public Relations,* a volume devoted to "the use of personal letters to vitalize and personalize public relations"—that he should sign his letters personally and avoid hackneyed phrases such as "Yours of —— came to hand." [17] Waste, friction and confusion will be the price if the public relations director tries to do the work of other departments. He may be able to help them, but that is another question, to which we shall come back.

Those who hold that the public relations specialist should take part in formulating policy agree that his skill in the arts of communication is important, but maintain that he will not be effective unless he is a good deal more—in particular unless he is an expert in interpreting the public to his employers and in advising his employers how to shape their policies in order to enlist public support. He may do his most successful work when by a word at a board meeting he saves the board from a course which will bring public discredit or persuades it to adopt policies which with little or no publicity will evoke a favorable response.

The factor common to each theory is that the ultimate object of public relations activities is mass persuasion. The peculiar feature of the approach which has just been described is the stress which is laid on the part of the public relations specialist in shaping the product which the "publics" are to be persuaded to accept. Nobody in his senses would refuse to listen to an expert publicist when he suggests that it will be hard to put over a particular course persuasively, and that the same purpose could be secured in another way which it would be easier to make palatable to the public. That again is not the issue. The public relations practitioner's claim to advise on the presentation of policy to the public can hardly be challenged.

The issue which is posed by those who hold that the place of the public relations practitioner is in top management is whether he is also exceptionally qualified to advise on the

[17] William H. Butterfield, *How to Use Letters in College Public Relations* (New York, Harper, 1944).

substance of policy. It cannot be decided *a priori.* The onus is on the public relations specialist, whose status as a communication expert is acknowledged, to prove that he possesses this important extra qualification. And not because he personally happens to be specially gifted, but because his special training and experience fit him for the wider responsibility. It is the more difficult for him to do so because he cannot fail to arouse the jealousy of other specialists who will not gladly admit his superior claims, and because he may expect a lukewarm reception from those already in the top levels of management who are accustomed to take their competence in matters of general policy for granted and do not feel the need for help from the "new profession." "Management" is used here in a wide sense. What has been said is as true of heads of government agencies and of university presidents as of business executives.

It is only natural that, as Holcombe Parkes, public relations vice president of the National Association of Manufacturers, told the Fifth Conference of Business Public Relations Executives in 1948, "the lawyers, the accountants, the personnel boys frequently view [public relations activities] with alarm and veto with what seems to be a fiendish glee." [18] The attitude of the other specialists who resent the encroachments of the specialists in public relations was neatly focused by a spokesman of advertising, Henry Obermeyer, who was arguing that there was no fundamental distinction between public relations and advertising: "There have been a lot of fancy definitions of public relations, some of them arrogating even the prime functions of management. Business at large will reduce most of these high-flown conceptions to a common denominator, which is the skilled communication of ideas with the object of producing a desired result." [19]

There is no denying that the more ambitious definitions of public relations involve the participation of the public relations

---

[18] *Proceedings* of the Fifth National Conference of Business Public Relations Executives, February 5–6, 1948 (New York, National Association of Manufacturers, 1948, processed), 43. Quoted subsequently as *Business Public Relations Executives.*

[19] Henry Obermeyer, "Is Advertising Losing Out?" *Printer's Ink,* 222 (6), February 6, 1948, 136.

director or counsel in the prime functions of management. Not that their authors would wish to deny it. If, as Paul Garrett said in 1938, "public relations is not a specialized activity like production, engineering, finance, sales," but "runs through all these as the theme for each," and "is an operating philosophy that management must seek to apply in everything it does and says," [20] the only place for it is at the very top.

That is the logical conclusion even of such comparatively modest statements as this by the American Public Relations Association: "Knowledge of public interests + policies in the public interest + merchandising your good policies = profitable public relations." [21] According to a definition widely publicized by the editors of *Public Relations News:*

"Public relations is the management function which evaluates public attitudes, identifies the policies and procedures of an individual or organization with the public interest, and executes a program of action to earn public understanding and acceptance." [22]

Paul Garrett has said that public relations must help business to adjust its policy to political, economic, social, and other changes and the challenges which they bring.[23] Ben S. Trynin, research director of the American Council of Public Relations, described "the ultima thule" of scientific research as "study of the bases of social conflict—the occurrence of which the entire total of public relations efforts hopes, and strives strenuously, to avert." [24] "The function of the specialist on public relations," said Professor Harold D. Lasswell in 1941, "is nothing less than the discovery of how to adapt an enterprise to the total environment in which it operates. This means that he is a specialist on human attitudes as they are distributed in a given society." [25]

[20] Garrett, *Public Relations—Industry's No. 1 Job*, 8.
[21] *Your Public Relations Executive* (American Public Relations Association and Executive Service Corporation leaflet, 1948).
[22] Denny Griswold, 3.
[23] Garrett, *Public Relations—Industry's No. 1 Job, op. cit.*
[24] Ben S. Trynin, "Research in the Public Relations Field, 1946 A.D.," *Public Relations Journal*, 2 (1), January 1946, 36.
[25] Harold D. Lasswell, *Democracy through Public Opinion* (Menasha, Banta Publishing Co., 1941), 71–2.

So it is urged that one of the most important tasks of public relations men is to ensure that managements follow policies which are in the public interest and—what is not necessarily the same thing—in consonance with the dynamics of the age. It is ambitious doctrine. The difficulties of applying it in government are self-evident, and we can leave for the present how far it makes sense even as an objective in other spheres and how far it is likely to carry conviction with the hardheaded executive. Its exponents must first of all prove the special competence of public relations practitioners to discharge general management duties.

Hence the pains which have been taken to show that they are more than merely specialists in mass communication. In substantiating this claim they are faced with a difficult choice. They can try to show that they are experts in the social sciences which can make a special contribution to management problems; or they can rely on qualifications of personality and experience. The public relations counsel, advertised Edward L. Bernays in 1946, is "the modern technician in social sciences . . . who is qualified by education, professional training and experience to apply science to practical problems." [26] Bernays' own professional advice, another advertisement claimed in 1949, was "based on a rare combination of *knowledge* of theoretical psychology, sociology and other social sciences, and of *practical achievement*." [27] Verne Burnett, formerly vice president in charge of public relations for General Foods, recommended the would-be public relations counsel to study "history, literature, semantics, economics, sociology, religion, philosophy, psychology, psychoanalysis; business, finance, journalism, labor relations, and government." [28] Claude Robinson in 1949 was almost as ambitious—"economics, political science, sociology, psychology, philosophy, logic, literature, statistics, accounting, journalism, and public speaking." [29]

[26] Advertisement in *New Republic*, December 23, 1946.
[27] Advertisement in *New York Times*, December 6, 1949.
[28] Verne Burnett, *You and Your Public; A Guide Book to the New Career—Public Relations* (New York, Harper, revised ed., 1947), 182.
[29] Claude Robinson, "Education in Public Relations," *Public Relations Journal*, 5 (2), February 1949, 12.

Not the least of the difficulties which confront writers who describe the public relations practitioner as an expert in the social sciences (with a good deal more thrown in) is that their picture has no relevance to the qualifications possessed by the overwhelming majority of those engaged in public relations. The facts are against them. Most practitioners— in business, government, education, wherever they are—have graduated from journalism, and Sussmann found that only a handful of the group she studied had degrees with majors in social sciences, much less commanded a battery of the social sciences.[30]

Public relations has been described with much truth as a "safety valve against overpopulation in the newspaperman's world." [31] "It has been almost an unwritten law," said an old hand, Pendleton Dudley, in 1949, "that a beginner in the profession must have been a newspaper reporter." [32] It is also doubtful whether top management would be much impressed by a parade of high academic qualifications in the social sciences. The status of social scientists is neither so assured nor so elevated that all the doors would at once be thrown open. Their experience in Washington during and since the war is pertinent.

In the face of the facts it is tempting to fall back on the argument that personality and experience count for more than formal education. "Whatever his formal education," said Bernays himself, "the public relations counsel needs sensitivity, and self-propelled appetite for knowledge and experience, more than degrees . . . His textbooks are the facts of life—culled from newspaper and magazine articles; advertisements, billboards; smoking-room anecdotes; Wall Street gossip; legislative speeches; or theological discourse." [33]

[30] Sussmann, 700.

[31] Millard Faught, "Postwar Public Relations," *Tide*, 20 (10), March 8, 1946, 19.

[32] Pendleton Dudley, "Qualifications for Public Relations Management," in Griswolds, *Your Public Relations*, 56.

[33] Edward L. Bernays, *Public Relations* (Boston, Bellman Publishing Co., 1945), 15.

Pendleton Dudley thought that perhaps the most important requirements were "the gift of human sympathy and understanding, a rare mixture of integrity and courage, and a warm and genial personality which invites confidence while expressing conviction"; a college degree, though helpful, was not essential, but at the same time no profession demanded so broad a background of knowledge and culture.[34] The Code of Ethics of the American Public Relations Association bound members to "consider the practice of public relations as based upon broad general knowledge; logical and objective thinking; discretion; tact; imagination; talent of expression; an active desire to understand and help people; and, above all, absolute integrity."

Examples to the same effect could be multiplied. As a foundation for the more ambitious claims they share one serious limitation. Far from being distinctive, the qualities in question are just those which should be possessed by men who want to make a success of any job involving the handling of people. They are as likely to be found among advertising executives and "personnel boys" and other rivals as among public relations specialists. To rely on them in support of the claim to admission to higher management is to abandon the attempt to give it an objective foundation at all.

It is also a mistake to argue from the few outstanding public relations counsel and executives who have succeeded in gaining recognition as general advisers on policy by virtue of expert knowledge in the social sciences or personal qualities and experience. The presumption is that they are the aberration, and the vast majority are the norm. For this majority there is no future in a conception which subordinates their specialist qualifications to an ill-defined general role for which they are unfitted. And there is really no doubt that their special skills lie in the field of communication. This was the common denominator in the examples of public relations in practice which were given in the last chapter. It is the only view which is consistent with the facts about the men and women who constitute the

[34] Dudley, in Griswolds, 55.

"new profession." With few exceptions they share a common background of experience in mass communication, usually journalism; and this is as true of government, for example, as of business and private public relations practice. It is contrary to common sense that mere change of milieu should bring about any fundamental transformation of the former news- papermen and publicists.

What of the future? A glance at public relations courses in universities and colleges does not suggest that the picture is likely to change substantially. There is no prospect of the market being flooded by Mr. Bernays' social science tech- nicians. It is no wonder that, as Donald W. Krimel of the University of Ohio School of Journalism said in 1947, the pro- fessors who have to plan the courses "aren't finding it a partic- ularly easy case." [35] The siren song of the higher public rela- tions thought draws them in one direction. They are drawn in the other by the practical needs of students who will have to find jobs at a more prosaic level and by the impossibility of turning out publicity technicians who are also trained social scientists.

The dilemma is illustrated by the early history of the School of Public Relations at Boston University. It was based on the former School of Journalism. Three of the four divisions dealt with techniques of communication—Journalism, Radio and Speech, Motion Pictures and Visual Aids. The fourth was the Division of Public Relations. The School's prospectus for 1947– 1948 offered students the opportunity of learning "the science and art of public relations." Since the turn of the century, it explained, "a definite philosophy with systematic procedures" had been worked out, and the School would teach "the funda- mentals of public relations theory, its history and principles, its ethics and psychology." Most of the first year's courses were purely practical; in the second year a more even balance was struck, but instruction in communication techniques continued to predominate. Twelve hours were required in the courses dealing with the social sciences underlying public relations,

[35] Donald W. Krimel, "Problems in Public Relations Training," *Public Opinion Quarterly,* 11 (4), Winter 1947–48, 540.

twelve in basic courses in the arts of communication, and nine to eleven in elective courses which the students were advised to choose from one of the other three divisions so that they might have specialized training in a particular medium. Social sciences meant in this context such subjects as "Public opinion and propaganda," "Social patterns affecting public relations," and "Forecasting and planning public relations," including "the logistics of synchronized media use, attitude development and organizational extension." Subjects suggested for graduate study included the "dynamics of organization," "logistics of public relations planning," and "sociometrics and public relations."

Graduates of schools like this may be the better for seeing their jobs in a wider perspective and learning some of the ways in which the social sciences can help them. It is out of the question that they should be fully rounded social scientists or qualified to advise on management in general.

In fact few public relations practitioners outside a narrow circle think of themselves as social scientists, and, paradoxically, the most important practical application of the social sciences in the field of public opinion is tending to restrict the scope of public relations practice. Instead of the scientific methods of measuring opinion and attitudes becoming tools in the public relations kit, public relations practitioners, like others, have had to turn to a new and distinct category of specialists when they want to use them. They have not given up their own claims as interpreters of public opinion, but they base them on experience and intuition and not on skill in using scientific techniques. This does not mean that their role is passive, when use has to be made of research organizations. It falls naturally to the public relations department to provide the link with the outside specialist, and in present circumstances a very useful purpose can be served by an intermediary who can interpret the needs of his employer to the scientists and their findings to his employer.

It is, therefore, as an expert in using the techniques of mass persuasion that the public relations practitioner must be judged. According to Smith, Lasswell, and Casey, the public relations counsel is a "business communication specialist," along with advertising men, industrial relations experts, press agents, and publicity men.[36]

Generally speaking, there are two situations in which there is a prima facie case for employing specialists: (a) when special skills or aptitudes are required; and (b) when continuity of contact with particular groups is important.

A public relations specialist meets the need for special skill in mass persuasion, and for experts in handling the mass media. But how is he to be distinguished from other "communication specialists"? First, he is relatively unspecialized: he employs all or any of the media according to the needs of the particular case. Secondly, he works through media which he does not control and which do not control him, though this does not prevent him from going into direct production, as with employee magazines, exhibits, plant tours, motion pictures. Thirdly, he acts not for himself but for other people; whether he is paid by salary or by fee, he is a hired man. Taken separately, none of these characteristics is peculiar to him, but, taken together, they distinguish the public relations group from other categories of communication specialist—advertising men, newspapermen, writers, broadcasters, etc., not excluding the press agents from whom it is descended.

As for the much discussed question of where to draw the line between public relations and publicity, a study of actual usage provides little guidance, and suggests that there is a distinction without much significant difference. It is possible to turn to most public relations and to most publicity firms for the same services, and most public relations directors and most publicity directors are doing jobs which are hard to distinguish. It may be that the terms should be more clearly demarcated. If so, "publicity" might be used to describe the technicians who are actually responsible for the execution of publicity programs.

For the present, "public relations" and "publicity" overlap in practice, and we may sum up by saying that the public

[36] Bruce Lannes Smith, Harold D. Lasswell, and Ralph D. Casey, *Propaganda, Communication, and Public Opinion: A Comprehensive Reference Guide* (Princeton University Press, 1946), 255 seq.

relations-publicity practitioner is a communication specialist who is in the market for hire by anybody who needs expert but generalized help in conveying information and views to the public or sections of the public, and in persuading the public to do as he wants. In other words, he is an expert in managing communication with the public—communication in both directions. This does not mean that he is responsible for all such communication on the part of his employer: his services are needed only when specialist help is required. "This," said Averell Broughton (later president of the Public Relations Society of America) in 1943, "is really the field of public information, whether provided about an individual, a business corporation, a town or community, a nation or nations, or just a new idea." [37]

In modern conditions public information means mainly though not exclusively information through the mass media. The expert help which the public relations practitioner can give derives mainly though not exclusively from his knowledge of the mass media and how to use them. The purpose of information is almost always persuasion—even in government, which, as we shall see, is the marginal case—, and he will not do his job of mass information and persuasion with maximum effect if he is a mere publicity technician or works in a watertight compartment. His special qualifications do not entitle him to act as a general adviser on policy or to oversee every activity which impinges on the public. At the same time he must watch every facet of his employer's activities for opportunities to present them to the public, and he must not fail to draw attention to any aspects which make the task of interpretation more difficult, even where they involve questions of policy. He will be unwise to trespass on the fields of his specialist colleagues, but they will need his help on matters which call for his specialized skills.

Just as the labor relations department would naturally look to the legal counsel for advice on the legal aspects of an industrial dispute, so it would turn to the public relations di-

[37] Averell Broughton, *Careers in Public Relations: The New Profession* (New York, Dutton, 1943), 17.

63

rector when it came to communicating the management point of view to employees and the general public. It would not look to him as a matter of course before introducing improved conditions even though the object was to improve "employee relations." The sales department might ask for help in a campaign to introduce a new product: it would not ordinarily do so before appointing new sales representatives, though this might be of the highest importance to "dealer" and "customer relations."

We shall return in Part III to the reasons for the increased importance of "public relations" in the American society. Its development as a specialized function reflects the demands upon the system of communications by those who wish to speak to the public and can afford to hire experts for the purpose. That explains why it has come to be chiefly associated with relatively wealthy groups and institutions. These include big business corporations and trade associations, universities, public authorities, and to an increasing extent labor unions.

It would be a mistake to identify public relations with propaganda for the vested interests which can afford to use it most. In modern conditions it is an indispensable tool of administration for every public institution and many private ones. This is true even where it is not recognized and where no specialist is employed. It is necessary to tell a community about the facilities of its public library. It is good administration and good democratic practice for a city government to report regularly and intelligibly to the people. A settlement house needs the support and understanding of its neighborhood. A company will do well to keep its stockholders informed about its activities. A public transport system must tell passengers how they can help to make rush hour travel less uncomfortable. The public will get better service if the Post Office can persuade them to mail early at Christmas. These are just as much the province of public relations as campaigns to promote bowling, to revive the social prestige of cigar smoking, to evoke attitudes favorable to labor, or to achieve overdue recognition of historical personages.

In no area is public relations more important to the American democracy than national government. This is literally the field of "public information." Modern administration would come to a standstill if government could not constantly speak to the people as individuals and in and through the different groups to which they belong. It must do so mainly through the mass media. Public relations practitioners, said a leaflet prepared by the American University, "practice the arts of communication in the continuous, purposeful group relationships of modern society. The everyday problem of explaining purpose and action has grown into a specialized function of administrative procedure. The public relations practitioner who can make effective use of his tools—language and graphics—finds openings in many fields." [38]

The term "public relations" is out of favor in official Washington, but even the critics who view with distaste what they may publicly describe as the "army of federal propagandists" do not deny that it is an essential administrative function, for the discharge of which the federal government must employ specialists.

It will be assumed in this book that the director of information of the U.S. Department of Agriculture, the director of public relations of General Foods, and the typical public relations counsel differ in detail and not in kind, and that each reflects a universal response of American institutions to the demands of a highly complex society knit together by a highly complex system of mass communications.

[38] *Careers in Public Relations* (leaflet in use at American University, 1948).

PART II

THE PUBLIC RELATIONS OF THE
FEDERAL GOVERNMENT

CHAPTER 4

◇◇

PUBLIC RELATIONS AND
BIG GOVERNMENT

◇◇

WHEN in 1913 Representative Frederick H. Gillett—later to become one of the most distinguished Speakers of the House—drew attention to an open competitive examination for a publicity expert in the Office of Public Roads of the Department of Agriculture, he had no difficulty in persuading Congress that executive agencies should be forbidden to employ publicity agents without its express authority.

It was inevitable that the discoveries which press agents and publicity men were making should influence public administration, and that the process should raise questions which would affect the relationship between the legislative and executive branches. Gillett did not dispute the need to publish information about roads, and he agreed that farmers' bulletins should be readable and attractive. What made him apprehensive was that, as he thought, it was proposed to appoint "a person simply as a press agent to advertise the work and doings" of a government department and, as another Congressman expressed it, to "extol and exploit their virtues." He was particularly disturbed by the requirement that a candidate should have "affiliations with newspaper publishers and writers . . . extensive enough to ensure the publication of items prepared by him." This was nothing short of press agentry, and he believed that "anything which requires the knowledge of the public certainly finds its way into the press at this time." [1]

---

[1] Senate Committee on the Executive Agencies of the Government, *Preliminary Report* (1937), 531–32. Quoted subsequently as *Senate Report on Executive Agencies.*

The fact that Gillett's initiative resulted in legislation which is still in force has tended to overemphasize its originality. The conflict between Congress and the Executive which came to a head in 1913 had long been latent and had often become acute before. In the nineteenth century Congress had entrusted responsibilities for information and education to the Department of Agriculture and other agencies, and the employment of editorial and other information specialists was no novelty. According to the *Congressional Directory* for 1901, the Division of Publications of the Department of Agriculture was issuing, "in the form of press notices, official information of interest to agriculturists"; it was "also charged with the preparation and printing of Farmers' Bulletins, four-fifths of which are distributed upon the orders of Senators, Representatives, and Delegates in Congress." [2]

The new feature was the emergence of specialists who were akin to the press agents of business, as distinct from the personal aides who as part of wider duties had long helped their chiefs in cultivating the newspapers. According to *Editor and Publisher,* the development owed much to orders by Presidents Roosevelt and Taft forbidding officials to issue information direct to the press. "Formerly it was the custom of correspondents to call on department officials and gather up such information as they thought their papers would like to publish." Instead, news was channeled through specialists in press relations; and "quite a number of newspapermen in Washington" obtained "good berths in the different offices, their duty being to furnish 'stuff' to the correspondents." [3] One of them, Jesse L. Suter, a newspaperman who was "publicity agent" of the Post Office Department from 1909 to 1913, was so successful in his dealings with the press corps that on the change of administration the Washington correspondents took the singular course of petitioning the Postmaster General not to dismiss him. [4]

There was obviously a danger that the government press

[2] *Official Congressional Directory for 1901,* 240.
[3] *Editor and Publisher,* 13 (13), September 13, 1913, 257.
[4] *Editor and Publisher,* 13 (5), July 19, 1913, 91.

agents would be used to "extol" their departments. The matter which they furnished, *Editor and Publisher* alleged, "contained very little news; it was mostly exploitation of the department and officials of the department." [5] Congress had been restive before 1913. In 1909 it forbade the Forest Service to spend money on the preparation or publication of newspaper and magazine articles, though not on the issue of "any facts or official information of value to the public," provided that it was to "all persons, without discrimination, including newspapers and magazine writers and publishers." [6] This prohibition had been renewed annually, and was made permanent in 1913. In 1912 there had been several incidents. In May there was discussion of the possibility of clipping the press agents' wings by cutting appropriations, and Representative Nelson of Wisconsin called for a committee to inquire into the conditions, existence, and duties of the various press bureaus. In the same year the Senate struck from the Naval appropriation bill a provision authorizing the employment of an advertising agent for the Marine Corps. [7]

These are examples of a tension which can be traced back to the early days of government printing and is still familiar. It was bound to become more serious with the advances in mass education and mass communications, and as the scope of government increased. The fact that it has lasted so long and has so often broken into flame over trivialities is evidence that it is deep-seated. It is a fairly safe generalization that when there is constant friction over questions of little importance in themselves, and in particular over nomenclature, there is a major issue of principle in the background.

Modern techniques of mass information and persuasion are powerful tools, and all who seek to acquire or maintain power in a democracy must make use of them. Congress cannot view with equanimity their unfettered use by the Executive. On the

---

[5] *Editor and Publisher*, 13 (13), 257.

[6] *Senate Report on Executive Agencies*, 532n. This is the form in which the provision was made permanent in 1923.

[7] *Editor and Publisher*, 11 (48), May 18, 1912, 2; 11 (49), May 25, 1912, 8; and 12 (4), July 13, 1912, 1.

other hand, as the chief repository of power under the Constitution, the Executive cannot dispense with them. Representative Gillett is only one of many who have tried to resolve the dilemma, but an enduring solution seems as far off as ever.

The reasons go deep into the American political system. The controversy over the limitations which should be set upon federal government public relations springs from the fear lest programs undertaken in the name of administrative efficiency should result in an excessive concentration of power in the Executive. This fear is shared by Congress, the states, and the pressure and other groups which, though unrecognized by the Constitution, compete with the constitutional organs in the *de facto* exercise of power. What is more, government public relations threatens the member of Congress not only in Washington but in his constituency, where he has traditionally been the chief spokesman of the central government and the chief medium of communication with the capital. The controversy over government public relations is one facet of the perennial controversy over a strong central Executive. Those who wish to stimulate it find convenient support in the aversion of the average man from being exploited by irresponsible manipulators behind the scenes.

The tension is in some respects the greater because Congress and the Executive have tacitly agreed over a wide area, and the fiercest disputes have turned on the application of principles which neither side would openly deny.

Congress does not in practice challenge the right of executive agencies to have an information division of some sort nor the right of that division to engage in press and radio relations and to issue publications. Even the House Propaganda and Publicity Subcommittee, which could not be suspected of undue sympathy toward government public relations, acknowledged in 1947 that it was not "unlawful or improper for officials or employees of the federal government to express opinions or to impart factual information, if distinguished from propaganda." "Information" was "the act or process of communicating knowledge; to enlighten:" "propaganda: a plan for the propagation of a doctrine or a system of principles." [8]

For its part the Executive agrees that information divisions must not engage in party propaganda, personal promotion, or lobbying. Government officials would endorse the remarks of Milton S. Eisenhower, director of information of the Department of Agriculture under both the Hoover and Roosevelt administrations:

"The Office of Information is in no wise a publicity agency in the usual sense of that term. Its purpose is not to acquire prestige for itself or for the Department as a whole, not to 'sell' the Department to the public or to advertise the achievements of Department workers, but to make public the results of the Department's manifold activities." (*Annual Report*, 1929) [9]

"We have never used one penny for propagandistic purposes. We make no attempt to publicize the Department as an institution, or as a group of individuals. We do not propagandize the Department's functions or activities. Our job is far different. Our function, as set out in the organic act of the Department, is to take the results of scientific research, put them into an understandable form, and distribute them." (Evidence before House Appropriations Subcommittee, November 18, 1932)

It is one thing to say in general terms what government information divisions may and may not do. It is not so easy to interpret the generalizations in practice or to guarantee that the boundaries of the admittedly legitimate are not transgressed. Experience has shown how frequently discussion of government public relations is colored by differences over the policies which it is being used to further. There will always be room for argument about the point at which its proper use shades into the acquisition of prestige or popularity for the

[8] House of Representatives, Committee on Expenditures in the Executive Departments, Publicity and Propaganda Subcommittee, *Investigation of Participation of Federal Officials of the War Department in Publicity and Propaganda, as It Relates to Universal Military Training*, July 24, 1947, House Report No. 1073, 7.

[9] Quoted by T. Swann Harding, "Genesis of 'One Government Propaganda Mill,'" *Public Opinion Quarterly*, 11 (2), Summer 1947, 232.

department; and it is impossible to escape the fact that information activities are more likely to enhance than to diminish a department's reputation. The danger that public relations will be misused for party advantage is greater under a system without a strong civil service tradition and where the distinction between the government as a permanent going concern and as the party in power is imperfectly established.

It came naturally to a political publicist like Charles Michelson to criticize the Navy Department under Secretary Knox for not employing a Democratic advertising agency in its recruiting campaign. He took it for granted that no advertising agency could fail to be in some measure biased in favor of its own party:

"Democratic agencies of equal repute felt, and still feel, that they were entitled to the advantage of such advertising by a Democratic Administration. To be realistic on this subject, I know that if I had had the placing of such a contract, it would have redounded to the benefit of the Democratic cause, and I do not mean by this that an agency controlled by the members of our party would have been any more partisan in the discharge of its function than was the Barton agency in the other direction. It would have motivated a Democratic agency to more emphatic friendliness to the Administration, and such Democratic publications as got the advertising would have been encouraged in their support."

Michelson also took a different view from Eisenhower of the proper limits of departmental publicity. When he joined the NRA: "Naturally, I wanted to start off my new job with a bang. I conceived the glowing thought that a sky display was the thing. I visioned squadrons of airplanes over each great population center flying in N.R.A. formation—ground demonstrations would, of course, be taking place at the same time,—perhaps a fireside talk by F.D.R. over the radio to a multitude of meetings celebrating the theme of the new organization that was to launch the recovery of industry." [10]

How, too, draw the line between legitimate information ac-

[10] Charles Michelson, *The Ghost Talks* (New York, Putnam, 1944), 201, 122.

tivities and lobbying? As the *Washington Post* acutely observed, "there is a fine and sometimes indistinguishable line between what constitutes informing the public on a vital issue and what amounts to bringing pressure on legislators. In some cases the former results in the latter." [11]

Take, for instance, the criticisms which the House Publicity and Propaganda Subcommittee leveled against the War Department and the Federal Security Agency for alleged propaganda to secure legislation in favor of compulsory military service and "socialized medicine." It charged the War Department with engaging in "activities calculated to build up a federally stimulated public demand upon Congress for enactment of legislation for universal military training." The Department had sent speakers round the country; it had shown a film in support of universal military training to 680,000 people; the Women's Interests Unit had been at work on the women's organizations; much of the material issued was "unworthy of any department of government." [12] In reply, Secretary Royall denied that there had been "any effort to influence legislation by illegitimate means," but said that he would be less than frank if he did not admit that some of the statements might influence Congress.[13]

The Surgeon General, Dr. Thomas Parran, similarly denied that his staff had done anything illegal, but he drew attention to the difficulty of their position in the face of a law which was not clear and had never been tested in the courts. "Certainly I am confident that there has been no such violation if any reasonable interpretation is put upon that statute." Had he violated the statute in an article "Why Don't We Stamp Out Syphilis?" which the *Survey Graphic* and the *Reader's Digest* had published in 1936? "This article and many others were not 'designed or intended to influence' any member of the Congress. They were designed and intended to inform the people of this country concerning this unnecessary burden of

[11] *Washington Post*, January 17, 1948.
[12] Publicity and Propaganda Subcommittee, *Report on Universal Military Training, passim.*
[13] *Washington Post*, January 15, 1948.

sickness, death, and economic loss then laid upon our people by syphilis. The result has been national, state, and local action in terms of laws and appropriations backed by public senti-ment." Had he violated the statute by his advocacy of tuber-culosis control, and by the six-point national program which the Public Health Service had sponsored in conformity with his annual report to Congress of 1944? "It has got so far that a government official can hardly explain the work of his depart-ment in the normal course of his duty without being charged with propagandizing." [14]

Incidents such as these have kept alive the always smolder-ing fear that the official information services will be misused. Whether justifiably or not is beside the point. The fact is that it has colored the policy of Congress on aspects of government public relations about which there is no disagreement of prin-ciple and where there is little risk of abuse.

Two main arguments can be advanced for government pub-lic relations. The first may be called the reportorial argument. A democratic government must report to the people. This does not necessarily involve any element of persuasion. The second may be called the administrative argument. Certain adminis-trative measures will not succeed unless the public or sections of the public are adequately informed about their rights and duties, or unless—foreign policy in some of its aspects is a good example—the public understands and acquiesces in them. Sometimes it may be necessary to go further and to persuade the public to cooperate. Where voluntary cooperation can be secured, it is not only to be preferred to compulsion from the point of view of administrative efficiency. It has positive demo-cratic advantages. The case for overseas information activities is different, but they are outside the scope of this book.

The first view is orthodox enough. Pendleton Herring stated it clearly in 1936: "Popular government rests on the assump-tion that the people are capable of passing a verdict for or against the administration in power. The accuracy of this ver-

[14] *Department of Labor—Federal Security Agency Appropriation Bill for 1949, Hearings before Subcommittee of House Appropriations Committee,* 1948, 183–4.

dict depends upon the public's knowledge of what the government has done or failed to do." [15] Robert Fraser, director general of the British Central Office of Information, stated it in
essentially similar terms in 1947. The British government was
"consciously accepting some measure of responsibility for seeing that a fully enfranchised people, confronted with manifold and difficult problems, received all the information they
needed in order to enable them to make up their minds about
the answers, and generally to act as intelligent citizens." [16]

The task force appointed by the Hoover Commission to report on departmental management said in 1949 that there
could be little doubt of the "basic obligation" to keep the public informed about the activities of the executive agencies.[17]
George Washington summed it up long ago in his Farewell
Address of 1796: "In proportion as the structure of a government gives force to public opinion, it is essential that public
opinion should be enlightened."

It has been argued that in the United States the need of the
Executive for its own channels of information to the public is
the greater because, unlike the cabinet under a parliamentary
system, it cannot use the legislature as a forum. Professor Carl
J. Friedrich has gone further. He has argued that—whatever
the system—modern conditions make it impossible for large
areas of administration to be controlled in detail by the traditional processes. In such areas government information services provide a method of making the administrator responsible
to the people. It helps him by keeping him in touch with the
sections of the public whom his activities most affect. It is democratic because it enables them to bring their influence to bear
on the administrator. "Through . . . informational services,
administrative officials have begun to tap independent sources
of insight into the views and reactions of the general public

[15] E. Pendleton Herring, *Public Administration and the Public Interest*
(New York, McGraw-Hill, 1936), 363.
[16] "How to Tell the People," in *The Changing Nation* (London, A Contact Book, 1947).
[17] Commission on Organization of the Executive Branch of the Government ("Hoover Commission"), *Task Force Report on Departmental
Management* (1949), 57.

which are increasingly important in guiding them towards the making of public policy in a responsible fashion. . . . [Along with the outflow] an ever increasing quantity of intake . . . of all sorts of communicable views, opinions, facts, and criticisms is becoming a potent factor in the shaping of public policy, particularly in areas where the government is entering new or experimental ground." [18]

"Big government," said Samuel A. Stouffer, "can be responsive and responsible to the people only if there are efficient channels of communication between the governed and the governors." [19]

That the reportorial obligations of government are taken for granted is shown by the complaints when the government fails to supply information. In his report on *Government and Mass Communications* (1947) for the Commission on Freedom of the Press, Zechariah Chafee, Jr. expressed concern at "the enormous recent expansion of the subjects which officials are seeking to hide from publication until they give the signal." [20] One of the stormier episodes in the stormy history of the Agricultural Adjustment Administration turned on its refusal to publish some of its payments; in 1947 the Department of Agriculture was criticized for withholding information about an offer of potatoes to relief agencies. The State Department is periodically charged with undue reticence: Secretary Byrnes was praised for unusual frankness. The Armed Forces are suspected of sheltering behind security when their real reasons for holding back information are administrative. "Too much of official Washington," wrote Hanson W. Baldwin in 1948, "apparently believes that slickness and secrecy are a clever substitute for frankness and truth. But this is playing with fire." [21]

[18] C. J. Friedrich, "Public Policy and the Nature of Administrative Responsibility," in *Public Policy*, ed. C. J. Friedrich and Edward S. Mason (Harvard University Press, 1940), 16.

[19] Samuel A. Stouffer, "Government and the Measurement of Opinion," *Scientific Monthly*, 63 (6), December 1946, 435.

[20] Zechariah Chafee, Jr., *Government and Mass Communications. A Report from the Commission on Freedom of the Press* (University of Chicago Press, 1947), I, 13.

[21] *New York Times*, January 7, 1948.

In these circumstances the only question is how the reportorial duty is discharged. The central issue, as will be shown later, is the extent to which the government needs its own machinery to supplement the privately owned mass media. Can it not do the job without the apparatus of press releases and information specialists and more information and periodicals than "Carter had pills? Why not close this thing out now?" [22]

The case for public relations as an aid to administration is exemplified by the agencies which the Congress has long since charged with responsibilities for public information. The Department of Agriculture is the outstanding example. It was set up in 1862 expressly "to acquire and diffuse among the people of the United States information on subjects connected with agriculture in the most general and comprehensive sense of that word." In 1867 the U.S. Office of Education was established with the duty of diffusing "such information respecting the organization and management of schools and school systems and methods of teaching as shall aid the people of the United States in the establishment and maintenance of efficient school systems, and otherwise promote the cause of education throughout the country." The legal obligation of the Public Health Service to publish health information goes back to 1893. The publication of economic data as an aid to business has always been an important function of the Department of Commerce. The Federal Coal Mines Inspection and Investigation Act of 1941 directed the Secretary of the Interior to "compile, analyze, and publish" the information about conditions in the mines which was disclosed by inspections; it gave him no power to enforce improvements—the sole remedy was to be public opinion. In these and other agencies the dissemination of information is part of their reason for being.

There is a certain philosophical primitivism in talking about "information" and "facts." It may be sufficient to supply experts with more or less undigested information—to publish

[22] Representative Albert Thomas, *Independent Offices Appropriation Bill for 1947, Hearings before Subcommittee of House Appropriations Committee,* 1946, 47.

the scientist's own account of researches to other scientists or trade statistics to businessmen. To publish information which the members of the general public cannot understand is certainly to "diffuse" information, but it is not to inform those who receive it.

What is more, the reason for publishing the information is seldom the dissemination of knowledge for its own sake; it is to get people to act. It may be necessary not only to make the information understandable, but to attract attention to it and to show how it can be applied in practice. The facts may be simple and may only need to be stated to be understood. They will not be understood unless they are first listened to. The Veterans Administration wanted veterans to write to regional offices instead of to Washington and to forward full particulars of themselves with their letters: it made use of all-star radio programs to secure audiences for these simple messages. The reason for telling the farmer how to conserve his soil is to prevent its erosion; and it would not greatly further the national interest if he treated it as an irrelevant addition to his general knowledge. Thus information merges into persuasion.

It may, therefore, be necessary to popularize information— to select the facts which are most likely to interest the audience; to state them in the language of the mass circulation magazine; to repeat them; to use other media than the printed word such as broadcasts, motion pictures, comic strips; and to follow up with personal contacts. It may, in short, require a fully developed public relations program.

Here, for example, is part of *A Hasty Glance at the Information Program of the Federal Extension Service:* "Out of every 100 farm families adopting better farm and home practices, about 38 said this was due to popularized scientific information read, seen, or heard in bulletins, newspapers, on the radio, or in other mass media.

"As the number of channels for reaching people increased from one to nine, the percentage of families adopting better practices increased from 35 to 98. So, repeated impressions *via* many channels and methods are important."

The media to which the families owed their better practices were analyzed:

"METHOD FOR MASSES (37.4%), INDIRECT

News stories	Exhibits
Radio	Bulletins
Magazines	Posters
	Circular letters

METHODS FOR INDIVIDUALS (17.5%), DIRECT

Farm and home visits	Correspondence
Office calls	Demonstrations
	Telephone calls

METHODS FOR GROUPS (26%), DIRECT

General meetings	Extension Schools
Method demonstration meetings	Leader training meetings
	Tours
Discussion meetings	Motion pictures

OTHER INFLUENCES (19.1%), INDIRECT

Not traceable, probably mostly from neighbor to neighbor." [23]

There are some who go further and say that the case for such methods does not depend solely or mainly on administrative expediency. They think that it is the democratic way. It is the way of active democracy, the modern equivalent of the town meeting, one answer to the problem of making "Big Government" popular. "A government continually at a distance and out of sight," said Alexander Hamilton in the *Federalist*, "can hardly be expected to interest the sensations of the people." "An essential part of any successful action on the part of the United States," said Secretary George C. Marshall in his Harvard speech on June 5, 1947, "is an understanding on the part of the people of America of the character of the problem and the remedies to be applied." The Hoover Commission

[23] *A Hasty Glance at the Information Program of the Federal Extension Service, Part I—The Cooperative Extension Service* (U.S. Department of Agriculture, Extension Service, processed, 1947), 20.

thought that "the State Department must not only estimate and evaluate the views of the American public in foreign affairs matters but must also win its acceptance and support on the paramount issues." The same theme has been elaborated in a number of recent books on foreign policy and the American people.[24]

David E. Lilienthal based the "grassroots" administration of the TVA on the view that popular understanding and participation are the foundation of administrative efficiency and a bulwark of democracy. "Technicians must learn that explaining 'why' to the people is generally as important . . . as 'what' is done. To induce the action of laymen . . . 'why' is almost always the key. Experts and managers at central business or government headquarters, isolated and remote, tend to become impatient of making explanations to the people. From impatience it is a short step to a feeling of superiority, and then to irresponsibility or dictation. And irresponsibility or dictation to the people, whether by experts or politicians or business managers or public administrators, is a denial of democracy."[25]

Alfred D. Stedman, assistant administrator of the Agricultural Adjustment Administration, gave the American Political Science Association in 1934 what is still one of the best analyses of the part which public relations can play in an administrative program calling for active cooperation by the people.[26] His starting point was that Congress had by law directed the operation of a national farm program. "How far can a federal government agency go as a matter of wise and sound public

[24] Hoover Commission *Report on Foreign Affairs* (1949), 54–55. Recent books which are relevant include Gabriel A. Almond, *The American People and Foreign Policy* (New York, Harcourt, Brace, 1950), Thomas A. Bailey, *The Man in the Street* (New York, Macmillan, 1948), Leonard S. Cottrell, Jr. and Sylvia Eberhart, *American Opinion on World Affairs in the Atomic Age* (Princeton University Press, 1948), and *Public Opinion and Foreign Policy*, ed. Lester Markel (New York, Harper, for Council on Foreign Relations, 1949).

[25] David E. Lilienthal, *TVA, Democracy on the March* (New York, Pocket Books, 1945), 137.

[26] Reprinted in Agricultural Adjustment Administration, *Agricultural Adjustment 1937–38* (1939), 226 seq.

policy in publicizing favorably its own activities and in seeking widespread public participation in its programs? How does the dissemination of information by such an agency affect the operations of the democratic system?" It would not have been enough if the AAA had simply told "the what, the why, and the how" of its program. It was necessary to arouse a favorable response on the part of farmers and to encourage them to take part in the plan, and, "with full respect for the facts," to give them "an extensive presentation of one course of action as being more desirable than others. The process involves picking and choosing as between sets of facts, placing more emphasis upon some than upon others according to a judgment of their relative importance. Thus it does involve a departure from the objective attitude. It involves active support of a positive plan of cooperative action which is intended to improve the economic condition of agriculture."

The fundamental question was whether the information activities could be "carried on constructively in our country" or were "in some way inimical to democracy." Stedman replied that they were an important safeguard of democracy. Through Congress the majority of the people had insisted on action, and the danger to democracy would lie in failure to act on their mandate. "Informed public opinion is the basis of democracy. Adequate information is all that stands between democracy and the complete inefficiency and ineffectiveness which hitherto have paralyzed the people during a depression."

This is a cogent statement of the case for persuasive public relations by government. It would not have convinced some of the opponents of the Roosevelt agricultural policy. Opposition to government publicity, as we have seen, often springs from opposition to the particular purpose for which it is being used. Complaints about publicity are favorite tactics of defeated minorities in fighting the rearguard actions against adverse decisions which are so familiar in American politics. But the views which Stedman expressed are tacitly accepted by all who acquiesce in public persuasion to sell savings bonds or to prevent forest fires or to recruit for the Army or to promote food conservation. When President Truman set up the Luckman Committee, the criticism was not that a public relations campaign was improper, but that it would be ineffective.

The fact is that, as Walter Lippmann said in 1922, "persuasion has become a self-conscious art and a regular organ of popular government," [27] and nobody questions its propriety when the object has broad national support. It is noteworthy that the Advertising Council, one of the main instruments of persuasive publicity for the federal government, takes Stedman's criterion of Congressional approval as a condition for deciding whether it should help.

Tacitly, at any rate, Congress acknowledges the right of the government to use mass persuasion to further programs which have general approval. Is it, however, legitimate for government to use all the techniques of commercial public relations? Is it legitimate, as Robert K. Merton asked, to rely on fallacious arguments or to play upon mass anxieties? How far may government publicity be addressed to the emotions? Or to certain emotions—greed or fear or sex? Should it adopt mass standards of taste? Should it renounce the flashier techniques even at the price of sacrificing effectiveness to dignity? Under the heading "cheesecake," the public relations manual of one of the War Assets Administration Zones included the following instruction in 1947: "Cheap glamour photographs and publicity will be avoided. The dignity of the federal government and of WAA as a government agency must always be kept in mind."

Stedman partly answered some of these questions: "The educational effort must be truthful and factual in character and not a mere campaigning of ballyhoo and bunkum. It must not be high pressure promotion. It must not depend on the shallow and artful tricks of publicity. It must not rely on stirring dangerous fires of fear or hate."

These careful generalizations are safe but not very helpful. They leave most of the points in doubt. What, for example, of the tricks of publicity which are not "shallow and artful," and of promotion which is not high-pressured? Or even—as in

[27] Walter Lippmann, *Public Opinion* (New York, Harcourt, Brace, 1922), 248.

time of war—playing on fear and hate? These are important questions, to which we shall come back, but it cannot be said that they have excited much attention in practice, perhaps because, on the whole, lack of restraint is not a failing of official information services.

Enough has been said to show how large is the area of superficial agreement. Yet the tensions remain. The following analysis of newspaper comment on federal government public relations activities between February and August 1947 may help to illustrate them. It is based on clippings from 139 newspapers in 40 states and the District of Columbia.

Most of the comment was adverse. The *Wall Street Journal* (March 28) expressed the main danger as seen by the more extreme of the critics: "Of course a government propaganda machine is the instrument of dictatorship." Several papers quoted Representative Forest A. Harness when he complained of 45,000 propagandists on the federal payroll at a cost of $75 million a year. The *Florida Times-Union* (February 4) made its own calculations. It differentiated between "information specialists" and "public relations counselors"; because of their ramifications, 23,000 government public relations counselors cost some $700 million a year. The *Chicago Tribune* (April 15), under the headline "New Deal Ballyhoo," reported a Senate investigation into "the multi-million dollar annual New Deal propaganda expenditure." The *Springfield* (Mass.) *Union* (May 24) complained of "government-made opinions," and quoted a statement by Representative Harness that every department had "a propaganda bureau to protect itself from budget cuts." The *Topeka Capital* (July 9) condemned the bales of worthless handouts with which business as well as government inundated the newspapers; most were "nothing but propaganda so ineptly disguised that a glance is sufficient for most editors. They look, then throw away."

Several newspapers drew attention to alleged lobbying by government agencies. "The Government Lobbies While the People Pay" (*Philadelphia Inquirer*, June 1). "Army Grinding Out Propaganda in Large Doses," said the *Chicago Tribune* (March 12). The *Oklahoman* (February 8) criticized the

Department of Labor for sending it an editorial from the *Washington Post* which answered Representative John Taber's complaint that public relations staffs were excessive. The *Montana Standard* (June 11) objected to a Department of Agriculture statement that droughts and duststorms would return sooner or later to the Great Plains on the ground that it was propaganda against a proposed cut in the appropriation for soil conservation. The *Chicago News* (May 13) said of a Department of Labor pamphlet, *Women's Stake in Unions*, that the unions should do their own propagandizing over their own names and at their own expense.

A favorite complaint was that government information offices were wasteful and their output poor in quality. Most of it was fit only for the wastepaper basket. It was "wastebasket fodder" (*Post Journal*, Jamestown, N.Y., June 3); "hog-wash" (Representative Harness); "low-grade press agentry" (*Southwest American*, Fort Smith, Ark., February 11); "useless" (*Telegraph*, Macon, Ga., April 23). It was wasteful of the Department of Agriculture to issue a release pointing out that "people often notice that when one four-leaf clover is found, others usually are growing nearby. Plant scientists explain that some white clover plants have the characteristic of producing leaves with more leaflets than the usual three" (*Star*, Indianapolis, Ind., July 7). Under the headline "An Easy Way to Save 75 Millions," the *Chicago Tribune* (April 20) blamed the U.S. Office of Education for using expensive pictorial charts to say what could be said clearly in a few words. There was a minor furor in May when Representative Dirksen drew the attention of Congress to a Department of Agriculture booklet on eating better breakfasts. Why spend the taxes on telling Americans to "eat plenty but eat right" and that "a breakfast should taste good and give you a lift"?

The friendly comment was also revealing. A favorite counterattack was to tell Congress to put its own house in order first. The House of Representatives, wrote Royce Brier in the *San Francisco Chronicle* (July 10), published "trillions of tons of tripe." About half the crumpled documents in the wastepaper basket of the columnist Fred Othman came from "the talented pens of Congressmen." There would be no heartbreak if Congress cut down its speechmaking to save paper (*Journal,* Flint, Mich., July 1); and the *Congressional Record* was a frequent target as an alleged depository of junk. Other newspapers made the point that if there were too many official press releases, business and other private organizations were as bad or worse.

More positively, some specific items were singled out for praise. The *Labor Information Bulletin,* said Edwin A. Lahey (*Chicago News,* April 15), showed "a peculiar facility for compressing significant activities into an informative and readable little package, which is something good in government . . . and worth encouragement." Books in the series "Armed Forces in Action," the Social Security pamphlet on infant care, and the Department of Commerce magazine, *Federal Science Progress,* also received commendation.

Lastly, there were two newspapers which vigorously championed government information services. In the *Capital Times* (Madison, Wis., May 7) William T. Evjue said that it was true that the *Times* filled many wastepaper baskets with useless publicity from Washington, but this was much better than that the sources of information should be dried up. "This thing we call democracy is based on the assumption that the people shall have full information on which to build an intelligent public opinion." "After all," said the *Beacon Journal* (Akron, Ohio, May 29), "the publicity men are the people's chief source of facts about government bureaus, and now as always the need is for more facts, not less."

Most of the criticism lay either against "propaganda" and lobbying or against extravagance and inefficiency. There was no criticism of the principle of government information or of the use of persuasive publicity in support of an administrative program.

This is characteristic. Critics like Representatives Harness and Miller have admitted the need for information services but have alleged that they are used for "propaganda" and are extravagant. Politics aside, the problem is to discover methods of control which will prevent abuses and waste without hampering administration. In practice, politics cannot be excluded, but it would be common ground that the problem has not been satisfactorily solved. As Representative Miller said, Congress needs "a definite policy with respect to publicity, and . . . appropriations should be confirmed by this policy." [28]

The lack of a definite policy has clouded the history of government public relations. The fear that the executive branch may use the information services to strengthen itself against the legislature has always been uppermost in the mind of Congress. Except during periods of national crisis its approach has always been negative. Even in the crises its acquiescence has been half-hearted.

The result—as one information officer expressed it to me— is that there has never been a meeting of minds between administrators and legislators on this important subject. Congress has come to piecemeal decisions, and it has never clearly distinguished between the different categories of publicity. The departments have sometimes responded by evasive measures such as the use of misleading or nondescript descriptions of information work, and Congress has been strengthened in the suspicion that they are up to no good.

The need for information staffs has grown, and Congress has found itself in the frustrating position of King Canute before the advancing tide. It has struck hard but blindly at those activities which it is easiest for it to check. It used its control of appropriations to eliminate most of the radio and motion picture activities of the early Roosevelt days. It has been more difficult to control the staffs engaged on duties such as press liaison and publications for which it is accepted that provision should be made. It has been hard to enforce rules of conduct like abstention from self-advertisement and propaganda, and practically impossible to distinguish effectively between different kinds of publications.

Congress has mostly relied on the scrutiny of departmental budgets to keep information staffs down. It has reinforced this by two major prohibitions. The ban imposed by the Act of

[28] Quoted by Dick Fitzpatrick, "Public Information Activities of Government Agencies," *Public Opinion Quarterly*, 11 (4), Winter 1947-48, 539.

1913 on employing publicity experts without its express authority has had a considerable psychological effect, but it has not prevented similar appointments under other names with or without Congressional approval. The Act of 1913 was mainly directed against self-advertisement by government agencies.

The so-called "gag law" of July 11, 1919, was directed against lobbying. It prescribed severe penalties for using appropriations for services, messages, publications, or other devices designed to influence any member of Congress in his attitude toward legislation or appropriations. Officials could, however, communicate with members of Congress at the request of the latter, and could communicate direct to Congress through official channels requests for legislation or appropriations which they deemed necessary for the efficient conduct of the public business. Literally interpreted, the law of 1919 would forbid many contacts with Congress which take place in practice and cause offense to nobody. It is difficult to enforce and has never been tested in the courts. None the less it is important as the statement of a principle which the Executive itself would endorse, and, like the law of 1913, exerts a considerable psychological effect. It has been invoked on several occasions—for example, during the controversy over the Copeland food and drug bill in 1933, and by the Propaganda Subcommittee in its reports on the alleged propaganda of the War Department and the Federal Security Agency.

Congress has experimented with several methods of controlling publications. In 1861 it set up the Government Printing Office under its own control instead of under the Executive, and a joint resolution of June 23, 1860, had laid down that all printing should be done at the GPO unless otherwise provided by law. It did not, however, prove easy to eliminate the departmental presses, and the process of elimination was overtaken by the introduction of mimeographing and other new methods of reproduction. Neither Congress nor the Public Printer has yet discovered how to bring these new processes under effective control. An Act of March 1, 1919, literally applied, would have meant that practically all duplicating which was not typewritten would have to be done by the GPO. No attempt was made to enforce it strictly until 1936, when the Comptroller General gave a broad interpretation of its provisions. By this time the problem was beyond handling so simply; it was made worse by the proliferation of departmental presses all over the country during the war; and it still remains unsolved.

Various expedients have been tried for controlling the volume and the content of government publications. Sometimes the controls have taken the form of general injunctions. The General Printing Act of 1895 forbade agencies to print any matter "except that which is authorized by law and necessary to the public business." An Act of March 3, 1905, had a similar purpose, but applied only to the executive departments: except with express authority, they were not to publish any book or document "not having to do with the ordinary business transactions" of the department. Another act of the same date provided that printing or binding appropriations must not be used to pay for illustrations until the head of the establishment certified that the illustration was "necessary and relates entirely to the transaction of public business."

In 1919 (Act of March 1) Congress embarked on the experiment of directly controlling the initiation of new periodicals, when it required agencies to discontinue all periodicals which it had not specifically authorized. It soon, however, realized that it was not well equipped for the detailed examination of proposals to start new periodicals, and a joint resolution of May 11, 1922, transferred the responsibility for approving new periodicals to the director of the Bureau of the Budget, with the stipulation that the head of the agency must certify that the periodical was "necessary in the transaction of public business required by law."

Congress came to rely more and more on the Bureau of the Budget. Between 1937 and 1947 it made no less than nine requests of the Bureau for investigations relating to publications. To give some examples, in 1942 the Joint Committee on Printing asked its cooperation in eliminating publications which were not essential to the proper conduct of public business or to winning the war. In 1943 the Byrd Committee asked for a report on methods of controlling penalty mail, with the reduction of publicity material as one of the objects. This was a form of control with which Congress had experimented several times in the nineteenth century but had found unsatisfactory. On this occasion the outcome was the Penalty Mail Act of 1944, under which upper limits were set to mailing costs. In 1946 the chairman of the House Appropriations Committee asked for an analysis of the effectiveness of the penalty mail law, and a report on the control of publications. In the same year the Joint Committee on Printing called on the Bureau and the Public Printer to report on agency printing and duplicating plants. In 1948 the Penalty Mail Act was repealed; another experiment in controlling publications through mailing costs had failed.

The difficulty which more than any other stands in the way of effective Congressional control of government publications is the absence of criteria by which it can distinguish between publications, such as departmental instructions, which are needed for purely administrative reasons, publications of an informational character which are required for the execution of programs which it has approved, and publications serving purposes which it would not endorse. In an organization so vast as the federal government, with its two million employees, it is bound to happen that periodicals survive after they have ceased to be useful, that publications are sometimes issued without full regard to administrative need, and that extraneous considerations occasionally cloud decisions about the initiation or the cessation of departmental publications. The very vastness of the organization makes detailed Congressional scrutiny impracticable.

Congress has succeeded neither in devising adequate machinery of control nor in evolving a definite policy for settling information appropriations. Probably it never got nearer to such a policy than in the report of the Byrd Committee of 1936 on the Executive Agencies of the Government. Even so the committee mainly concerned itself with the prevention of extravagance, and its conclusions lacked precision: "The furnishing of facts is undoubtedly a proper duty of a Government agency, but the expenditure of over $500,000 a year for personal services for publicity work and the issuance of 4,794 releases in 3 months seems to indicate that, if possible, some controlling mechanism should be set up." The Committee doubted if either legislation or organization offered an adequate remedy, and thought that budgetary and administrative control by a superior executive authority was "the most feasible method of keeping Government publicity agencies within reasonable limits." [29]

The Hoover Commission had very little to say on the subject of public relations, but did go so far as to recommend by a majority that the President should give a responsible official in the Office of the Budget the duty of supervising and coordinating publications, with a view, for instance, to eliminating redundancy and duplication.[30] This proposal had the merit of according with the tendency of Congress to use the Budget Bureau as its agent. It is a role which the Bureau has been willing to accept. Its objective, it told the Senate Appropriations Subcommittee in 1946, was "to eliminate abuse of publicity media as tools of executive management. The only sound approach lies in constant particularized examinations of each operation of Government with a view to correction of abuses if or whenever or wherever they are found." [31]

One difficulty is of course the reluctance of Congress to place all its trust in an instrument of the Executive when the danger which it fears is that information activities will be used to strengthen the Executive. Such a situation contains the makings of continuous friction, and the frustration felt by Congress in default of really effective machinery of control of its own helps to explain why it has so largely fallen back on harassing tactics—ceaseless strictures on alleged government "propaganda," the establishment of the Subcommittee of Propaganda and Publicity to keep a general eye on what was going on, budg-

---

[29] Senate *Report on Executive Agencies*, 538.

[30] Hoover Commission *Report on Budgeting and Accounting*, 30.

[31] *Second Urgent Deficiency Appropriation Bill for 1946, Hearings before Subcommittee of Senate Appropriations Committee*, 1946, 18.

etary cuts made without any precise calculation of their effect, the grilling of witnesses from the information offices, repeated requests for analyses of publicity staffs and expenditure. It is of course as well to remember that public relations is not unique among government activities in being the object of the unfriendly attentions of Congress, but it has had more than its share.

Yet the common denominator of agreement between the executive and the legislative branches is high. "Everybody in Washington," said Representative Harness in 1948, "recognizes that certain information services are an essential part of any institutional operation. . . . But Congress insists that there is a clear line of distinction between legitimate information services and those additional operations which tend to build up public opinion in favor of more projects, broader programs, or Federal invasion of new spheres of public service. It is primarily the latter operations which our subcommittee seeks to itemize as to cost and scope." [32]

Representative Harness and the Propaganda and Publicity Subcommittee have been more concerned with the dangers of extravagance and abuse than with the positive advantages of government public relations. The Commission on Freedom of the Press thought on the other hand that the dangers were secondary. "Doubtless some governmental officers have used their publicity departments for personal or partisan aggrandizement. But this evil is subject to correction by normal democratic processes and does not compare with the danger that the people of this country and other countries may, in the absence of official information and discussion, remain unenlightened on vital issues." [33] That is about the measure of the open difference between the critics and the advocates of government public relations.

That the apparently small gap between the two views has not been bridged is not merely due to the difficulty of devising effective controls. It is not merely that there are no objective criteria by which in borderline cases legitimate and illegitimate,

[32] *Congressional Record*, 94 (15), January 26, 1948, A 428,
[33] Commission on Freedom of the Press, 89.

useful and unnecessary information activities can be differentiated. The Executive is bound to be under a constant temptation to err in the direction of laxity, and its opponents to be unreasonably strict. Every administration will be tempted to "sell" itself and its programs to the people with the aid of the official publicity machine: the most conscientious official may be led astray by an excessive zeal for the public welfare which blinds his sense of constitutional niceties, the less conscientious may be influenced by personal ambition or outside pressures. Legislators and political opponents, even if they try to be dispassionate, start with a predisposition to suspect any activity which may strengthen the Executive: where they are less careful, their judgment may be warped by partisan motives or influenced by outside interests which are not seriously exercised about constitutional propriety.

It is here that another distinction becomes important—the distinction between what is a proper use of tax-supported information services and what it is proper for responsible departmental heads to say on their own account. It is the duty as well as the right of the departmental head to tell the public how he proposes to develop his policies and to test public reactions to them. He is entitled to answer his critics and to justify himself to the people. Under a parliamentary system the parliament would be the main though not the only forum in which he would meet his critics, account for his administration, and make major statements of policy. In the United States he must mainly rely on the press and the radio.

This is the point at which administration merges into politics, and the obligation to desist from partisanship ceases. As Stedman said, "the speeches, letters, and public statements of the executives are recognized by everyone as being expressions of policy. . . . They contain personal and official philosophy, argument, defense, and also at times, viewpoints attacking or disputing the reasoning or citation of facts by critics. Nevertheless, while they are clearly persuasive, that is almost never taken as grounds for criticism of these expressions of policy." [34]

[34] Stedman, 233.

In a stimulating examination of "Executive Leadership and Government Propaganda," Harold W. Stoke argued in 1941 that if, as had been happening under President Roosevelt, the Executive had increasingly to take the risk of acting first and seeking popular support afterwards, it must have the means of persuading the people to approve its actions. "Official publicity, or, more bluntly, governmental propaganda" was the new instrument of political power which was being developed for the purpose. It was not a matter for moral judgment. It was an inevitable response to the evolution of new functions of government.[35] Against the immediate background of New Deal experience, this proposition must have seemed more plausible than it does in the light of experience under the less active Administration of Mr. Roosevelt's successor. It has some substance, but there are several reasons for questioning whether it is of more than limited validity.

Government publicity is far from new: even under Mr. Roosevelt most government information activities were associated with well-established programs. It is easy to exaggerate the extent to which the Executive needs positive support from a largely uninformed and indifferent public in the detailed execution of policies which have had the broad approval of the electors and Congress. It may need the understanding and cooperation of certain sections of the public, but that is another matter.

The objection which is more relevant here is that Stoke failed to distinguish sufficiently between publicity as a political instrument and publicity as an administrative aid. The use of publicity to enlist support for universal military training or socialized medicine is entirely different in principle from its use to foster savings or to instruct the public in taking precautions against forest fires. It may well be that modern conditions oblige politicians to make more use of publicity in the exercise of political leadership, and that more active leadership is required of them. It may be, too, that, as the *Washington*

[35] Harold W. Stoke, "Executive Leadership and the Growth of Propaganda," *American Political Science Review*, 35 (3), June 1941, 490–500.

Post pointed out, the line between the two uses is sometimes blurred. But in theory the distinction is clear enough, and it is important that it should be as clear as possible in practice.

On a conservative view, said Leonard D. White, "an administrative agency should be considered only as a means of executing policy, and its public relations efforts directed solely to facilitating the achievement of predetermined ends." That, as has been shown, is the view on which Congress has acted and in which the Executive has acquiesced: it is the only view which is consistent with classical interpretations of the American Constitution. "An intermediate view," said White, "would yield to the public agency the same privilege allowed any other group or organization to have a program and to explain, defend, and encourage its adoption by direct appeal to public opinion." [36] That, on the view taken here, is the role of the politician and not of the civil servant, up to the point when the program has been adopted through the appropriate constitutional processes. It would then become proper for the agency to use official information services to explain it, encourage its adoption, and even—though this may require some qualification—defend it.

The want of clear demarcation between the politician and the civil servant in the organization of the executive branch thus explains much of the difficulty over the public relations of the federal government. The official information services must not be partisan, but the publicity conducted by the political chief and his friends without their aid is free from this restraint. Anything which sharpens the distinction between the politician and the civil servant and fortifies the tradition of civil service impartiality will reduce the risk that government public relations will be abused for partisan ends. But it will not eliminate the need for Congress to be vigilant against abuses and extravagances. It will provide no escape from the difficulty that the more efficient the official information services are in facilitating administration and increasing popular understanding of government policies the more they will add to the reputation of

[36] Leonard D. White, *Introduction to the Study of Public Administration* (New York, Macmillan, 1948, 3rd ed.), 227.

the administration of the day. The same is true of other civil service activities, but there is none whose impact on opinion is so direct and obvious.

The danger of abuse and the tendency of all publicity to give an unduly favorable picture of the administration are among the reasons for using unofficial instruments of information and persuasion wherever possible. The relations between the federal government and the mass media are central to the question of the proper role of the official information services.

"Anything which requires the knowledge of the public," said Representative Gillett, "certainly finds its way into the press at this time." If this were true the government would need no press liaison machinery. If it were true of the other media it would not need specialized information machinery at all.

The classical view has been that the press should be the chief medium of information on public affairs. "The way to prevent these irregular interpositions of the people," said Thomas Jefferson in 1787, "is to give them full information of their affairs thro' the channel of the public papers, and to contrive that those papers should penetrate the whole mass of the people." "The newspapermen—publishers, editors, reporters—," said Theodore Roosevelt in 1910, "are just as much public servants as are the men in the government service themselves." [37] "The spotlight of publicity," said Michael J. McDermott, special assistant for press relations to the Secretary of State, "must be trained through an unbiased, objective press on the developing facts" of foreign policy problems.[38]

The assumption that it is the duty and privilege of the newspapers to inform the people on public affairs is one of the foundations of the First Freedom. The admission that they share this duty is one of the arguments of the radio and motion picture industries for sharing the benefits of the First Freedom. The Commission on Freedom of the Press blamed the motion

[37] Quoted by James E. Pollard, *The Presidents and the Press* (New York, Macmillan, 1947), 53, 594.

[38] *Department of State Appropriation Bill for 1949, Hearings before Subcommittee of House Appropriations Committee*, 1948, 31.

picture industry because it had not done more "to help the public to understand the issues that confront them as citizens of the United States and of the world." [39] Mr. Justice Murphy said of the radio in 1943 (National Broadcasting Company v. United States, 319 U.S. 190, 228): "Although radio broadcasting like the press is generally conducted on a commercial basis, it is not an ordinary business activity like the selling or the marketing of electrical power. In the dissemination of information and opinion, radio has assumed a position of commanding importance, rivaling the press and the pulpit."

It is generally accepted that the press, the radio, and the motion picture industries—in descending importance—have a special responsibility for informing the public on matters of government. The same applies in lesser degree to other media. The Advertising Council represents the acceptance by advertisers of a somewhat similar conception of their responsibilities. Some book publishers would feel that the obligation extended to them, and during the war it was formally recognized by the establishment of the Council of Books in Wartime. In 1948 the Treasury Department asked the cartoonists' society to be the keystone of a voluntary program to carry the Security Loan Drive to wage earners. Even the pulpit retains some of its importance as a medium of official information; the churches, for example, collaborated in the food conservation campaign of 1947. In his report for the Public Libraries inquiry sponsored by the Social Science Research Council, McCamy took the view in 1949 "that public libraries as agencies of government supported by taxation have a natural and strategic role to play in the conservation and distribution of information which aids communication between the government and the citizen." [40]

Here, then, is a most important principle which has underlain the development of official information activities in the federal government, and has been implicitly accepted by Congress, the Executive, and the mass media. The first object

[39] Statement by the Commission in Ruth A. Inglis, *Freedom of the Movies: A Report on Self-Regulation from the Commission on Freedom of the Press* (University of Chicago Press, 1947), v.

[40] Robert D. Leigh, Foreword to James L. McCamy, *Government Publications for the Citizen* (Columbia University Press, 1949).

should be to facilitate the dissemination of information by the mass media, and the information services should inform the public direct only where the mass media fail to do so adequately.

The Commission on Freedom of the Press stated this principle in the form of a policy to guide the relationship between government information agencies and the mass media: "We recommend that the government, through the media of mass communication, inform the public of the facts with respect to its policies and of the purposes underlying those policies and that, to the extent that private agencies of mass communication are unable or unwilling to provide such media to the government, the government itself may employ media of its own." [41]

Three examples may be enough to illustrate the general acceptance of this conception of the respective roles of the media and the information offices.

(1) It was one of the grounds on which in 1947 the publishers of popular scientific magazines successfully protested against the Department of Commerce periodical *Federal Science Progress,* which was threatening their circulations. They maintained that a federal agency ought not to compete on ground which they were already covering.

(2) In November 1947, David E. Lilienthal told the American Society of Newspaper Editors: "The facts of atomic energy must be known to the American people. But the agency to inform the people must not be the agency of Government in whose hands they have placed responsibility for the conduct of their atomic energy program. That is a responsibility of a free press—to disseminate facts, to interpret them and give them meaning, and to hold public servants accountable for their conduct of the people's business." [42]

(3) Arthur Krock in the *New York Times* (December 9, 1947) took the occasion of a mistake by which an item of State Department news was broadcast exclusively by the "Voice of America" to lay down some principles for the handling of government news: "One function of the government is to pass on

[41] Commission on Freedom of the Press, 88–9.
[42] *New York Times,* November 30, 1947.

to the public through established channels of information the news its agents gather, subject to restrictions of policy and national security . . . The State Department last week became a competitor with the vehicles of public information which are operated under the guarantee of the Constitution by the daily and periodical press and, through government license, by the radio."

The Commission on Freedom of the Press spoke of "facts." It is possible to go further. The mass media also accept the responsibility for cooperating in persuasive publicity in support of nationally approved policies. In war the acceptance is explicit. If the issue were raised in normal conditions, there might be argument. The fact is none the less that in varying degrees all the mass media make a considerable contribution to public persuasion on behalf of the federal government. The savings campaign is the outstanding example out of many.

The mass media are thus partners of the official information services. Since they are also rivals, the relationship contains elements of tension, but it is to the mass media that both the Executive and Congress naturally look first. The primary function of the information machinery is to help the media; its second is to supplement them. Most of the information which the average person gets from the federal government reaches him through unofficial channels. Far and away most of it. But this does not mean that the government's own output is small. There is much indispensable information which the mass media cannot handle. It may be too voluminous; it may be of limited interest; it may be important that it should be on record in an official publication.

To speak of public information and persuasion as involving a partnership between government and the privately owned mass media still does not give the whole picture. As will be shown later, there are many other channels through which the people are informed about government activities and persuaded to cooperate in them. They include trade associations and individual businesses which have a stake in the success of a project, states and municipalities which are partners in federal programs, and voluntary groups which are interested in particular phases.

The Office of Education and the Public Health Service, for example, largely depend on states and municipalities to publicize their programs. The Foreign Policy Association, the Council on Foreign Relations, and other voluntary organizations play a major part in public information on foreign affairs. The Consumers Union helps to keep the public informed about the steps taken by federal agencies to protect them as consumers. Trade associations inform their members of laws and decisions which affect them. Railroad companies, fertilizer manufacturers, and makers of agricultural machinery conduct propaganda for soil conservation: they do so because it is good for business, but the value to the Soil Conservation Service may be much greater than if it conducted the same propaganda on its own account.

The actual publicity material issued by federal agencies is thus only a small part of a complex picture. It is natural that it should receive most of the attention, but the public relations of the federal government will be understood only if the press conferences and handouts and other outward manifestations are seen against the background of the mass media and of all the groups and interests which are contributing to public information and persuasion on governmental affairs.

As Stedman said of the information policy of the AAA, the official information services exist "primarily, not to create new media for spreading information, but to supply information . . . to the agencies constituting the immensely valuable machine already existing in this country for dissemination of human intelligence." [43]

[43] Stedman, 229.

CHAPTER 5

◇◇

MEN AND MACHINERY

◇◇

MEMBERS of Congress, administrators, and students have spent much energy with little reward on the elusive problem of calculating the staff and resources employed in what those who are unfriendly have called the "propaganda mill" of the federal government.

The problem is insoluble because it involves a series of impossible distinctions. Where draw the line between research studies and popular leaflets based upon them? How apportion the time of regional officers, military commanders, forest rangers, and other government employees whose public relations work is incidental to their main duties? What of contacts between civil servants and private groups, or of Army bandsmen who help with recruiting, or of postmasters at whose stations publicity material is distributed? What of the public speeches of administrative chiefs and of the ghost writers, personal assistants, and other officials who brief them? What of the time they themselves devote to planning and overseeing public relations policy? What of the time which information staffs spend on purely administrative functions such as controlling the printing and binding appropriations of the whole department? In particular, how deal with agencies like the Extension Service and the Office of Education, whose reason for existence is to carry on public relations in a broad sense?

The difficulties of even rough measurement are illustrated by the much quoted statement that in 1946 the federal government was employing 45,000 "propagandists" at an annual cost of $75 million. It was based on a memorandum circulated by the Bureau of the Budget at the request of a subcommittee of the Senate Appropriations Committee.[1]

The statement covered "educational, informational, promotional, and publicity activities." To include education was inevitably to blur the picture. To exclude it would have involved an arbitrary distinction between education and information. Secondly, the figure of 45,000 was misleading. Only 23,009 people were in fact engaged full-time on the activities in the fiscal year 1946. The remaining 22,769 devoted more than one week but less than a full year to them, and even so the "total man years of both full-time and other employee service" came to no more than 14,757.

There were on the other side an indeterminate number of exclusions. The Bureau explained that "there are found in almost every public service activity public relations aspects which require the use of publicity, education, information, and promotion as ordinary working tools, inseparable from other means and methods," and that they had never, "except in isolated instances, been distinctively treated in the accounting, budgeting, or appropriating systems and procedures of the federal government." As activities which would be severely handicapped without the full use of publicity, the Bureau cited the work of the Department of Agriculture, "the administration of regulatory statutes, the postal service, the financing of the Treasury, the advancement of public health, the protection of natural resources." Thirdly, the fact that most of the expenditure went on overseas publicity, defense, and the sale of savings bonds is a warning against overhasty deductions from global figures. Lastly, the Bureau took a broad view of the activities on which it was asked to report. It included all published material, except administrative forms, stationery, and official circular letters or other correspondence; salaries and expenses of employees attending meetings of nongovernmental groups, whether or not addresses were made; correspondence relating to the activities; and "individual contacts."

The full list was as follows: publications; press service; radio

[1] *Second Urgent Deficiency Appropriation Bill for 1946, Hearings before Subcommittee of Senate Appropriations Committee, 1946, 17-19.*

broadcasting; group contacts; paid advertisements; exhibits; motion pictures; lantern slides and lecture material; photography; correspondence; individual contacts; educational cooperation with schools, and civic or special interest organizations; posters; miscellaneous and other. It gives a useful bird's-eye view of the media in use at that time. Yet, the Bureau concluded, "the fact remains that 'the publicity set-up' of this government cannot be successfully or accurately segregated or isolated from the other elements of countless governmental functions of which publicity is an essential integral part."

The less spectacular figures presented by the Bureau of the Budget to the House Appropriations Subcommittee in 1947 were not so frequently quoted. These showed a total of 3,199 employees engaged full-time and 1,304 part-time in "public relations and publicity activities" in the fiscal year 1947: the estimated annual salary rate, including full annual cost of part-time personnel, was $13,313,196. The estimate for 1948 was 2,485 full-time and 1,117 part-time employees at a cost for salaries of $11,183,214.

Corresponding information was submitted to the Subcommittee in 1948. It was estimated that in the 1949 fiscal year 2,423 full-time and 1,243 part-time employees would be engaged on public relations and publicity work at an annual salary rate of $13,539,008; 2,025 of the full-time total were accounted for by the National Military Establishment: Department of the Army, 1,011; Department of the Air Force, 672; Department of the Navy, 333; Office of the Secretary of Defense, 8; the Panama Canal, 1. The Military Establishment also accounted for nearly half (511) of the part-time total.

For all non-military activities there remained 398 full-time and 732 part-time employees: the estimated annual salary bill was less than $5½ million. The Veterans Administration reported 100 full-time employees and none employed part-time; the Department of Agriculture 69 full-time and 447 part-time; Commerce, including the Civil Aeronautics Board, 52 and 11 respectively; Treasury 41 and 2; Labor 27 and 3; the Department of State 23 and 23; the Atomic Energy Commission 23 and 4; the Housing and Home Finance Agency 16 and

20. No other agency reported as many as ten full-time employees, and only three more than ten in both categories; these were the Federal Security Agency 0 and 89; the Interior Department 3 and 78; the Tennessee Valley Authority 0 and 14; and the Civil Service Commission 0 and 11.

If the earlier statistics were of little value because they covered too wide an area, these figures suffered from the opposite defect. Yet both were collected under direction from Congress with the same object—to measure the effort which the federal government was expending upon "public relations and publicity." And possibly the chief value of each is to illustrate the difficulty of disentangling the activities which the inquiries were intended to measure from "educational" and other work undertaken as an integral part of an administrative program.

The omissions from the later figures are as significant as what was included. The President's press secretary and his staff were left out, presumably on the ground that they were engaged not on publicity or public relations but on press relations. The Advertising and Motion Picture Liaison Divisions were omitted, presumably because they were engaged on coordination and liaison. The State Department partly or wholly disregarded its overseas information activities. There was a nil return for the War Assets Administration.

Departments also differed in their interpretation of the material they were to furnish. A necessarily artificial, if proper, distinction was sometimes drawn between public relations and administrative duties in the case of officers who were obviously information specialists, with the result that even the heads of information divisions were sometimes counted in the part-time category, on the ground that they spent part of their time on administration.

In view of the difficulties, no attempt will be made here to estimate the total expenditure on government public relations or the total staff employed, nor to isolate "information," "publicity," and "public relations." In official usage the terms are for the most part interchangeable. "Information" is generally preferred because it lacks the promotional connotations of the alternatives; the Hoover Commission favored "information and publications officer." [2] However, in 1947–1948 a few agencies which were more daring or felt more secure than others were employing staff which were described as engaged on "public relations": the Treasury, Justice, and Post Office Departments were some which had "directors of public relations."

Who are the public relations or information staffs? Most of them are, naturally, publicity technicians—experts in writing, radio, graphics, films, exhibits, and other media. In official parlance, they are many different things—"creative writer," "research writer," "editor," "visual information specialist," "motion picture sound engineer," "chief of graphics unit," "exhibits specialist," and so on. Substantial numbers are also employed on routine duties connected with the physical preparation and distribution of information material, and with the operation of the administrative controls imposed by Congress and the Bureau of the Budget.

The men and women in the middle and lower strata are doing in government service the technical jobs which they might be doing in a commercial office—editing, designing posters, taking photographs, mounting exhibits, attending to secretarial and clerical routine. They contain some of the information chiefs of tomorrow, but with few exceptions they are craftsmen who will never have to handle policy.

The top men are the nearest counterparts to the business public relations executive and the public relations counsel. They include the directors of information or public relations of the principal agencies, a few personal advisers to administrative heads, some of the deputies in the more important offices, and the information chiefs of some of the semi-autonomous bureaus within the departments. Whether their assignments are large or small, their common feature is that they are the principal public relations advisers of the top executive. They are the key people on whom more than any of their colleagues the quality of the Federal information services depends.

[2] Hoover Commission *Reports, passim.*

Let us look at a few of the top men in 1948. Charles G. Ross, press secretary to the President, was a boyhood friend of Mr. Truman and a former Washington correspondent who had won the Pulitzer Prize in 1932. The Assistant Secretary for Public Affairs at the State Department was a career diplomat, George V. Allen, who had been ambassador to Iran and was appointed ambassador to Yugoslavia in 1949, when he was succeeded by E. W. Barrett, editorial director of *Newsweek* magazine. Under Allen, in charge of the public relations program at home was Francis H. Russell, a lawyer, who had served under another lawyer, John S. Dickey, when systematic liaison between the State Department and the public was being developed. Press relations was separately organized in a staff office under Michael J. McDermott, special assistant for press relations, who had been doing this work for many years: according to a task force report to the Hoover Commission he did not participate in the high-level decisions, and the Commission itself recommended the assimilation of press relations into the general information machinery of the Department. The chief of public information in the Department of the Army was a regular soldier, Major General F. L. Parks. Keith Himebaugh, director of information at the Department of Agriculture, had been engaged in newspaper and radio work before he joined the Department's field information service in 1934. Herbert Little, director of information at the Department of Labor, was formerly Washington correspondent for the *Buffalo Times*. Carlton Skinner, director of information at the Interior Department, had been on the Washington staff of the United Press and later with the Maritime Commission.

These examples illustrate the heterogeneity of talent at the higher levels, but the State Departments and the defense departments are not typical. They do less than justice to the most noticeable characteristic of the group as a whole—the marked preponderance of newspapermen. In some cases newspaper experience has been short or specialized, but with few exceptions the Washington information chiefs look upon themselves as newspapermen by profession and most have known the workaday life of the newspaper reporter. In short, they are the same kind of people that become public relations counsel and public relations executives elsewhere.

The preponderance of newspapermen is understandable. Press liaison and publications are the main information activities of the federal government, and the choice of newspapermen is less likely to offend either Congress or the press itself than the obvious alternatives. It is also argued that it is impossible to turn anywhere else with the same assurance of finding certain essential qualifications—skill in writing, a sense of news, ability to work to a deadline, experience in collecting information and interpreting public reactions.

Others think that, far from there being any presumption in favor of newspapermen for the higher information posts, the contrary is true. While they are well fitted to handle press relations, their experience is a hindrance when it comes to planning and carrying out an integrated program. They do not think in administrative terms. Their highly developed news sense preoccupies them with the events of the moment, and they are apt to suppose that when they have got their material into print they have done with it. They are unaccustomed to scientific research, impatient of social psychology and sociology, prejudiced against the other media, uninterested in group relations.

Fortunately it is unnecessary to take sides in this argument. The facts are that, as in other public relations appointments, experience of one of the mass media is normally regarded as essential, and that of the mass media the press is by a long way the most important from the point of view of government public relations.

Formally the information chiefs have a high status. As McCamy found before the war, they usually have a staff position near the top executive, on a par with the staff officers responsible for personnel management, law, and finance. This was also the recommendation of the Hoover Commission, who thought that they should be responsible to the Administrative Assistant Secretary whom the Commission advocated for each of the departments.

There may sometimes be intermediaries between the director of information and the head of the department—he may have devolved some of his responsibilities to an Under or Assistant Secretary, as the Hoover Commission envisaged, or one of his personal entourage may take a special interest in public relations—but in the ordinary course the director of information retains the right of access to the top administrator and is in close touch with him. He handles his press relations, arranges his press conferences, covers his speeches, collects material for them, sometimes prepares them. How much this means in practice depends on the volume of top-level press relations, the methods of work of the two men, their congeniality one to another. Where their personal relations are close, the director of information may be taken into the wider counsels of the department, and his status will grow correspondingly. But this is exceptional, and the government information chiefs have not in general secured the share in policy making which is one of the goals of the public relations group as a whole. The intake of leading figures from outside during the war made no permanent change in this respect, and, as things are, there would be no place for high-powered public relations advisers. The suspicions of Congress would be deepened, and the political chiefs do not feel the need.

Most of the top information officers have civil service status, and the impression which they make is of conscientious public servants who are anxious to observe the constitutional proprieties. They look forward with varying degrees of assurance to holding their jobs if the political color of the administration changes. They believe that they can make an important contribution to administration, and they want to show that their work can be done in a spirit of civil service impartiality. On the whole they are unsympathetic alike to the more flamboyant and the more scientific aspects of commercial public relations, and its "mumbo jumbo" has little place in their vocabulary. They feel frustrated by the atmosphere of hostility and suspicion in which they have to operate and by the often arbitrary cuts in appropriations which most departments have experienced. They are not greatly preoccupied with the question of professional status, many of them feel little affinity with their confreres in business, and few of them belong to the public relations associations, partly but not only because the associations have been backward in cultivating their support.

It is characteristic that, except on the job, nothing is done to train recruits in the theory and practice of their duties. Such organized training as there was in 1948 was directed toward the equipment of other people to help in government public relations. The Armed Forces had systematic arrangements for the instruction of officers and enlisted men in public information duties. One of the main purposes of the information activities of the Department of Agriculture has been the training of field representatives, employees of the Extension Service, and others in the effective use of the various media. The experiments of the Office of Information under Morse Salisbury in the 1930's did much to raise the general level of radio speaking: its Radio Service held 34 radio schools in 1947–1948. The enterprising readability program of the Extension Service will be described later.

For the ambitious federal information specialist who wants to improve himself by study out of office hours there are—or were in 1948—only the courses provided by the Graduate School of the Department of Agriculture and the American University. In 1948 neither had much to offer beyond a few courses in specialized publicity techniques, such as editing, radio script writing, and "visual presentation in federal information work" ("primarily for information workers, but will be useful as background for subject matter specialists and junior executives"). The only noteworthy exception was an advanced course on "government-public relationships" which was to be given in the Agriculture Graduate School by R. L. Webster, associate director of information of the Department of Agriculture, and others. It was "designed to give federal administrators and those who look forward to executive positions an appreciation of the scope and fundamental nature of public relationships of a government agency." It promised to be most interesting. It did not take place because of lack of enrolments, and a similar course suffered the same fate in the following year.

What of coordination—both within agencies and over the government as a whole?

The federal government is distinctive for the independence enjoyed by its individual units, and this independence extends beyond the separate units to the bureaus within them. The President is the sun which keeps the whole system alive. The departments and agencies circulate around him like planets, and the planets have their satellites in the shape of the bureaus. Formal coordinating machinery is conspicuously lacking, and the main coordinating factor is the personality of the administrative head, whether it is the President or one of the lesser luminaries. The checkered stories of the most recent attempts at the systematic coordination of information work—the Office of Government Reports, and the wartime experiments culminating in the Office of War Information, whose chief, Elmer Davis, was as conciliatory as his predecessor of the first war, George Creel, had been provocative—are a vivid reminder of the difficulties which the would-be coordinator must overcome, whatever his field.

A theoretical case can be argued for government-wide coordination of information work for two purposes.

There may be coordination to ensure that an integrated picture of government activities is presented to the people and that inconsistencies and overlapping are avoided. This was one of the reasons for setting up the Office of War Information.

Or the purpose may be economy and efficiency—to make limited resources go further, to pool talent, to promote uniform standards, to facilitate interchange of staff and the circulation of ideas, to plan the publicity releases of the different departments to meet the convenience of the media and the public. Centralized production and distribution of films may save money and raise the level of technical achievement; it may enable better use to be made of an exceptionally talented producer. Central issue or supervision of press releases, such as was exercised by the OWI, may help the newspapers by regulating the flow of government material, and avoid clashes between important stories from different departments. As for the radio, Jeanette Sayre reported in 1941 that some broadcasters thought that if government radio activities were better coordinated, "programs would be improved, stations would be happier, and more people would listen to federal programs." [3] The Fulbright-Aiken Bill of 1947 proposed a central clearinghouse for technical information under the Department of Commerce as a service for the convenience of the public.

There is no government-wide machinery for the coordination of information policy with a view to presenting an integrated picture to the public. Whether this result is achieved—as indeed in other branches of federal administration—depends upon the extent to which the different units of the government share a common outlook and upon the informal contacts which the different information offices make with one another as a matter of commonsense administration.

Of coordination in the actual execution of public relations programs there is on the other hand more than might be expected. The outstanding example is the Government Printing Office, and, though the motives of Congress have been political, a case for centralized printing can be made out on grounds of economy and efficiency. The suggestion has even been made that, with the double object of relieving the fears of Congress and of enabling the Executive to make more effective use of publicity, the production of other publicity material should be centralized in bodies modeled on the GPO. McCamy's investigations for the public libraries inquiry led him, however, to the conclusion that its transfer to the Executive was badly needed.

The other examples of administrative coordination are minor, but cumulatively not unimportant. The regulative functions of the Bureau of the Budget operate to produce uniformity of standards as far as publications are concerned. The coordination exercised by the Advertising and Motion Picture Liaison Divisions in the Executive Office of the President

[3] Jeanette Sayre, *An Analysis of the Radio Broadcasting Activities of Federal Agencies* (Littauer Center, Harvard University, Studies in the Control of Radio, No. 3, 1941), 116.

has been more positive. They were almost the only survivors of the OWI, and the reason was that outside interests which had services to give the government found it convenient to deal through one office rather than many. On the film side there was very little to do, but the Advertising Liaison Division has acted as the link with the Advertising Council in programs worth many millions of dollars to the taxpayer. *The United States Government Manual,* a directory of the Executive Branch, also survived the liquidation of the central services rendered by OWI, and ultimately found a home with the National Archives; the Government Information Service, which rendered a comparable service, was granted a short reprieve, but was abolished in 1947. The Motion Picture Service of the Department of Agriculture has been widely used by other agencies. The Federal Reports Act of 1942 had as one of its incidental consequences that all opinion research projects required the approval of the Bureau of the Budget. Recruiting is coordinated through the Civil Service Commission with the result that there are supposedly common standards of entry at the junior levels.

But the formal arrangements do not tell the whole story. It is true that in the United States more respect is paid to formalized rules and procedures than in some other countries, notably Britain, and that informal arrangements tend to be crystallized in black and white before they are very old. None the less, under any system the dynamic is less likely to be found in the letter of the office manual than in personal relationships, in the mores of the organization, in its *esprit de corps,* in the unexpressed assumptions of those who belong to it. So with the information services of the federal government.

To the extent that coordination depends on formal machinery—the keeping of centralized records, the pooling of physical resources, the provision of common services to the public—little can be done to fill the gap by informal means. There is a big area, however, in which machinery is less important than good will, personal relationships, and a common approach.

As far as the methods and outlook of federal information staffs are concerned, the observer will be struck less by the disparities than by the similarities. This may be attributed to several causes. First is the fact that so many information officers are former newspapermen. Sharing the same background, they think on the same lines and set about their work in the same way. The problems which they have in common call for similar solutions, and the mass media, which are their common clients, have to be handled in the same way. The information chiefs are few enough to have a corporate feeling which is strengthened by their sense of unity in the face of their critics, and by the restrictive effect of the attitude of Congress upon any tendencies to exuberance and extravagance. They know one another as friends and former newspaper associates. They mix in the same circles; many of them belong to the National Press Club.

What of coordination within agencies? The details vary, but the pattern is similar. The information offices of the bureaus and subdepartments enjoy a degree of autonomy which is usually substantial. As was said by Wayne Coy, a former assistant director of the Bureau of the Budget: "Generally speaking, the departments are weakest in the continued translation of the drives coming from their component parts—the bureaus, divisions, branches, and sections—into a work plan truly agency-wide. Each bureau is likely to think of itself as a world of its own, filled with a feeling of its own importance, and eager for self-sufficiency." [4]

The information office is unlikely to be stronger than the department itself in its relations with the component parts. Its strength lies in its close association with the Secretary or other administrative chief, and in the position which it usually occupies as the channel of communication with the Government Printing Office and the Bureau of the Budget on publications. It normally clears all releases—whatever the medium. It may —as in the Department of Agriculture—provide some central services, though the bureaus may duplicate them to some extent. It will certainly be charged with a general responsibility

[4] Wayne Coy, "Federal Executive Reorganization Re-examined: A Symposium, I," *American Political Science Review*, 40 (6), December 1946, 1129.

for "coordinating" the information activities of the department as a whole.

In terms the authority of the departmental director of information may be considerable. The Administrative Regulations of the Department of Agriculture provided as follows in 1948: "The director of information is responsible for coordinating the informational work of all agencies in the Department. All such informational work shall be cleared with the director of information. To correlate information arising in different agencies, and to make it more effective, the director of information shall have general charge of all informational work of the Department. He shall supervise the issuance of publications, press releases, and radio releases to meet the current needs of farmers, homemakers, and other groups. . . . The director of information is authorized to cooperate with agency heads in coordinating all phases of the Department's work that affect the informational programs and will keep policies and procedures responsive to current needs. He shall allocate printing funds and otherwise manage the Department's informational work in a way most effectively to fulfill the Department's obligations to the public."

The responsibilities of the Division of Publications of the Department of Commerce were similar. Its "objective" was "to coordinate and direct all informational activities of the Department"; and in addition to specific responsibilities it was charged to "form the closest possible working relationships with the staffs carrying out informational activities in the constituent offices and bureaus of the Department . . . and . . . exercise such functional supervision over these staffs as is necessary for policy coordination, quality control, press room direction and distribution."

The centrifugal tendencies are strong. If the departmental director of information shares in the authority of the head of the department, the bureau information chief is in a similar relationship to the head of his bureau—appointed by him, in practice irremovable except with his consent, responsible to him, and operating with bureau appropriations. He may draw the same salary as the departmental director of information and may very well control a larger staff. Where there is resistance to central control, the latter can intervene effectively only with the support of the head of the bureau, who is unlikely to be predisposed to the centralization of authority. In practice he is no more than *primus inter pares*, and the most he can do—in the words of another and perhaps more realistic operations manual—is:

"To help safeguard policy for the Agency as a whole;

"To present a united front—considering each item in relationship to the broader agency picture, and avoiding any apparent contradictions on matters of fact, as well as policy;

"To facilitate effective distribution and timing;

"To help eliminate gaps and duplications, crossed wires and unnecessary delay;

"To maintain a central over-all list of all officially released informational material issued from the Agency."

To ask whether there should be increased coordination at any level is to ask a largely academic question. It will not be settled as a matter of operational efficiency. There seems to be no prospect of further experiments with a government-wide information agency except in an emergency. Even at lower levels what will happen will be determined by political, constitutional, and even personal considerations.

So far this chapter has been written almost exclusively in terms of Washington. Yet it is a platitude, often repeated to visitors from overseas, that the mistake of seeing the United States through the spectacles of Washington is second only to that of seeing it through those of New York. This is true of the federal government. It is not only that not more than one in six or seven federal employees are in the capital, but their direct impact upon the citizen is proportionately even less. Very broadly, Washington deals in ideas, and the field offices in action.

It might be supposed *a priori* that the majority of the information staffs would also be in the field, close to the main currents of regional opinion and in touch with the grass roots of American democracy. The contrary has always been the case. In 1937, McCamy learned of nine Washington offices with some form of regional publicity organization: Soil Conservation Service, 11 agents; Forest Service, 9; Farm Credit Administration, 12; Federal Housing Administration, 8; Reclamation Service, 2; National Park Service, 4; Public Works Administration, Housing Division, 4; Resettlement Administration, 12; Social Security Board, 12. The Works Progress Administration had a publicity official attached to each state office, and six regional officials who helped these officers with their programs.

The position after the war was similar. In January 1948, twelve civilian agencies had field information staffs which were recognizable as such from their designations: Soil Conservation Service, 25; Forest Service, 9; Production and Marketing Administration, 6; Bureau of Animal Industry (campaign against foot and mouth disease, etc.), 1; Commodity Credit Corporation, 8; Bureau of Domestic and Foreign Commerce, 5; Bureau of Reclamation, 7; Bureau of the Public Debt, 14; U.S. Employment Service, 1; Veterans Administration, 19; War Assets Administration, 131; Civil Service Commission, 1.

The field staffs are small for reasons that are partly administrative and partly political. With a staff function, the main concentration of effort is naturally at headquarters where policy is made; secondary concentrations will be found at points where policy making has been devolved. The ideal pattern for the information services will also be affected by the organization of the media through which they have to work. Some important media can be handled satisfactorily only at the center. This is broadly true of motion pictures, magazines, and official publications; it obviously applies to national advertising and national broadcasting; and it is true on all major issues even of the newspapers, who look to their Washington correspondents and the wire services to inform them of important news about the federal government.

On the other hand, if administrative efficiency were the test, most of the larger agencies could no doubt do their information work more effectively with the aid of regional and field representatives. Both the chief media—the newspapers and the radio—are highly localized. It is impossible for Washington to take full account of the multiplicity of local differences and idiosyncrasies. Ideally, almost everything issued from Washington would gain from being channeled through experts who are in touch with local conditions, and the closer their local contacts with the media, the greater the impact will be. It is one of the defects of federal publicity—as of much publicity of other national organizations—that it is imperfectly adapted to the needs of its audiences, to the Negro farmer of Mississippi, the hill folk of Kentucky, the Pittsburgh steel worker, the Puerto Rican immigrant. Nor is it just a matter of adapting news releases to different audiences. Motion pictures, radio features, advertising, posters, publications—theoretically all would gain.

To suggest that much more could be done would be unrealistic. Even if the political and constitutional difficulties did not exist, the cost of substantially extended programs would be prohibitive. That federal agencies would like to do more is shown by the record. Suspicious of any governmental publicity, Congress is exceptionally suspicious of field publicity. This is understandable. To the extent that there is a risk that official information services will be used to influence opinion in favor of the administration and against its opponents, the closer they get to the people the greater the danger, and individual Congressmen will suffer in their own territory. Field information activities also touch upon another sensitive spot in the constitutional system—the federal-state relationship itself.

Congress has left no doubt about its attitude. One of the New Deal experiments which it liked least was the establishment of state information offices by the National Emergency Council. The domestic field offices of the Office of War Information were an object of special attack, and were eliminated when the domestic branch was cut by two-thirds in 1943. The result was not in accordance with expectations—within a year there had been such an upgrowth of field activities among other agencies that the field staffs of the Office of Price Administration alone exceeded those formerly employed by the OWI—but the purpose was plain. The Department of Labor had a similar experience; regional offices which were set up in 1946 were swept away in 1947. The Department of Agriculture was expressly forbidden by law to have a regional information organization, though the ban did not apply to its bureaus. Other agencies had to abandon or reduce drastically their field information activities as a result of Congressional action. The armed forces are the only important exception to the general rule; and they are less susceptible to control by Congress, and do not so immediately affect states' rights or the privileges of Congressmen.

Where field information offices exist, the pattern is as might be expected. They are in a staff relationship to the chief local administrator, are responsible to him, and are subject only to a vague suzerainty from the director of information in Washington. As at headquarters, the information specialists themselves are mainly engaged in press and radio liaison, supplying information from their own areas and acting as a channel through which material from Washington is distributed and adapted to local needs. But they are a long way from the grass roots. A mere handful of men and women often responsible for areas larger than many independent countries, their own impact is only relatively less broad than that of their headquarters. And they cover a very small part of the activities of the federal government.

Where there are no information specialists, it does not follow that no information work is done. There are few offices which in modern conditions never have to issue news releases, arrange for a public speech, answer inquiries from the newspapers; and, in the absence of a specialist, the work falls to other members of the staff. This is apart from the agencies of whose line operations public relations is so integral a part that they look to their staff as a whole to act in a public relations capacity. With some it is difficult to say where information is to be demarcated from other activities. The most that can be said is that publicity is the specialty of the information staff, and it is to them that the agency would look where specialized techniques were important. With their colleagues it is secondary to agriculture or education or weather forecasting, or whatever the subject in which they are experts.

One duty of the security force of the TVA is to conduct visitors around the Authority's property. They are trained in public relations as well as in fire fighting and law enforcement. Rangers of the Forest Service are expected to look after their own public relations—to broadcast, to issue news releases, to arrange for visits by community leaders. The National Park Service takes just pride in its interpretative service: it is a nice point whether the naturalists who give lectures to visitors and the rangers who tell them of the facilities in the parks are federal "propagandists." The armed forces believe that every man should play his part in public information and in building prestige with civilians. And there are the agencies—like the Public Health Service and the Women's Bureau—whose primary purposes include public information.

There is in fact no stopping short of the conclusion that every official who comes into contact with the public is an agent of government information. Even the research workers emerge from their laboratories to report on their studies in talks to learned audiences or articles in learned magazines. In the equipment of departments which have to administer complicated laws affecting large numbers of people, explanatory literature is hardly less essential than telephones and typewriters. Obvious instances are the Veterans Administration, the Bureau of Internal Revenue, and the Post Office Department. Talks by officials on the radio and to local groups, film showings, exhibits, and other information activities are also important aids to routine administration which operating officials use as a matter of course in their everyday duties. The same techniques are applied on a large scale in the federal government's own "employee relations."

What is the relationship between the information specialists and the thousands of other officials who are engaged on information work in ways like these? Why, asked Representative R. B. Wigglesworth in 1948, did the Federal Mediation and Conciliation Service, with 241 people out in the field, need an information office at all? "Do you not have enough employees who can tell them what the objectives of your Service are?" [5]

The answer will vary. By and large, it is, first, that some media cannot be used at all, and others cannot be used to full effect, without employing experts. Experts are needed to put literature about social security into popular form, and to oversee the production of films shown by forest rangers; with their help press and radio can be used to better advantage. Representative Wigglesworth recalled his own days as a civil servant: "If the Secretary had something to say to the people, he called someone in, dictated a memorandum, and they gave it out to the press at noon." [6] The Secretary's own statements are still most important for his department's public relations, but the days are gone when occasional high-level press releases will suffice to put over departmental programs. Important though the part of the operating official must continue to be, under modern conditions the help of experts is indispensable. The Hoover Commission's task force on departmental management said that department heads needed specialized assistance on public relations problems. It may only be a question of arranging a press conference—who, for example, should be invited, and when and where would be best—or of editing an explanatory leaflet. It may involve the planning and oversight of a comprehensive public relations program.

Secondly, information divisions do not as a rule speak direct to the people. For good constitutional and practical reasons they prefer to channel their material through others. The privately owned mass media are the main channel. Another important channel is provided by the hundreds of thousands of officials who are in day-to-day contact with the people and with the public authorities and private groups whose collaboration is essential to the success of the public relations programs of federal agencies. Line officials everywhere play a positive part in government public relations through speeches, radio talks, press interviews, contacts with their communities, and otherwise. They also make a major if more passive contribution as

[5] *Urgent Deficiency Appropriation Bill for 1948, Hearings before Subcommittee of House Appropriations Committee,* 1948, 82.
[6] *ibid.*

distributors of the material which the information specialists prepare—issuing pamphlets, displaying posters, putting on movie shows, and so on.

State and other public authorities are also big consumers of federal information material, notably in their public health, educational, social security, and agricultural programs. They are often partners in its preparation. The forest fire prevention campaign, for example, is directed by a joint federal and state committee, and the cost is shared. The outstanding case of federal-state collaboration is the Extension Service.

In 1947 extension agents distributed 18 million bulletins, made 47,000 radio talks, and issued 725,000 news and advice stories. This was in addition to visiting 2 million farms, receiving 9 million visitors, conducting 800,000 demonstrations, and holding meetings which over 52 million people attended.[7] It is an almost unbelievable tally. Here is the end product of the principal information program of the Department of Agriculture. These are the ways in which material originating in the bureaus and research stations of the department finally reaches the farmer and his wife. On its way to them it has passed through the specialist information divisions, but it comes to them immediately from state and county officials, who combine their primary functions as expert agricultural advisers with important public relations responsibilities. In discharging these responsibilities they act as distributors for centrally prepared publicity, and they engage direct in public information by word of mouth and through the local media.

To move still further away from the official information machinery, similar aid is being received from thousands of private organizations and hundreds of thousands of private individuals. It is not proposed here to discuss their relations with the federal government in detail: to do so would require and deserve a whole volume. To say that their contribution to government public relations is great is understatement. It is indispensable to many information programs because it introduces the human element without which their impact will necessarily be diffuse and insufficiently related to individual circumstances.

[7] *Report of the Secretary of Agriculture,* 1947, 149.

It supplements the limited resources of the official information services with additional manpower and an almost infinitely flexible machinery for adapting generalized material to the needs of particular sections of the population.

It is not inconsistent with this to add that some of the most important help is purely coincidental. The motive for enlisting outside collaboration may be political or administrative, and have nothing specifically to do with information as such. It may manifest itself in the different aspects of so-called "clientele government." An agency may set up an advisory committee to placate critics or to pool expert opinion. Whether those concerned are aware of it or not, a by-product is that influential people are the better informed and the better able to explain government policies to their constituents and associates.

Conscious or unconscious, this is public relations addressed to opinion-forming groups. Much the same result may flow from some of the unwritten rules of the American Constitution which puzzle the stranger and test the ingenuity of those who try to rationalize them—for example, the convention that two of the Assistant Secretaries of the Department of Labor should be representatives of labor unions, and the *de facto* veto which John L. Lewis has reputedly exercised over the appointment of the chief of the Bureau of Mines. So also with the relationship between Congress and the Executive. Perhaps without generally knowing it, Congressmen are important agents of government information. Their contribution is not confined to distributing publications on a large scale. In their speeches, correspondence, and personal contacts, they are constantly passing on material which originated in a government department.

This may seem to be laboring the obvious. That is not necessarily a fault—the obvious is too easily taken for granted. Information about federal activities and programs is being carried all the time along all the antennae which start in Washington and end in the home of the plain American citizen. Whether the carriers act from a sense of public duty or out of self-interest is incidental and makes little difference to the result. It may be asked again why it is necessary to have specialized information services when there are plenty of unofficial channels. The first answer is of course the need for experts to prepare and process much of the material. The second is that the transmission of information through normal administrative and constitutional processes is necessarily haphazard. Specialists are required to organize the contacts with outside groups and to systematize the help which is received from them as far as this is practicable.

Among the most interesting information programs are those in which federal agencies have looked beyond the mass media and have deliberately set out to enlist the help of unofficial groups and private citizens as voluntary agents of government public relations.

The armed forces, with the special problem of breaking down the barriers which seal them off from civilians, have for many years cultivated a large number of important voluntary organizations; in 1947 the War and Navy Departments had special branches devoted to liaison with these groups. First there are the organizations interested specifically in service questions. In 1947–1948 the Navy Council was acting as a channel for the flow of information in both directions between the Navy and eighteen bodies of the type of the Navy League, the Friends of the Navy, and the Navy Mothers Clubs of America. Industry was reached through the Navy Industrial Association. Special attention was given to veterans', women's, and youth organizations, but no relevant category was neglected. Washington can keep in touch only with the national representatives of the larger groups. At the regional and local level, one of the responsibilities of naval commandants was to maintain contacts with individuals and bodies who can make a significant contribution to the public relations of the Navy. Their interest was stimulated by "open days," by invitations to attend Navy Day and other celebrations, by the provision of speakers, by the loan of films, and by other well-tried public relations methods. Navy civilian indoctrination courses at Columbia University catered to legislators, business leaders, writers, educators, and other opinion makers. The main purpose of these activities was to foster the prestige of the Navy.

The Army has used essentially similar methods for the same purpose, but it has also had to pay more attention to recruiting. The postwar recruiting drive, started in 1945, made extensive use of advertising and other publicity methods, but these were supplemented by a grassroots program which was intended to get the cooperation of community leaders in influencing possible recruits and their parents. The goal was the establishment in some 2,000 localities with recruiting stations of Military Manpower Committees under the chairmanship of a leading citizen, and including representatives of the local press and radio, civic groups like the Kiwanis and the Elks, women's clubs, and educational and other community organizations. There were three main objects: (a) to enlist practical help— for example, in helping recruiting officers to gain a hearing in quarters where they might otherwise be received with suspicion; (b) to cultivate the general good will of the community through its leaders and organized groups; and (c) to mobilize the cooperation of community leaders in Army publicity, by persuading the editor to keep the recruiting campaign before the public, the businessman to sponsor advertisements, the department store to display promotional material, the clubs to organize special events with the object of furthering the campaign.

Voluntary organizations have also been important in the domestic public relations of the State Department. Since the war, liaison with organizations interested in foreign affairs has been, next to press and radio relations, the Department's chief method of informing the American public. The task force appointed by the Hoover Commission thought that it might be more fully developed, but in 1947–1948 the Department was in touch with about 300 bodies—by means of conferences, publications and periodicals, speakers, and personal contacts. Under arrangements first made in 1946 and extended later, a number of regional organizations formed distributing centers which were among the principal outlets through which State Department publications reached the public.

The Department did not adopt a mass approach. It lacked the resources, and it is arguable that the attempt would not have been worth making. It concentrated on a relatively small number of people who were influential in forming opinion, and looked to them to supplement the press and the radio in interpreting its activities to a wider public. As Secretary Acheson when he was Under Secretary urged women's groups to do with respect to the British Loan,[8] it relied on them for help in translating the technicalities of foreign policy into simple language which the people generally understand.

These are three examples of a public relations method of which Federal agencies make wide and important use. Here briefly are a few more:

(1) Two from agriculture. (a) In 1944 M. L. Wilson, director of the Extension Service, defined the grassroots organization which was one of the principles of extension work. It was "sponsorship of local programs by local groups of rural people in cooperation with the resident agent." Over a million voluntary local leaders were helping in 1947.[9] (b) In 1948, seven lumber companies, ten railroads, seven food processing companies, and seven gas and oil companies were among over a hundred business organizations cooperating in the information program of the Soil Conservation Service. Teachers helped through systematic school courses in soil conservation.[10]

(2) An inter-agency committee of federal and private agencies organized the third annual "National Employ-the-Physically-Handicapped Week" in 1947. Official publicity was reinforced with community programs embracing civic, business, veterans', women's, and other groups. Ministers, priests and rabbis were asked to cooperate by making announcements from their pulpits and in their church bulletins.

(3) In 1946–1947, the Apprentice Training Service of the Department of Labor published 97,000 pamphlets, 35,000 reprints of articles, and 5,600 copies of speeches for distribution through its field staff and other channels to employers, labor unions, veterans' organizations, and so on.[11]

[8] *Washington Post*, January 31, 1946.
[9] M. L. Wilson, "Thirty Years of Extension Work," *Land Policy Review*, Fall 1944: and *Report of the Secretary of Agriculture*, 1947, 149.
[10] Information obtained from the Soil Conservation Service.
[11] *Annual Report of the Secretary for Labor for 1947*, 50.

(4) The small central and state staffs of the savings bonds campaign served mainly to supply policy guidance and publicity material to millions of voluntary helpers. This is another campaign in which the share of the teachers is important. It is illustrated by the *School Savings Journal,* published by the Savings Bond Division of the Treasury Department and mailed to all principals of public schools. In 1948 they could get classroom aids (such as "Lessons in Budgeting" and elementary arithmetic work books), "play and program materials," a quarterly clipsheet for high school papers, films, free mats, booklets, the School Savings Charter. In each issue of the *Journal* there was a poster for classroom display: the Minute Man, "symbol of security and peace," was the central figure in the poster for spring 1947.

(5) Even the Customs Service—in most countries traditionally backward in such matters—turned to public relations after the war. John S. Graham of the Treasury Department told Congress in 1948 that an illustrated pamphlet in popular language had been prepared for the guidance of the traveling public, but it was to be published and distributed through the agency of the American Automobile Association.[12]

It would be easy to give more examples, but enough has perhaps been said to emphasize the importance of the aid which is being received, though, as McCamy showed in 1949 in his study of the role of public libraries in the distribution of government publications, by no means all the possibilities have been fully developed. The extension agents, the rabbis who tell their congregations about the work for the disabled, the teachers who displayed the Minute Man poster, the AAA men who explain the customs regulations to tourists, the civil servants who hand out leaflets or speak to local groups—these are the field officers who count for most in government public relations. No information specialists can fill their place. For those who like the term, these are the army of federal propagandists, but it is propaganda which rightly does not stir the anxieties of

[12] *Supplemental Treasury and Post Office Departments Appropriation Bill for 1949, Hearings before Subcommittee of House Appropriations Committee,* 1948, 42–3.

Congress. Call it "active democracy," or the "American way," or what you like; it is arguable that it is no substitute for a more dynamic relationship, but few will dispute that citizen participation in government on such a scale is healthy. It is also good administration.

One reason for thinking that it is good administration is that it facilitates the flow of information and opinion to as well as from government. The service groups do not merely listen to the defense departments; they also seek to influence them. The State Department looks to the voluntary bodies with which it is in touch for advice and criticism as well as to disseminate information.

This is important. It is a commonplace that a public relations program should be based on an analysis of public attitudes and that the interpretation of the public is one of the duties of a director of public relations. Too often, however, actual practice is but a pale reflection of the textbook theory. Even where public relations is highly organized, interpretation of the public is commonly much more rudimentary than interpretation to the public. It has a subordinate place in the typical federal information office. Administrators do not turn as a matter of course to their information divisions when they want to assess opinion, though they may turn to a trusted information chief, as they would to others, for his personal view of what opinion is and what opinion will stand. He will no doubt say that it is part of his job to keep abreast of public opinion but in no more precise a sense than a politician or a newspaperman might say the same thing. He may offer a few concessions to system, such as collecting press clippings, studying newspapers with different points of view, or sounding his friends at the National Press Club. In the last resort, like the newspaperman that he usually is, he relies mainly on his intuition.

On the whole, federal agencies are still using the methods of assessing opinion that served Abraham Lincoln. They are not necessarily the worse for being traditional and unsystematic. At least they are well tried. They are also diverse. Some are formal and expressly provided by law: Presidential and Congressional elections, and hearings on the Hill are the classical means by which opinion is brought to bear upon the Executive. Others are part of the unwritten constitution. Instances are lobbying and clientele relationships with government departments. There are hundreds of advisory bodies. Deputations are heard, and interviews are granted. On controversial issues mail pours in from the public and from Congress. Political managers, old friends, valued assistants, sympathetic and unsympathetic Congressmen, express their opinions. Information about public reactions travels to Washington from the field offices, and some of it percolates to the makers of policy. High officials read the newspapers of their choice, listen to their favorite radio commentators, attend cocktail parties, play bridge, talk to barbers, have wives—in short, are subject to the same influences as other people. In addition, some of them possess a flair for sensing and weighing opinion which is born of natural aptitude and political experience.

Wisely or not, "Big Government" has made less use than big business of the more scientific methods of gauging opinion which became fashionable when George Gallup achieved a world-wide reputation by predicting Roosevelt's victory in 1936. Gallup and the other pollsters have been energetic in promoting the new tool, and it does not look as if the setback which was suffered after the Presidential election of 1948 will be lasting. Rapid progress has been made in solving some at least of the outstanding technical problems. Social scientists have been eager to exploit one of their few tangible contributions to practical affairs and to earn a share of the recognition which their rivals in the natural sciences have all but monopolized. Along with a due measure of skepticism, opinion research acquired an aura of science, mystery, and novelty which assured it a profitable vogue during the postwar inflation.

At the same time, as leading opinion analysts recognize and were reminded in 1948, the sky is not wholly blue. The cautions with which the more scrupulous qualify their claims are sometimes overshadowed by the enthusiastic salesmanship with which competing organizations—particularly the commercial ones—press their services. The risk is that competition for markets may lead to lower standards, and that disillusionment may follow exaggerated expectations. Opinion research may be oversold. Cheap and shoddy methods may be used in order to cut prices. Results may be oversimplified for the sake of clients who are impatient of reservations and refinements.

The future of opinion research in the federal government will largely depend on the progress it makes elsewhere. So far most politicians and administrators have remained cool to the blandishments which have persuaded many of their business friends.

A small study by Martin Kriesberg in 1944 showed that 88% of the Congressmen and 53% of the top-line federal officials who were interviewed thought that the government should not be interested officially in polls.[13] It is natural that, like newspapermen, members of Congress should be suspicious of a development which threatens their position as interpreters of public opinion to the Executive. In Kriesberg's survey, the legislators ranked polls fifth in usefulness as a method of ascertaining public opinion—after personal mail, visits to the public, newspapers, and visits from the public. Their attitude was summed up by a Representative from the Middle West: "[Polls] create an impression that is misleading. A poll is supposed to represent the people; the Congressman represents them; he should know what the people think. Polls are in contradiction to representative government."

The hesitations of the administrator are due to different causes. Kriesberg's group, though on balance opposed to the federal government using polls, were much more sympathetic to polls in general than was the group of legislators, and placed them first as a method of ascertaining opinion. Nearly twice as many (63%) thought that they were helpful to the democratic process, and 60% that they were usually accurate. But the administrator is bound to be sensitive to the attitude of Congress, and administrators who acknowledge the value of opinion surveys in their place are skeptical about their extended use. They doubt the accuracy of existing techniques for measuring the subtler aspects of opinion, in particular quality as dis-

[13] Martin Kriesberg, "What Congressmen and Administrators Think of the Polls," *Public Opinion Quarterly*, 9 (3), Fall 1945, 333–37.

tinct from quantity. Many decisions cannot wait while surveys are taking place. The high cost limits their usefulness. Where opinion is fluid, a survey may be out of date soon after it has been completed.

The main reason for caution is more fundamental. Advocates of opinion research argue that, whatever its limitations, it gives more accurate results than the traditional methods. One of their favorite examples is the wrong impression which Congress formed of public opinion on selective service in 1941. Whereas members of Congress were misled because 90% of their mail was hostile to compulsory military service, polls showed that the majority of the people were in favor. Allowing that it may sometimes be right to reject majority opinion, it is surely better to know what the majority think instead of relying largely upon guesswork. At the very least a scientific survey should be a useful supplement to what can be learned from other sources.

Avery Leiserson summed up like this in 1949: "The great rationalizing influence that the scientific opinion polls can contribute to this [political] process is not to tell the policymakers what their decisions ought to be, but to clarify for the politicians looking for reasonable, constructive adjustments the extent and area of agreement between the varying shades of opinion in the community or population as a whole. . . . If we can agree that public policy decisions are more apt to be made in the line of public interest when more precise information is available as to the extent of agreement and disagreement among opinion segments of the population than when they are made solely on the basis of group pressures and politicians' hunches, then public opinion research needs no higher justification." [14]

This reasoning is plausible and hard to answer. It presupposes that in competent hands opinion research is sufficiently reliable to add useful information to other material. Some might dispute this, but it would be generally conceded. A more serious difficulty arises at the next stage: in the use to

[14] Avery Leiserson, "Opinion Research and the Political Process," *Public Opinion Quarterly*, 13 (1), Spring 1949, 33.

which the findings are put. In American political conditions they may have more authority than is desirable. Being supposedly scientific, they will certainly be represented as the true voice of the people. Gallup himself has advocated "advisory referenda" using sample survey methods. In doing so, he quoted with approval the Massachusetts law under which "questions of public policy" could be referred to the voters of any electoral district, and the statement by Lord Bryce that the next stage in the development of democratic government would be reached "if the will of the majority of citizens were to become ascertainable at all times." [15]

The danger is that, even if they are in terms advisory, officially administered polls on controversial issues will have an authority which is not far short of mandatory. They are open to the objections which have hitherto led Congress to reject the referendum itself. These objections may be illustrated by two stories. There is the old story of the ship with the drunken skipper and the intoxicated first mate. It ran into a storm. The compass was out of order, so a vote was taken of the passengers to decide which direction was north. This was the wrong way of answering a question which only an expert could answer: the right way would have been to sober up the skipper. The other is a story about Franklin D. Roosevelt. On one occasion he angrily dismissed a poll "with the announcement that the state of public opinion would be different after he had discussed the problem with the people." [16]

In other words, some advocates of opinion research come dangerously near to the populist fallacy of an omniscient electorate. The mere fact of taking an official poll of opinions about a question of policy implies acceptance of the competence of the voters to judge the issue, and publication of the findings will add greatly to the difficulty of rejecting them. This is one reason why political leaders hesitate about the use of opinion research as an aid in deciding controversial questions. There are many matters on which the electorate lack either the knowl-

[15] George Gallup, *A Guide to Public Opinion Polls* (Princeton University Press, 1944), 85 and 3.
[16] Raymond Moley, *After Seven Years* (New York, Harper, 1939), 395.

edge or the experience to reach decisions, and all that democratic principles require is that they should be free to choose the
experts to whom they will entrust the responsibility for deciding them. The same line of thought may also result in an un-
democratic deference to the transient and weakly felt views of
apathetic majorities, when, as artists in the practicable, politicians know that it is often wrong to override the more strongly
held views of minorities. And it is at least arguable that, as some
have urged, "ambiguity of political symbols is a primary instrument of political leadership" in a complex society like the
United States.[17]

With this preface it may be easier to understand the place
which opinion research occupies in the organization of the
federal government. What has been said applies primarily to
the higher levels—the levels at which national leadership is
exercised and national opinion is assumed to be awakened. It
applies much less if at all to the use of scientific methods to
collect information about attitudes which are relevant to the
formulation of policies and programs, and their execution once
the main questions of policy have been decided. In fact the
suspicion of polls in general colors the attitude to the use of
opinion research at all levels, and it has played a comparatively
small part in federal administration. Where it has been used,
this has been almost entirely on specific problems connected
with the user's relationships with particular "publics" and not
on testing opinion at large.

The story begins in 1936 when Henry Wallace, as Secretary
of Agriculture, adopted a suggestion of the head of the Extension Service, M. L. Wilson, that the experience of farmers
with the agricultural programs should be studied systematically. The small unit which was set up was unique until immediately before Pearl Harbor; and up to that time, total
federal expenditure on opinion research never exceeded
$100,000 a year.[18]

[17] David B. Truman, "Public Opinion Research as a Tool of Public Administration," *Public Administration Review*, 5 (1), Winter 1945, 63.

[18] Waldemar A. Nielsen, "Attitude Research and Government," *Journal
of Social Issues*, 2 (2), May 1946, 3. This number of the *Journal* contained
several important articles on opinion research and government. Other sources

With the war came the brief efflorescence in which, like other social scientists, practitioners of opinion research blossomed forth in welcome and unexpected glory. The Department of Agriculture's Division of Program Surveys under Rensis Likert shared with the Surveys Division of the Office of War Information the responsibilities of a common service agency to the civilian departments. The War Production Board conducted studies through its Office of Civilian Requirements. The Army was particularly active, the Navy less so. Many of the leading men in opinion research today spent some time in government employment.

Some conclusions of interest for the future of opinion research in public administration can be drawn from the wartime experience. In the first place, the relationship between the survey units and the operating officials was never satisfactorily defined, and for the most part they were struggling against relegation to impotence and obscurity. The formal status of the Surveys Division of the OWI was inferior, and it depended for its influence upon the personal relationship which its chief was able to establish from time to time with key officials. It was comparatively easy to obtain funds for research. It was harder to sustain interest, and to secure a flow of carefully considered projects. It was hardest of all to persuade high officials to make what the researchers thought was good use of the results.

----

which I have found of special use are: Leonard W. Doob, *Public Opinion and Propaganda* (New York, Holt, 1948), and "The Utilization of Social Scientists in the Overseas Branch of the Office of War Information," *American Political Science Review*, 41 (4), August 1947, 649–67; Quinn McNemar's study for the Social Science Research Council, "Opinion-Attitude Methodology," *Psychological Bulletin*, 43 (4), July 1946, 289–374; Laszlo Radvanyi, *Public Opinion Measurement, A Survey* (Mexico City, Instituto Cientifico de la Opinion Publica Mexicana, 1945); Hans E. Skott, "Attitude Research in the Department of Agriculture," *Public Opinion Quarterly*, 7 (2), Summer 1943, 280–92; "Report on the Analysis of Pre-Election Polls and Forecasts for the Social Science Research Council," *Public Opinion Quarterly*, 12 (4), Winter 1948–49, 599–622: Truman, *op. cit.*; Stouffer, *op. cit.*; and Martin Kriesberg, "Opinion Research and Public Policy," *International Journal of Attitude and Opinion Research*, 3 (3), Fall 1949, 373–84. I also had the great advantage of meeting many people with experience of the field both during and since the war.

In the second place, the wartime experience disappointed both partners. Perhaps each hoped for too much. War relaxed financial restraints and made for readier acceptance of new ideas. On the other hand, it did not provide the conditions in which an inexact science could show itself off to advantage. Busy men were impatient of the inevitable delays, of findings hedged with reservations and hard to apply to specific problems, and of the detailed work which was expected of them both in planning and in interpreting a survey.

Opinion research exponents can point to a few important achievements, and it may be assumed that they have made the most of the record. What is remarkable is not how much but how comparatively little was accomplished in relation to the potentialities. The following are some of the highlights:

(1) The War Production Board carried out a series of surveys to assess the need for consumer goods in short supply, and used the results in planning allocations for their production.[19]

(2) A federal conservation agency found that there were difficulties in applying in the South some methods which had been successful elsewhere. A survey showed that the methods conflicted with habits of living in Southern communities.[20]

(3) Surveys were used by the War Department as an aid to what in civilian life would be called personnel management. The views of soldiers were periodically ascertained on food, clothing, entertainments, promotion practices, the deficiencies of leadership, and the administration of discipline.[21]

(4) Studies made by Rensis Likert's Division of Program Surveys led to an important change in war bond policy. They showed that most redemptions were for emergency expenses and that the difficulty of redemption was a deterrent to some prospective investors. The division advised the Treasury Department that it could safely increase the ease of redemption and that this was likely to produce higher net receipts. The advice was taken, and the prediction was fulfilled.[22]

[19] Angus Campbell, "The Uses of Interview Surveys in Federal Administration," *Journal of Social Issues, op. cit.,* 21.

[20] Truman, 66–67.

[21] Nielsen, 5.

[22] *ibid.,* 18, and information obtained orally.

(5) The point system for demobilization was based on an investigation by the Research staff of the War Department into the attitude of soldiers on the weight which should be given to different reasons for priority of discharge. It made an important contribution to the solution of an inherently difficult problem.[23]

The factor common to these examples is that they dealt with matters on which the attitude of a particular group was relevant for efficient administration. They told how the group behaved or thought on subjects connected with programs whose success depended on the group's participation. They were the governmental equivalent of market research rather than public opinion polling.

Such survey work as was being carried out by the federal government after the wartime activities had been largely eliminated fell into the same category. In 1948 the Bureau of the Census and the Bureau of Agricultural Economics were alone in having their own units. Other agencies made use of outside organizations such as the National Opinion Research Center and the Institute for Social Research of the University of Michigan. The emphasis was on behavior and preferences.

The Department of Agriculture was mainly concerned with actual market research—on, for example, women's preferences among textile products, the consumption of citrus fruit and potatoes, and the factors motivating hog farmers in producing and marketing their animals. The Federal Communications Commission wanted to discover the quality of radio reception in rural areas and whether listeners were satisfied. The Federal Reserve Bank employed the Institute for Social Research on regular surveys of liquid assets. There was no question of referenda on issues of policy.

Comparatively little use has been made of survey methods for a purpose to which they are *prima facie* particularly well suited—namely, as a guide in planning information programs and in testing their effectiveness. The Office of War Information made a few studies, including one of doubtful utility to discover whether people thought that they were being adequately informed about the war, and surveys were a valuable

[23] Stouffer, 438–39.

aid in the war bond drives. Two studies made by the Bureau of Agricultural Economics for the Extension Service and published in 1947 and 1948 illustrate the possibilities. The first was a survey taken in Vermont which showed that radio and the newspapers—other than farm papers—were the least effective media for extension purposes, while the most effective—for those who actually met him—was the county agent himself. The second showed that after years of educational work half of the homemakers in a selected "urban community" had little or no information on nutrition: only 4% had "adequate" information.[24]

At the time of my investigations in 1947–1948 only the traditionally conservative State Department seemed to be making systematic use of opinion studies as an aid in the planning of general policy. It had no polling organization, but Congress was told in 1948 that the Division of Public Studies in the Office of Public Affairs collected information about public opinion "partly from newspaper editorials, partly from positions that are taken by the great national organizations, partly by following the public opinion polling operations showing public opinion in general; from the mail that comes into the Department showing what people are interested in; newspaper articles, and addresses by leading citizens. They correlate all that, and they then report to the Secretary and to the missions abroad." [25] At that time the Division sent a summary of its findings to the Secretary of State daily, and to heads of missions at frequent intervals.

The methods used were a compromise between the older and newer techniques, and corresponded with the reaction against a largely quantitative approach to the assessment of opinion. It was not the purpose of the Division to take periodical referenda of the mass public on subjects about which they knew

[24] *The Extension Service in Vermont* (U.S. Department of Agriculture, Extension Service, in cooperation with Bureau of Agricultural Economics, processed, 1947), and *Home Makers' Acceptance of Nutrition Information in an Urban Community* (U.S. Department of Agriculture, Bureau of Agricultural Economics, processed, 1948).

[25] *Department of State Appropriation Bill for 1949, Hearings before Subcommittee of House Appropriations Committee*, 1948, 130.

little and felt less, but rather to help the higher officials of the Department to understand the forces which were shaping opinion on specific issues, to assess the weight of different expressions of opinion, and to plan the domestic information program.

The enthusiast for opinion research might have been encouraged by the mere existence of the Division of Public Studies, but he would have been unwise to build high hopes upon it. It was several tiers below the Secretary of State, and did not enjoy the same status as the geographical divisions. Nor should its part in shaping policy be exaggerated. In an important study of State Department home information services W. Phillips Davison concluded in 1949 that the Division of Public Studies was making no significant contribution to the formation of policy. He illustrated its subordinate role by citing a recent analysis which showed that 95% of all policy documents were not even shown to the public opinion officers.[26]

It may seem that disproportionate space has been devoted to an activity of insignificant dimensions, which is conducted in the main without reference to the information divisions and in large part has nothing directly to do with their work. There are, however, several reasons for thinking that it should have full treatment. The fact that government has made less use of these new techniques in its public relations activities than American business calls for some explanation. Secondly, it may very well be that the present phase will not last long. It is noteworthy that some of those who are suspicious of the pollsters have also been among their clients. Congressmen are said to have made extensive use of polls in their constituencies: one of them, Representative J. K. Javits, has described how he conducted a Congressional election with the aid of a poll.[27] Thirdly, the progress of opinion research poses some fundamental questions for all who are interested in public relations

[26] "More Than Diplomacy," Chapter 6, in *Public Opinion and Foreign Policy*, ed. Lester Markel, *op. cit.*
[27] J. K. Javits, "How I Used a Poll in Campaigning for Congress," *Public Opinion Quarterly*, 11 (2), Summer 1947, 222–6.

as a method of bridging the gap between big government and the governed. "Through systematic contributions to the governing process, opinion measurement partially fills the gap between governor and governed, widened by the virtual elimination of daily and intimate contact between the two." [28]

That is the argument which is put forward by advocates of opinion research. To be dogmatic would be foolish, but it is at least safe to say that federal agencies are only on the verge of discovering how survey methods can be used to full advantage as an aid to administration, including in the forefront their public relations. All the same, it is possible that, perhaps for the wrong reasons, they are right in going slow with the new techniques at present. Some major sociological and psychological problems will have to be solved before these techniques will be perfected. But if those who use them are fully alive to their limitations, they can already provide valuable aid, particularly where the need is for information of a primarily factual character. A survey of opinions about the relative merits of different taxes for raising the same amount of revenue might be worthless or worse as a guide to deciding between them. A survey of the state of knowledge about existing tax procedures might suggest where changes should be made or indicate the points of misunderstanding on which publicity should be concentrated; the Treasury Department has in fact made use of survey methods in designing income tax forms.

Carefully used, survey methods can add to the data which is relevant in settling policy and shaping its administration, and provide an index to its impact when it has been introduced. They are particularly well adapted for use in planning and testing the effectiveness of public relations programs.

[28] Truman, 71.

CHAPTER 6

◇◇

THE PRINTED WORD

◇◇

THE recognition of the press as a Fourth Estate carries with it the implication that it has the special responsibilities to the public which have been discussed in Chapter 4. This is the conception of its constitutional role which was expressed by Theodore Roosevelt when he said that publishers, editors, and reporters were all public servants.

The way in which the press is discharging its responsibilities for public information and persuasion is thus the first question to ask before the government's own arrangements for informing the public through the printed word are considered. Theoretically, the newspapers, periodicals, and book publishers might do the whole job.

It is not always recognized that as a corollary of their exceptional status newspapermen like other public servants should be prepared for criticism when they fall short of what the public is entitled to expect of them. In their relations with government they are inclined to assume the virtue for themselves. Politicians and administrators, forced to rely on the press as their chief medium for speaking to the people, are on the other hand only too conscious of its deficiencies. In turn they sometimes fail to make due allowance for the difficulties of the newspapers. As Paul Mallon once said: "The Administration wants to know why doesn't the press say 95 per cent or 98 per cent of WPA or PWA is all right? The objection is entirely true and valid, explainable only by the fact that reporters energetically pursue news and a negative fact is rarely as important to the public mind as an affirmative fact." [1]

A balanced statement of both points of view came from Viscount Bennett in 1932 when he was Prime Minister of Canada: "Your business is to get news, I know, but mine is to see that you do not get any that will hamper the negotiations in progress. Your business is to find something to write about. Ours is to work for the benefit of the Empire as a whole." [2]

The truth is that the relationship between the Executive and the press is inherently difficult; in some ways it is similar to that between the Executive and the Legislature. The Executive must cultivate the press but cannot control it, and that is a potentially explosive state of affairs. The press is privately owned, and private ownership of an organ of opinion means the private ownership of political power. Newspaper owners and publishers are, therefore, rivals at the politician's own game. The press is run for profit, and experience has shown that profitmaking by organs of mass communication often means sensationalism and levity and bad manners.

These are some of the circumstances which make for tension and misunderstanding in government press relations and explain why many newspapers fall short of the performance which is expected of them. Some American newspapers discharge their obligations for public information in exemplary fashion. Nobody would claim this on behalf of the majority, or that with the best intentions they could rise to the standards of the small minority. In 1947 the *New York Times* published the texts of 359 documents of public importance. It was a great achievement, but even the *New York Times* could only skim the surface of the information which the federal government had to make available to different sections of the community.

On the whole, however, the tendency is to underestimate the contribution of the press to government publicity. It is easy to overlook what is done by trade and technical publications to

[1] Charles Fisher, *The Columnists* (New York, Howell, Siskin, 1944), 289.
[2] Leo C. Rosten, *The Washington Correspondents* (New York, Harcourt, Brace, 1937), 66.

inform their readers of administrative decisions and of the results of government research. And less credit than is due has been given to the major help which is received in the editorial as well as the news columns for persuasive programs of an uncontroversial character—fighting tuberculosis, Army prestige, savings, rat control, law enforcement. The Luckman Committee recorded that in two months it held four press conferences and issued 81 press releases, and that "a majority of newspapers cooperated in three major ways. (1) By using stories in their news columns. (2) By commenting at length on their editorial pages. (3) By using the advertising material supplied to them by the Committee. Newspaper columnists contributed to the advancement of the program, and this was also true of both editorial and comic-strip cartoonists." [3] Even where, on questions like eggless days and the closing of distilleries, all the newspapers did not agree with the committee, they helped to keep the purpose of the campaign before the public. The cooperation of the New York newspapers in the smallpox epidemic of 1947 is a good example of the same thing on a smaller scale.

Yet there remain severe limitations upon the amount of help which the press can give. It is not only that it would be physically impossible to reproduce more than a small part of the material which the government has to publish, and that most of it is of limited interest. Most is not "news." And where it is "news," it is "news" only once; however, repetition is usually essential to successful publicity.

The two tasks of government press relations are to help the press to collect the information which it needs if it is to do its own part well, and to supplement the work of the press with publications of the government's own.

Every President had his press relations long before formal machinery developed: James E. Pollard has surveyed the subject in a monumental volume of over 800 pages, *The Presidents and the Press* (1947).[4] Some Presidents have been aloof. Some have cultivated favorite publishers or editors or corre-

[3] Citizens Food Committee, *op. cit.*
[4] Pollard, *op. cit.*

spondents. Some have played politics with the press. Most have been suspicious. All have been exasperated. Few have understood the press. "I came to Washington," said Woodrow Wilson, "with the idea that close and cordial relations with the press would prove of the greatest aid. I prepared for the conferences as carefully as for any lecture, and talked freely and fully on all large questions of the moment. Some men of brilliant ability were in the group, but I soon discovered that the interest of the majority was in the personal and trivial rather than in principles and policies." [5]

Little was done to systematize the relationship until the present century. President McKinley introduced a seemingly unimportant innovation which is significant in retrospect when he provided a table and chairs for the newspapermen who waited around the White House. That is about all that was done by way of formal arrangements before Theodore Roosevelt. Today some of the major departments have special press rooms with telephones, typewriters and tape machines for the use of newspapermen.

Theodore Roosevelt saw that under modern conditions organized press relations were essential to good administration, and he gave impetus to the more or less simultaneous evolution of the three institutions which now exist for the management of government press relations—the press conference, the press release, and the press officer. Each has, however, arisen in response to the practical needs of newspapermen and administrators in the face of big and complex government rather than from conscious planning or any theory of the principles which should determine the relationship between the Executive and the Fourth Estate. The history of each has reflected the tensions which spring from the relationship, but each is now accepted as indispensable.

An indispensable part in the system is also played by the skilled and experienced corps of newspaper correspondents who are assigned to Washington specially to cover government. They get to know the leaders of the administration and

[5] Robert W. Desmond, *The Press and World Affairs* (New York, Appleton-Century, 1937), 310–11.

of Congress on hardly less than equal terms, and—according to personal deserts—enjoy their respect and confidence. In return for the confidence which is placed in them, they accept a voluntary code of conduct and discipline without which the relationship of trust could not continue.

The Washington correspondents are the main but not the only channel through which officials communicate with the press. The President and his colleagues from time to time meet publishers and editors as individuals and in groups. The War Department organized tours for publishers and editors in the American Zone of Germany. The Treasury Department met the cartoonists about their collaboration in savings bond publicity. Feature writers and columnists have their own contacts with officials. Some think that they do not always have enough. President Franklin D. Roosevelt once said of the columnists: "In most cases their columns are based either on the pure imagination and invention of the writer or on untrue gossip." [6] Westbrook Pegler, justifying himself against the charge that "veteran capital correspondents cannot recall ever having seen him at a State Department press conference," said in 1948 that he had spent not less than two months a year in Washington in the last fifteen years, but he did not run to press conferences, "because mostly they are worse than futile." [7]

Still the Washington correspondents are the chief link with the press, and the administrative arrangements are built around them. For most purposes government press relations means the contacts between officials from the President downwards to junior information specialists, and men like Arthur Krock of the *New York Times*, Bert Andrews of the *New York Herald-Tribune*, and so on down the line in the Washington bureaus of the newspapers and press agencies. [8]

The press conferences of administration leaders—particularly the President's—have been likened to Question Time in

[6] Franklin D. Roosevelt, *Public Papers and Addresses* (New York, Random House, 1938), II, 28, quoted by Pollard, *op. cit.*

[7] *PM*, March 7, 1948.

[8] Rosten, *op. cit.*, is out of date on the details, but continues to be most valuable for the insight which it gives into the role of the Washington correspondents.

the British House of Commons as a forum in which spokesmen of the public as a whole can call the government to account. That the comparison should be made is a striking acknowledgment of the quasi-constitutional status of the American press, but it does not bear examination. The purpose of the press conference is administrative convenience, not accounting to the public. It is called, conducted, and ended by the administrator who gives it. The newspaperman has no right to answers to his questions, and little or no redress if he gets none or does not like what he is told.

None the less it has become an unwritten rule of the Constitution that the President and other top administrators should periodically submit themselves to interrogation by the press, and the press relations machinery of the federal government assumes its most spectacular shape in the President's own press conferences. This is mainly due to President Franklin D. Roosevelt, though irrespective of personalities the crises of the 1930's and 1940's would have made it necessary for the President to meet the press more often. Mr. Hoover held 66 press conferences. Mr. Roosevelt held nearly a thousand in his four terms. On taking office Mr. Truman announced that he intended to follow Mr. Roosevelt's example of holding frequent press conferences, though once instead of twice weekly. And in 1950 Mr. Truman made two changes whose symbolical significance and long-term implications exceed their intrinsic importance when he moved his press conferences from the crowded office where Presidents had held them for nearly forty years to a bigger room across the street; and introduced—not to everybody's satisfaction—the requirement that correspondents must state their identity before putting a question.

Of President Truman's cabinet in 1947–1948, only Secretary Marshall was holding regular as distinct from *ad hoc* press conferences. Either he or one of his chief assistants met the press weekly, as well as *ad hoc* when the occasion arose; in addition the Press Relations Office was holding briefing sessions almost daily, there were spot news conferences for matters of urgency, and background and off the record conferences were organized as required. Yet the Hoover Commission described the relationships between the State Department and the press and other media of publicity as "extremely weak." [9]

The effective use of the press conference depends upon there being "news" to talk about; this may be why the press conference flourished in the radical phases of the Roosevelt Administration. Personalities also count for much. As was said by the *Washington Post* (March 20, 1948): "We underrate the great gift that the wise conduct of a press conference calls for. There are few masters of it. The gift calls for a quality of reticence and openness at the right time which amounts to genius."

From his early days as Assistant Secretary of the Navy, Mr. Roosevelt showed this genius. At Albany he had "family conferences" with the newspapermen, and it was certain that the White House conferences would take on new vitality in his hands. The men around him included several whose dramatic personalities made news of much of what they did and said. "The N.R.A. set up was the realization of a publicity man's dream. Our picturesque chief with his pungent speeches, with his talk of being the target of dead cats, etc., made headlines in the papers without any effort from me." [10] James Farley was well known for speaking frankly at off the record conferences. On the other hand newspapermen complained of Miss Perkins that she was dull and uninformative. Similar complaints were made of the Truman Administration. In fact, said James Reston, in the *New York Times* (December 11, 1947), "Mr. Truman and Secretary of State Marshall tend to look on the press conference as a difficult chore, which admittedly it can be; Mr. Roosevelt looked on it as an opportunity."

There could hardly be criticism of the principle of holding press conferences. There has been some criticism of alleged abuses. Going off the record is said to be used as a device for silencing the press on subjects which it would be embarrassing to have discussed in public. Friendly correspondents are asked to put prearranged questions and to guide the conference along congenial lines; President Hoover was supposed to have

[9] *State Department Appropriation Bill for 1949, Hearings,* 31–2; and Hoover Commission *Report on Foreign Affairs,* 15.
[10] Michelson, 122.

"trained seals" who would perform at his will. Trial balloons are flown, and intentional leakages occur. More often, however, the criticism is that particular press conferences are a waste of time because the official is dull or impatient or evasive. Or because of the deficiencies of the newspapermen. "That diabolic institution known as the press conference," wrote a woman journalist in 1947, "is geared to the lowest and slowest mentality present (not hers)." [11]

The press release is sometimes said to have come into governmental use during the First World War as a device for dealing with the enormous volume of war news. It would be more accurate to say that it was not used on a really big scale until then. As we have seen, the practice was much older, and in 1913 *Editor and Publisher* was complaining that exclusive stories had been killed by the Roosevelt and Taft orders forbidding officials to supply the press with information direct, and that the departmental press agents issued news to all papers. "In fact, it was typewritten, duplicated, and mailed to every correspondent." [12]

This invaluable device has not shared the relative immunity from criticism which the press conference has enjoyed, but it has survived all attacks because the newspapers could not cover the vast quantity of official news without its aid. The objections to "handouts" increase in geometrical progression with the distance of the critic from actual newsgathering, whether it is distance up the newspaper hierarchy or distance from Washington. It is naturally the publisher and not the working newspaperman who says that handouts make correspondents lazy and stifle their initiative. The further the editor is from Washington the more likely he is to complain that handouts are useless by the time they reach him or that he has had all that he needs on the subject through the wire services. But the Washington correspondents, even if they belong to a large newspaper bureau, know that left to themselves they would find it impossible to collect, let alone discover, the "news" which arises from the activities of two million federal employees.

[11] India McIntosh, in Herzberg, *Late City Edition*, 48.
[12] *Editor and Publisher*, 13 (13), September 13, 1913, 245 and 257.

The criticism most frequently heard is that there are too many releases for the time and patience of busy editors. In reply it is said that everything practicable is done to fit the distribution lists to the recipients' needs, that there are at least as vociferous complaints if newspapers do not get the handouts they want, and that the releases are in fact extensively used. When the OWI checked an allegation that it was a "handout heaven" because it had issued 52 releases in a single day, it found that of the 44 which were intended for immediate use the *New York Journal of Commerce* alone had used 32.[13] Like public relations practitioners generally, government information officers are, however, conscious of the damage which may be done by issuing releases indiscriminately, and do their best to keep the number down.

A more serious criticism is that press releases are vehicles of propaganda. This has nothing to do with them as a piece of machinery. It is undeniable that, as is sometimes said, they contain "channeled" news. There is no such thing as complete objectivity in selecting and presenting information, but there are substantial safeguards against abuse. The releases are prepared in the knowledge that they will be exposed to the expert scrutiny of other newspapermen and of watchful Congressmen.

Thirdly, the press officer. There must be men to work the press liaison machinery, and, just as happened in business, it proved to be most efficient to employ experts who understood the mentality of newspapermen and the workings of the newspaper world. A War Department press release in 1948 misled many newspapermen into thinking that General Eisenhower had not closed his mind to the possibility of running for President: it was said that the fault lay in the drafting, and that if the draftsman had had newspaper experience he would have realized that the language used would sound deliberately ambiguous.

There are disadvantages in a situation in which the operating official—the actual source of the news—is several stages removed from the newspaper reader. But the press officer adds

[13] *National War Agencies Appropriation Bill for 1944, Hearings before Subcommittee of House Appropriations Committee,* 1943, 33.

only one link to a chain which is already long, and most of the links are in the newspapers themselves—through the correspondent, the copy desk, the make-up man, the caption writer, the editors, all who may have a hand in the story as it finally appears on the breakfast table. It is rather like the party game in which an anecdote is whispered along the line, and it is no wonder that it sometimes emerges in a strange form.

Federal information officers are alive to the importance of avoiding grounds for the charge that they act as barriers between newspapermen and operating officials. "Representatives of newspapers and magazines," stated the Administrative Regulations of the Department of Agriculture in 1948, "often wish to obtain, by interview, information direct from specialists or officials who are best qualified to supply accurate details; such informal interviews are encouraged."

Newspaper correspondents are naturally jealous of their right of direct access to officials. If the information office is a barrier, said Joseph Loftus of the *New York Times*, the newspaperman is reduced to being a messenger boy.[14] Common sense and restraint have to be shown on both sides. The correspondents recognize that there are many other demands upon a busy administrator. Information officers have no wish to interpose themselves on matters which are highly technical or raise important questions of policy. They know the public relations value of direct contacts between the policy makers and the press, and of statements in the official's own words. At the same time, they are careful not to play favorites and not to issue exclusive stories to individuals. It is one thing to give background information to an inquirer, and quite another to single one man out for an exclusive item of news or statement of policy. The memory still survives of a much criticized interview which President Roosevelt gave to Arthur Krock in 1937: there were echoes of it as long afterwards as 1950, when President Truman gave an exclusive interview to the same correspondent, and the press corps "sizzled with rage" at the favoritism.[15]

[14] *Nieman Reports*, January 1948.
[15] *Time*, Atlantic Edition, February 27, 1950, 26.

The press conference is one method by which all the correspondents can be treated equally, and the convenience of the administrator reconciled with the desire to meet him personally. In practice, however, the Washington official is readily accessible. Joseph Loftus said that the Department of Justice was the only agency of which he had heard the complaint that the information office was a barrier: [16] and Bert Andrews of the *New York Herald Tribune* commented in 1947 that: "State legislators or town councilmen are usually harder to approach than top-flight men in government agencies. The latter realize what some of their small-town brethren never learn—that they must be affable, polite, and helpful, even to correspondents of papers vehemently opposed to them." [17]

What has been said of the press generally applies to particular sections. Each agency is in close touch with the technical periodicals interested in its work. Outside Washington the local newspapers are in much the same relationship to local federal officials as the Washington correspondents to their headquarters: and where there is no information specialist a member of the general staff does all that is necessary by way of organized press liaison. There seem, on the other hand, to be few systematic attempts to cater specially for the newspapers of foreign born and other minority groups. A Negro information specialist employed by the Department of Agriculture in 1948 to help the Negro press was, as far as I could ascertain, quite the exception. In general it was left to minority group papers to adapt to their readers information received through the normal channels.

In all these cases the traffic is two-way. The press offices are as busy answering the questions of newspapermen, putting them in touch with other officials, getting information for them, arranging visits for them, as with organizing the outflow of information which the department itself is anxious to disseminate. In 1948 some thirty to forty correspondents were covering the State Department daily, and about a hundred

[16] *op. cit.*
[17] Bert Andrews in Herzberg, *Late City Edition,* 74–5.

more called at the Department at least once a week: the Press Section answered 400 or more telephone calls a day.[18]

The relationship with other representatives of the press—feature writers, columnists, cartoonists—is more passive. Departments are always ready to help them. An article in *Life* or the *Saturday Evening Post* may be more useful than fifty routine press releases: the Office of Information of the Department of Agriculture congratulated itself in its Annual Report because the *Ladies' Home Journal* with its circulation of over 4 million had published four major articles about Department activities in 1947–1948. An article in a learned periodical may be read by more specialists than could be reached by any official publication. But, on the whole, agencies cannot do much to stimulate the publication of feature articles in the mass circulation magazines. It sometimes happens that appeals are made for their cooperation: the Luckman Committee reported on the considerable help which magazine publishers gave in the food conservation campaign, despite the difficulty that they went to press weeks or months before publication. Sometimes it may be possible to suggest subjects for articles by friendly writers. General Parks sent a memorandum to all former war correspondents asking them to persuade their editors to let them turn their favorite war story into a feature for Army Day, 1948. "If you are like everyone else, I'm sure nostalgia comes to grips with you many times at your typewriter." [19] There is more scope for placing feature material with the smaller newspapers and magazines, and technical and scientific periodicals will be ready to publish articles based on the results of government research. It is also common for leading officials and experts to be asked for signed articles. But none of this is important relatively to press relations activities as a whole.

The public speech is another major tool of government press relations. Under modern conditions top administrators often direct their speeches less to the immediate audience than to the

---

[18] *State Department Appropriation Bill for 1949, Hearings,* 33.

[19] Memorandum to all former war correspondents from the Chief, Public Information Division, Department of the Army, March 12, 1948.

wider public which can be reached through the press. It would be interesting to trace the history of speaking from a written text—George Washington is said to have done so with his Farewell Address—but it has now become general. With important speeches one reason is that the exact words may be quoted as an authoritative statement of policy, and it would be unwise to rely on the inspiration of the moment. Another is that without a handout speeches will not be as adequately or as accurately reported. A third is that many officials lack the time or the flair to prepare their own speeches. "Few candidates . . . can write their own speeches," said Shepard Henkin in discussing "political" public relations.[20]

It is for reasons such as these that a ghostwriter is so often in the background when a public figure speaks or writes. Far from being peculiar to government the practice is at least as common in business. It has fascinating possibilities. There is a well-known story about the predicament of two Congressmen who made identical speeches because they had employed the same "ghost." I met an Army officer who had prepared both the speech of welcome to a distinguished visitor and the visitor's reply.

The constitutional implications of this interesting institution received some consideration after the death of Charles Michelson. "Senators and Cabinet members, Representatives and lesser fry," said the *Washington Post* (January 11, 1948), "waxed eloquent with words put into their mouths by this former reporter. . . . To the extent that he put words into the mouths of public servants, the principle of representative government was distinctly blurred."

It is, however, questionable if there is any logical distinction between the ghostwriter and the other specialists—research workers, statisticians, advisers—who help in providing the material out of which speeches are built. The essential point is that the speaker retains full responsibility for everything that is in the speech. And Charles Michelson was an exceptionally gifted "ghost"; the strength of most ghostwriters lies in research rather than oratory. Instead of enlivening

[20] Henkin, 27.

public speaking they have tended to make it duller. They may have improved the content but they have flattened out the individuality.

Ghostwriting may mean many things—from the complete writing of a speech or article to preparing ideas and facts which can be used for the purpose. In one form or another it is inevitable in any large organization, and it is a job which any public relations specialist must be prepared to undertake. The extent to which top federal administrators use ghosts from their information divisions, from their own personal entourage, from other parts of the agency, or no ghosts at all will vary greatly, but assistance with speeches is among the duties which will fall from time to time upon the information staffs.

Whoever writes them, speeches are important for the public relations of most government agencies. The Annual Report of the Secretary of Labor for 1947 recorded that 45 speeches were written for representatives of the Women's Bureau. A hundred high Army officers and civilian officials were scheduled to speak on Army Day, 1948; [21] 225 officers of the State Department made 813 speeches in 1947.[22] It may fall to the information division to make the arrangements for the speech; it will almost certainly be their duty to see to the press coverage and to subsequent publicity in the shape of reprints for distribution to interested organizations and individuals.

When all that can be done through the newspaper and periodical press has been achieved, there remains the large area which can be covered adequately only by publications of the government's own. Despite the efforts of Congress to curb government publications, the Government Printing Office is the largest publishing house in the world. As long ago as 1899 it was printing 475 documents a month.[23] In 1948 the customary stock in hand averaged 30 million copies of more than 70,000 titles. Without advertising, its biggest best-seller had sold 4,645,590 copies, or approximately the world sales of

[21] Army Department release to press for Army Day, 1948.

[22] *State Department Appropriation Bill for 1949, Hearings*, 129.

[23] Leroy Charles Merritt, *The United States Government as Publisher* (University of Chicago Press, 1943), 80.

Gone With the Wind. This was *Infant Care,* a 15 cent Children's Bureau pamphlet: in one year more than a million copies were sold, and another million were given away. Next in popularity came two other Children's Bureau pamphlets, *Prenatal Care* (2,599,423 copies, 5 cents) and *Your Child from One to Six* (2,002,489 copies, 15 cents).[24] In addition to the output of the Government Printing Office, agencies produce large quantities of processed material themselves. Leroy Charles Merritt found in 1939 that almost half as many publications were processed as printed, though most of the processed material never reached the public.[25]

Few of these publications have anything to do with "information" in the specialist sense. They include official forms, judicial and legislative proceedings, specifications, directories, histories and historical documents. Merritt calculated that only 54 out of 1,672 printed documents published in October 1939 were "informational," i.e., "issued in the interest of informing the public about the nature and activities of its government." [26] This definition is, however, too narrow to be very serviceable; and there are few publications to which there is not a public relations aspect.

No attempt will be made here to classify government publications according to whether or not they are "informational." No hard and fast line can be drawn. An important practical distinction is between periodical and non-periodical publications. The Government Printing Office has succinctly explained the reasons for preferring periodicals in some cases: "Various bureaus of the United States Government have found that the only adequate way to get official information before the public while still fresh and valuable is to publish it in periodicals instead of holding it for annual reports or occasional volumes." [27]

Ninety-three official periodicals were on sale in March 1948,

[24] Interview with the Public Printer, John J. Deviny, *Washington Post,* May 2, 1948.

[25] Merritt, 131.

[26] *ibid.,* 80.

[27] *Government Periodicals, Price List 36* (Government Printing Office, March 1948).

but they included the *Congressional Record,* a number of judicial reports, and various works of reference like the *Post
Office Guide* and *Climatological Data.* There were only
twenty or thirty—such as the *Department of State Bulletin*
(weekly, 15 cents), the *Journal of Agricultural Research*
(semi-monthly, 10 cents), and *Child* (monthly, 10 cents)—
which were at all comparable to privately published magazines.
All of these were addressed to highly specialized audiences.

There are obvious difficulties about differentiating between
government publications according to the purposes they are
meant to serve. Even forms and reports of proceedings and
specifications may have the incidental effect of informing the
public, and they shade imperceptibly into those publications
which are produced in the discharge of the government's responsibilities for reporting to the public, and the larger number
which are produced because better public information is the
goal of an administrative program or essential to its success.
Some, like the *Department of State Bulletin,* are mainly directed to a small group of opinion makers. Most will never be
read except for reference purposes. Others contain information
of practical value to the reader. This is true of the pamphlets
on child care; the Health Education leaflets, telling in plain
language about serious diseases like cancer, minor ailments like
sunburn and hayfever, and the elementary rules of hygiene;
the Farmers' Bulletins, presenting the results of scientific research "in language easily understood and used by the average
farmer and housewife"; the Industrial (Small Business)
Series of the Department of Commerce, telling how to set up
small businesses like beauty shops, bookstores, and shoe repair
establishments.

Even where mass circulation is desirable, there is no question of indiscriminate distribution. Though the vagueness of
the law has fostered evasion, Congress has circumscribed free
issue. It has also forbidden sales except through the Government Printing Office, and forbidden the GPO to advertise.
Constitutional considerations aside, however, large free distri-
butions would not necessarily be wise; publications are likely
to be valued more highly and studied more attentively if they

have to be paid for. But from a purely publicity point of view there can be nothing in favor of making it difficult to buy them, as is sometimes charged against the Government Printing Office. And the attitude of Congress is a brake upon the adoption of aggressive selling methods. McCamy was critical of the sales policy in 1949. There was no rational division between sales and gifts; it was needlessly difficult for prospective purchasers to trace publications of interest to them; the procedure of distribution was cumbersome and wasteful.[28]

There is no test by which to decide whether a government agency is publishing too little or too much, and it is difficult to measure how effectively a particular publication is achieving its purpose. Recent years have, however, seen growing skepticism about the effectiveness of the method. In government as well as outside it is less readily assumed that the job is done when the facts are in print. It is being increasingly recognized that many people to whom printed material is addressed cannot read it with ease, and that many more do not want to read it if they can. Hence the increased attention which is being given to the popularization of printed matter, and to alternative methods of reaching the plain man—motion pictures, plant tours, slide films, advertising, comic strips.

Among the chief tasks of a publications section is to present technical information in the form best suited to the audience. It is at times delicate as well as difficult. The busy official may have to be wooed before he will put pen to paper; and he is apt to respond negatively to tactful criticisms of his style, or to suggestions that, despite the jeopardy to his professional reputation, he should sacrifice pedantic accuracy to readability. But the risk of offending him must be taken in the interest—as the Office of Information of the Department of Agriculture said in its Report for 1948—of the "elimination of less pertinent matter and clarification of obscure and highly technical passages." [29]

The really interesting problem is how to get official informa-

[28] McCamy, *Government Publications for the Citizen, passim.*

[29] U.S. Department of Agriculture, Office of Information, *Annual Report for 1948* (processed).

tion over to the man in the street—the man who does not want to read serious publications, does not like reading, cannot read except perhaps at the level of *True Story Magazine*. As far as publications are concerned, there are, broadly, three possibilities: (a) to use pictures; (b) to improve the physical presentation; (c) to popularize the style and the content.

Little need be said about pictures. Government information offices would make more use of them if funds and Congressional restrictions permitted. Official photography has a distinguished history, going back to the much admired work of Brady during the Civil War, under contract with the War Department. Most agencies have small graphics units, and are alive to the value of pictures as an aid to the understanding of printed matter. "During the year," reported the Office of Information of the Department of Agriculture in 1948, "the staff devoted much attention to ways and means of improving the quality of illustrations appearing in Department publications." Standards have risen considerably in the last twenty years, but the improvements have not been remarkable by comparison with outside, and there has been little to compare with the advances in pictorial journalism exemplified by *Life* and *Look* magazines.

Government publications also reflect recent advances in book production, and the format and typography are generally, though by no means uniformly, good. Financial and other restrictions have, however, limited the use of color, pictorial statistics, and similar aids to the attractive and intelligible presentation of difficult material.

As for content and style, it must be tempting to take refuge in the thought that so much of what goes into official publications is necessarily highly technical and addressed to small specialized audiences as to make it unprofitable to spend time and effort upon its popularization. The temptation is not always resisted: annual reports, for example, are too often poorly assembled compilations of imperfectly digested detail. Yet the problem is indivisible. The most effective long-term solution will be a general rise in the quality of official English: if this came about, half the battle would be won.

Not that there is any short cut to the eradication of what Representative Maury Maverick expressively called "gobbledygook." Its roots are deep in the sociology of the large-scale organization, and the variety found in Washington is one subspecies of a world-wide genus. Information staffs cannot do much to stamp out "gobbledygook" except by rewriting it in simple English when it comes their way, and setting a good example in their own writing. Few attempt more than this, or are entirely free from the disease themselves. At least as difficult is the task of putting official information into language which the majority of readers will not find it difficult to understand or be too lazy or indifferent to assimilate.

One reason for employing newspapermen is their skill in writing for mass audiences, but the newspapers have been learning how much of what they publish passes over the heads of many of their readers. Millions are at the comic strip level or not much above it, but it may be important to reach them with material which is intrinsically difficult. It is all the more necessary that its presentation should be adapted to their needs. Special interest, therefore, attaches to the few experiments which have been made with methods of popularization which are based on scientific research.[30] They have a qualitative importance which is out of proportion to their quantity.

Thorndike, Dale and Tyler, Gray and Leary, Lorge and Flesch, are some of those who since the early 1920's have engaged in the research which has led to the development of techniques for measuring and controlling the readability of printed matter. Starting on school textbooks, the pioneers went on to examine the reading capacity of adults, and to discover

[30] This account of work in connection with readability is based upon interviews and correspondence as well as upon published material. Mrs. Amy Gronna Cowing of the Extension Service of the U.S. Department of Agriculture was especially helpful, not only for what she told me herself but as a guide to other sources. I am also particularly indebted to the Bureau of Educational Research, Ohio State University; the Research Interpretation Service, Alabama Polytechnic Institute, Auburn, Ala.; and the Prudential Insurance Company of America, for supplying material. Of the leading students of readability Rudolf Flesch has in particular interested himself in government writing; see, for example, his "More About Gobbledygook," *Public Administration Review*, 5 (3), Summer 1945, 240–4.

what made the difference between ease and difficulty of reading printed material. The formulae which they have evolved for the guidance of writers take into account such factors as vocabulary, sentence length, the number of affixes, and the use of abstractions.

Gladys Gallup of the Extension Service seems to have been the first to apply the results of this research systematically to the popularization of government publications. When she came to Washington early in the war, the service was faced with the greatest information program in its history, and she knew from her experience in the West that much extension writing failed because it used the language of the universities to speak to farmers of little schooling. She began to experiment with the application of readability research as a guide for extension writers and as a yardstick by which the suitability of extension publications to their audiences might be measured.

The interest of other agencies was also aroused, and in 1946 the Civil Service Commission published a pamphlet, *To Government Writers. How Does Your Writing Read?* This was addressed to government officials generally, and is itself an excellent example of plain writing—agreeably illustrated with amusing drawings—which deserves to be better known.

The Extension Service used tests which had been worked out by Lorge and Flesch. By July 1947 they had been applied to more than 1,600 publications from forty-eight states, Hawaii, and Puerto Rico. In collaboration with the states, the service supplemented these tests with readership studies to measure the reading capacity of farm audiences.

Both methods produced illuminating results. Analysis of 712 random samples in agricultural and home economics bulletins from 13 Southern states showed that over half were at least of the standard of *Harper's* magazine and likely to be hard reading for three-fourths of the people for whom they were meant. Thirteen per cent were up to college level, or the standard of the *Yale Review*. Similar analyses elsewhere gave similar results, with an average reading difficulty slightly higher than in the South. The readership studies showed that farm people did not understand words such as "consumption," "minimum," "maximum," "specified," "sufficient," but understood "use," "lowest," "largest," "fixed," and "enough."

In other words, they would not understand this—from the Bureau of Home Nutrition and Home Economics:

"Vitamin A is a fat soluble compound, the function of which is concerned with the maintenance of the epithelial structures of the body and the preservation of normal physiology in the eye. The carotenes which constitute the chief precursors of the vitamin A of normal human nutrition are formed in plants and must be converted by the body into vitamin A before it becomes available either for immediate nutritional needs or for storage in the body. Certain animal products are excellent sources of the free vitamin."

But they would understand this from the Bureau's popular leaflet, *Vitamins from Farm to You:*

"Vitamin A—in fact, all vitamins—help to protect against infection. A is one of the vitamins needed for growth and for healthy teeth, bones, and nerves. Vitamin A is important for good skin and good linings to nose, mouth, and organs throughout the body.

"You get vitamin A by eating ripe yellow and green vegetables and some red-colored ones—tomatoes, for example—, also from liver, butter, and eggs. Bright colors in food are often —though not always—like flags, signaling with yellow, green, orange, or red, 'This way for vitamin A.' "[31]

There are many skeptics about the value of this work. There are healthy disputes among the readability experts, and there is not as yet the material on which it can be conclusively judged. In particular, it is difficult to make due allowances for style, content, and the reader's interest in the subject. By readability tests, some of the Psalms rate as easy to read as comic strips. If a farmer really wants to know about a plant disease, he will worry out the meaning of a pamphlet which in the ordinary way would be beyond his capacity: it may be too difficult for

[31] Amy Gronna Cowing, "Readable Writing," *Journal of American Dietetic Association,* 23 (12), December 1947, 1036–41, and Address before the Alabama Publications Workshop, Auburn, Ala., May 28, 1946 (Extension Service, processed).

somebody of higher educational attainments who is less familiar with the subject.

The Extension Service has, however, been encouraged by its experience. Tests have shown that extension publications were simpler to read after the readability program had been in operation. When 3,000 passages in bulletins issued in 1947 were compared with 3,000 similar passages published several years before, it was found that the proportion which were above the level considered easy reading for farm adults had fallen from 55% to 43%.[32] The presumption is that the improvement was due to the program, but the evidence is not final. Other factors may have been responsible. It is certainly likely that, irrespective of the methods used, the fact that attention was concentrated on the problem would have produced improvements.

It may be that at the present stage the chief value of readability tests is as a reminder to writers that in order to make the maximum impact they must take pains to adapt what they write to the reading capacity of their audiences. The popularity of these methods with businessmen is also inconclusive: American business is prone to passing enthusiasms.

Nor is the problem entirely one of mass audiences. Much remains to be done to improve the ease of reading of material addressed to the better educated. To be able to understand the *Political Science Quarterly* or the *Yale Law Review* is not necessarily to find it easy or inviting to read. An analysis of ten State Department publications which was made at Ohio State University showed that all but one (which was of high school standard) were above the level of the average reader who had not been to college. Two—*Expansion of World Trade and Employment* and *The Defense of Peace*—were "very difficult materials—above the college level in difficulty. Comfortable reading for specialists in the field." [33] These publications were not intended for general readers. None the less, it gives cause for thought that the large majority of Americans could not be

[32] *ibid.*, 1039.
[33] Sig N. Guckenheimer, "The Readability of Pamphlets on International Relationships," *Educational Research Bulletin* (Bureau of Educational Research, Ohio State University), 26 (9), December 10, 1947, 231–38.

expected to read without difficulty nine out of ten official pamphlets on major questions of foreign policy.

Perhaps the fault does not lie with the writers. Perhaps more is expected of the common man than will ever be realized outside the textbooks of political theory, and the intricacies of foreign affairs and economic administration will always be beyond him. But these circumstances only reinforce the challenge which is presented to all who are responsible for public information. The challenge is serious. The task is difficult. Where existing methods have been found wanting, it calls for originality and enterprise. What seems eccentric and even quixotic today may be the orthodoxy of tomorrow.

CHAPTER 7

◇◇◇

MORE TOOLS OF PUBLIC RELATIONS

◇◇◇

REX F. HARLOW and Marvin M. Black listed the following as the more important publicity media: "newspapers, magazines, books and other printed materials, advertising, direct-by-mail pieces, motion pictures, newsreels, outdoor boards and signs, exhibits, radio, public speaking, word of mouth." [1] Professor Doob included the stage, art, sandwichmen, skywriting, rumor, and parades.[2]

Strange as it may sound, almost all these media have some place in government public relations—either direct or incidentally to the use of the major mass media. The stage— through dramatic features on the radio. Pictorial art—through posters, illustrations, advertisements. More specifically, an exhibition of paintings by war artists was taken on tour in 1946, partly as public relations for the armed forces; this was "Operation Palette." Music—through military band performances and as the accompaniment to radio programs and movies, while the Treasury Department, for example, has adapted the words of popular songs for use in promoting school savings: thus, it was optimistically suggested that to the tune of "My Bonnie Lies Over the Ocean," schoolchildren should sing:

> Buy Stamps! Oh, buy Stamps!
> Exchange all your Stamps for a Bond, a Bond.

[1] Rex F. Harlow and Marvin M. Black, *Practical Public Relations* (New York, Harper, 1947), 234.
[2] Leonard W. Doob, *Propaganda: Its Psychology and Technique* (New York, Holt, 1935), ix.

Government vehicles and buildings are used to display posters and slogans; outdoor advertisers help in the Advertising Council's campaigns. Parades and displays are traditional public relations activities of the armed forces. "Direct-by-mail" was an important advertising method of the War Assets Administration.

"Word of mouth" plays a large part in most programs, and it is by "word of mouth" that the thousands of official and unofficial collaborators in government information activities make their chief contribution. The House Propaganda and Publicity Subcommittee took exception to the employment of paid lecturers allegedly to promote universal military training. Attention has also been drawn to the importance to government public relations of public speeches, official interviews, and private conversations; this is true even at low levels, as was recognized by a Navy public information course in which the students were reminded that the private conversation of sailors and their wives might enhance or damage Navy prestige.

The press and "word of mouth" apart, the important uses of the different publicity media fall under four main headings: exhibits and "open house," radio, motion pictures, and advertising.

Exhibits are one of the oldest tools of government public relations, and for some purposes they yield to none. An exhibits specialist told me that they achieve each of the objects of good publicity: they "stop, hold, inform, persuade." In their proper place they have most of the advantages of the motion picture without some of its drawbacks. They share its capacity for arresting attention and giving realism and drama to information which would otherwise be dull. They speak a language which almost everybody can understand, and, more easily than motion pictures, can be combined with practical demonstrations and personal exposition. Most important of all, the spectator can take his own time.

It is not for lack of appreciation of the value of exhibits but because they are an expensive medium and the opportunities of showing them are limited that they do not take a bigger part in federal information programs. Their major use has been confined to the Department of Agriculture. Its appropriation for exhibits was $128,400 in 1947–1948; it had been $129,870 in 1932.

The Department of Agriculture was also a pioneer in using exhibits. An exhibits specialist was appointed in 1912, and the Department's Exhibits Service rapidly developed with the growth of extension work. Its chief activity has been to supply exhibits for the Extension Service and for state and interstate fairs. They have ranged from simple panels with photographs and legends to elaborate devices such as dioramas, the "talking cow," and the "mechanical hen." In 1947 the service had ten "exhibition groups," which went on tour to agricultural fairs. Among the subjects presented were farm and forest conservation, livestock and forage, and better living on the farm. "Better Living on the Farm" consisted of seven exhibits: "Screw Worms—Damage, Control, and Treatment," "A Veteran Earns His Farm," "Farm Water Supply," "Publications," "Nutrition," "Produce Your Own Food," and "Electricity for All." Over three million people visited Department of Agriculture exhibits at agricultural fairs in 1947–1948.

Looking back at the series of great fairs which preceded the war, McCamy predicted in 1939 that if the nation continued to be addicted to large fairs, "large-scale exhibits will be for some time an important avenue for federal publicity to reach the mass public." He based the prediction on experiences such as that of the Century of Progress at Chicago in 1933 when 15½ million visitors—equivalent to more than one-tenth of the population—passed through the Federal Building. It was a comprehensive exhibit, which was "a combination of teaching the public facts gathered by the agencies and of telling the public, sometimes directly and sometimes by implication, what the government did in its routine, day-to-day work." They watched the minting of coins, saw dioramas of national parks, were fingerprinted for identification purposes, examined naval guns. Even the State Department "mustered a compelling exhibit consisting of a world-map with flashing lights to show the location of diplomatic and consular offices, samples of diplomatic correspondence and ceremonial letters, documents showing the steps in amending the Constitution and in making a law, gifts traditionally given by the President to officers and men of foreign ships that rescue American citizens on the high seas, sample treaties, and a model of the United States government building in Paris." [3]

It remains to be seen whether McCamy's prediction will be realized. The Freedom Train with its exhibition of historic documents is, however, a postwar example of the capacity which the technique has for capturing the popular imagination. It was inspired by the Attorney General though not financed from government sources. What in business would be called the "open house" or the "plant tour" is essentially similar in approach. There are some who think that too little is done in the United States to interest the citizen by showing him the actual operations of his government and by extracting the drama and color from normal constitutional and administrative processes.

The opportunities have not been entirely neglected. Mixing pleasure with their business as citizens, millions of Americans have inspected the great dams and other federal projects. Open days for the general public and organized tours for civic leaders, newspapermen, and other opinion makers have been important features of the public relations activities of the military departments. The Soil Conservation Service is another agency which has made considerable use of organized tours for civic leaders. The Government Printing Office has long been a showplace for tourists in Washington, and many thousands take part every year in the conducted tours of the headquarters building of the Federal Bureau of Investigation. The Bureau is lucky to have what in the trade would be called a "natural," and the tours are a cheap and effective way of spreading the impression—so important for the success of its administration —that it is a supremely efficient machine which almost always gets its man.

Like exhibits, the radio and the motion picture are methods of reaching millions who learn most easily by listening or seeing. For government information policy, they raise essentially the same issues as relations with the press. With radio, an im-

[3] McCamy, *Government Publicity*, 100–1.

portant difference is that there is no alternative to using the privately owned media. It has sometimes been suggested that the federal government should run its own stations. Representative Reid of Illinois proposed in 1928 that the Departments of Agriculture, Interior, and Labor should be assigned clear channels.[4] Public ownership of stations for specifically governmental purposes is not inconsistent with private ownership of broadcasting facilities in general, but there is no prospect of the federal government going into station ownership as part of its domestic information policy. It would be bitterly resisted, and it would be ineffective and extravagant. A governmental network would be needed to cover the whole country, and the mass audiences would remain with the stations which catered to popular entertainment.

Federal broadcasting activities have, therefore, to be conducted through stations over which the government has only the remote and indirect control that they have to satisfy the Federal Communications Commission that they are conducting themselves according to law. At the time of writing, it means getting into the programs of more stations than there are daily newspapers, and through them into nineteen out of every twenty American homes.

The constitutional responsibilities of the radio for public information differ from those of the press in that radio stations are subject to the specific obligation—laid down in the Federal Communications Act of 1934—to operate in the public interest, convenience, and necessity. Among the items on which the Federal Communications Commission has required stations to supply information is the proportion of time devoted to government broadcasts. "Include in this item all municipal, state, and federal programs, including political or controversial broadcasts by public officials, or candidates for office, and regardless of whether or not the programs included under this item are entertainment, educational, agricultural, etc., in character." [5] Stations are not expressly required to broadcast pro-

---

[4] Sayre, 10.
[5] Federal Communications Commission, *Public Service Responsibility of Broadcasting Licensees* (1946), 13. This is the famous "Blue Book."

grams about or on behalf of government. The obligation which the Commission has imposed is that they shall make sufficient provision for educational, cultural, religious, and other broadcasts which they owe to the community as a public service. One element in a balanced output is adequate provision for broadcasts about public affairs, including government activities.

It is certain that but for the Federal Communications Commission there would have been less public service broadcasting. On the other hand, leaders of the industry have always acknowledged that like the press it has a moral responsibility to inform and educate the public. "Broadcasting represents a job of entertaining, informing, and educating the nation," said David Sarnoff of the Radio Corporation of America in 1922, "and should therefore be distinctly regarded as a public service." [6]

From the point of view of specialist public relations, the radio is firstly a news medium. This raises no important problem for government information policy. Broadcasters receive news through the same channels as the press. In 1943 the President's press conferences were renamed "press and radio" conferences. That is about all there is to it. The radio commentator is the counterpart of the newspaper columnist, and often doubles the roles. Field offices have to keep in touch with local radio stations no less than with local newspapers. The same machinery can be used for both purposes. And, as with the press, the news is broadcast on its merits.

The Department of Agriculture is the outstanding example of the systematic use of radio for the dissemination of news from government. Radio is particularly well suited to the needs of the farmer. He wants up-to-the-minute information about weather prospects, prices, epidemics, crop conditions. Farms are often inaccessible, and he might lose valuable time if he had to wait for the newspapers. Rural radio stations set out to cater for his needs, and over the years the Department of Agriculture has worked out arrangements for close cooperation with them.

[6] Thomas Porter Robinson, *Radio Networks and the Federal Government* (Columbia University Press, 1943), 22.

It was a Department of Agriculture official, William A. Wheeler, who as long ago as 1920 made the first broadcast from a federal agency.[7] An amateur radio enthusiast, he saw the possibilities of the new invention in his work of distributing market reports. The Department set up a separate Radio Service in 1926, and in 1947–1948 it was in touch with 358 radio farm directors, most of whom belonged to state extension services, land-grant colleges, and state universities. Through the wire services it informed them daily of prices and other matters of interest to farmers. A weekly newsletter from the Radio Service in Washington told them of national developments, and they were in contact with county agents, state Departments of Agriculture, and federal field representatives.[8]

As in other respects, the Department of Agriculture is *sui generis,* but it is only doing on a bigger scale the same work of radio liaison which is an everyday public relations job both in government and other spheres. What, however, of the contribution of American radio to the dissemination of information which is not news but which the government needs to communicate to the people in the furtherance of its administrative programs and in the discharge of its reportorial duties? And to public persuasion in the furtherance of programs which depend upon active popular participation? And how far has use been made of specifically radio techniques in government information programs—talks, discussions, "spots," "commercials," actualities, documentaries?

Radio accepts a responsibility for cooperating in public information and persuasion; and there are two ways in which the responsibility may be discharged. Radio stations can make the necessary time available to the government. Or they can do the job for the government. Both methods have in fact been used, but at any rate at the network level there has been a marked swing in the second direction.

Time can be made available either free or on payment. The federal government has rarely bought time, and it has rarely been suggested that it should do so. The pioneers of the 1920's

[7] Sayre, 9.
[8] *Department of Agriculture Appropriation Bill for 1949, Hearings,* 316.

established the principle that help should be given as a public service. The purchase of time by the Treasury Department in 1927 for announcements about the refunding of the Second Liberty Loan seems to have been an aberration.[9]

Payment for radio advertising—as in the case of postwar recruiting campaigns—has also been exceptional but does not raise the same principle. A somewhat similar issue is, however, posed by the inclusion of federal broadcasts in sponsored programs. The advantage to the agency is that it ensures a big audience. The objections are that it makes the agency in some measure dependent on a commercial undertaking, and that it involves government partnership with a particular private interest, though any other interest which is aggrieved has the obvious remedy of offering to render a similar service. The Department of Agriculture long resisted proposals that the Farm and Home Hour, its main national instrument of radio publicity, should be sponsored. It could not prevent the National Broadcasting Company from selling part of the Hour in 1938; in 1948 the whole Hour was being sponsored by Allis-Chalmers, manufacturers of agricultural machinery.

Jeanette Sayre has told the story of the rise and decline of the direct participation of federal agencies in broadcasting activities.[10] The heyday was the early New Deal period. The circumstances were propitious. The Administration had a positive and radical program, and needed every available medium to explain it in the face of powerful opposition. Many of its measures required the active cooperation of the people. It believed in talking direct to the people. To the President and other New Deal leaders the radio was still a new and exciting instrument of popular education of which the possibilities had hardly begun to be realized; the President himself was a supreme artist in the radio talk. The technicians were eager to experiment, and the broadcasters' feud with the newspaper publishers made them ready to help. Relief funds were available to supplement other resources, and the Federal Theater Project of WPA had a radio division.

[9] Sayre, 53.
[10] Sayre, *op. cit.*

The enthusiasts tried many techniques—drama, serials, question-and-answer games, interviews, lectures, living newspapers. Many of the programs were contributions to general education rather than to public information, but federal agencies—notably the Department of Agriculture, the Department of the Interior, and the new economic agencies—used the radio as never before or since to enlist the cooperation of the nation in their policies. With more zeal than discretion, the head of the Radio Division of the WPA Theater Project spoke of selling government "the way you sell soap." [11]

This remark crystallizes the main reason for the passing of the phase. The enthusiasm of the broadcasters grew cool. They began to complain that the administration was using them as instruments of propaganda. They also alleged that they had to rewrite much of the material with which they were supplied. Jeanette Sayre came to the conclusion that there was substance in the complaints of incompetence and inefficiency. She also doubted whether the governmental programs were effective. Few attempts were made to find out. "If the government is to use radio intelligently, it must study its listeners and find out how well it succeeds." [12]

The use of broadcasting with its supposedly exceptional powers of influencing public opinion was naturally suspect to Congress. In 1937 the Byrd Committee advised Congress to fix an upper limit for broadcasting expenditure. Federal radio activities were a target for successive economy cuts. At the same time the networks were increasingly uncooperative. Fewer programs prepared in government agencies were put on, and even during the war there was no return to the former system. The networks were glad to help in domestic information activities and to receive advice from the OWI and other agencies on subject matter for their own programs, but they looked upon the actual preparation of programs as their own responsibility.

The position after the war was in marked contrast with that found by McCamy. During four months in 1937 the na-

[11] *ibid.*, 113.
[12] *ibid.*, 117.

tional networks were presenting ten regular feature programs originating in Federal agencies. These included regular broadcasts by the Army, Navy, and Marine bands; a Federal Radio Project series based on the Bill of Rights; dramatic sketches about the Smithsonian Institution; weekly lectures on American industry from the Department of Commerce; a "Cabinet" series in which Secretaries of federal departments discussed their work and policies; and a daily feature which the Department of Agriculture supplied for the Farm and Home Hour.[13] This famous program had begun in 1928, and went on until it was discontinued by the American Broadcasting Company in 1945. It was soon resumed on the National network—but weekly instead of daily, and the regular contribution of the Department of Agriculture was reduced to five minutes of farm news. What is more, the only other regular contribution by a federal agency in 1947–1948 was a similar news feature in the American Farmer program of the American Broadcasting Company.

There has, however, been a remarkable increase in the volume of government advertising on the radio. This will be discussed later, when the Advertising Council is described. Though the broadcasters have cooperated, it is due chiefly to a change in the attitude of advertisers. With this exception, talks are now the main broadcasting method in use by federal agencies. How far the industry is entitled to congratulate itself on the considerable amount of time which is provided for talks by officials is a matter of argument. It would be bad policy and bad programming to refuse facilities for the President to speak to the nation, while local stations may be glad to fill empty spaces with talks by lesser officials which, at no cost to themselves, may earn them credit with the Federal Communications Commission. Still the record is impressive. To take two of the networks by way of example, the President, twelve cabinet members, 15 assistant cabinet members, and 18 chiefs of federal agencies were broadcast over the National network in 1946; and the President and 14 cabinet and assistant cabinet members

[13] McCamy, *Government Publicity*, 94–95.

over Mutual in the same year.[14] The networks understandably stress the value of this contribution to public service broadcasting.

Their public spirit is less apparent to those who are refused facilities. Oscar Ewing, administrator of the Federal Security Agency, complained in 1948 that when it was suggested that Secretary Schwellenbach, General Bradley, and he should broadcast in connection with Employ-the-Physically-Handicapped Week, the National Broadcasting Company would provide facilities only for Mr. Schwellenbach, notwithstanding that his interest in the subject was the least. The company explained that according to Crossley ratings there were sufficient audiences to justify broadcasting the President, members of the Supreme Court, and cabinet members—in that order—but not other officials.[15] This suggested that listener preference was the criterion.

The forum program is an invention of considerable significance for democracy, and for government public relations. It is akin to the public meeting and the press conference as an occasion on which officials and other political leaders can explain their policies and deal with points of doubt which are troubling the public. In "Meet the Press" on the Mutual system I heard an interview in 1948 between Secretary of Agriculture Clinton P. Anderson and four well known newspapermen, Lawrence Spivak of the *American Mercury*, Ernest K. Lindley of *Newsweek*, Bert Andrews of the New York *Herald Tribune*, and Edward T. Folliard of the *Washington Post*. Some of the questions were purely political. Was he ready to run for Vice President? What did he think of Henry Wallace running for President? But most dealt with Department of Agriculture matters. Would meat rationing be necessary? What steps were being taken to prepare for it? Was it legitimate for federal employees to buy and sell on the com-

[14] National Broadcasting Company, *Annual Review 1946–1947* (1947), and information supplied by the Company.

[15] *Department of Labor—Federal Security Agency Appropriation Bill for 1949, Hearings,* 245.

modity markets? Why not eliminate the production of whisky? Was the Marshall Plan feasible in terms of farm output? When would eggless days be stopped?

Programs of the documentary type also contribute to government public relations. A critic of American radio, Charles A. Siepmann, commended the CBS documentaries in 1947 as evidence that radio was starting to grow up.[16] Like the March of Time films, they represent a fruitful adaptation of their medium to the problem of making serious discussion palatable to the millions if not to the masses. Where they deal with matters in which government agencies are interested, they may give them valuable support. Early examples from CBS included "The Eagle's Brood," on juvenile delinquency; "A Long Life and a Happy One," on public health; "Report Card," on the shortcomings of public education. Each was on a theme on which information was one of the chief tools of government policy. Somewhat similar programs on the other networks dealt with venereal disease, school conditions, and conservation of national resources.

The results of these experiments exceeded expectations. Audiences for the early CBS documentaries were generally over five million. Thousands of letters were received. In some communities councils were set up to tackle the abuses to which the broadcasts had drawn attention. The Department of Justice asked CBS to arrange further programs in synchronization with its own campaign against juvenile delinquency.

Here were the nearest counterparts to the experimental programs prepared by federal agencies before the war. Here, said Siepmann, was "a tentative blueprint for collaboration among government, radio, and listeners: here, in fact, is promise of that working partnership on which the success of our system of broadcasting depends." [17]

For the rest, noteworthy feature programs on governmental themes were not numerous after the war. But there were some. Two series of weekly discussions on the United Na-

[16] Charles A. Siepmann, "Radio Starts to Grow Up," *Nation*, December 27, 1947, 697–9.
[17] *ibid.*

tions and on foreign affairs which CBS arranged in consultation with the State Department in 1945 and 1946 were a valuable aid to the Department's domestic information program. Radio has regularly cooperated in the celebration of Army Day and Navy Day. The Luckman Committee commended networks and local stations for their substantial help in support of food conservation. Virtually every station in the country carried "Here's to Veterans," a program of the most popular radio entertainments—started in 1946—in which messages from the Veterans Administration took the place of "commercials."

It is difficult to assess the contribution which the networks, not to speak of the industry as a whole, have made to public information on matters of government policy and administration. The central question—whether American radio is doing as much as it should to educate and inform the American people—goes beyond the scope of this book. But, whether or not it is doing all it should, who can say what is the proper allocation between the different claimants for a share in public service broadcasting—the churches, education, science, labor, business, government? And the ultimate test is not the volume of broadcasting but the number of listeners. This depends not only on the quality of the programs, but still more upon the times when they are broadcast, how many stations use them, and the amount of publicity which they are given. Without promotion, said two competent observers in 1948, public service programs "may constitute, in actual practice, little more than ineffective gestures of good will." [18]

And, as far as the networks are concerned, it is important to bear in mind that affiliates often reject public service programs, and that the number of subjects which lend themselves to treatment on a national scale is limited. There are fewer still which will not gain in their presentation by being adapted to local circumstances. It is through the local stations that broadcasting can be used to greatest effect in most information programs, and they are usually ready to provide opportunities for talks

[18] Charles A. Siepmann and Sidney Reisberg, " 'To Secure These Rights.' Coverage of a Radio Documentary," *Public Opinion Quarterly*, 12 (4), Winter 1948–49, 655.

by government officials. They are not so ready to provide peak listening time or to exert their energies and ingenuity to attract audiences. In other words, their help is, qualitatively, much less valuable than its quantity might suggest; it is largely unsystematic, fortuitous, and narrow in scope. And that would be a fair verdict on the contribution of American radio as a whole to public information.

Little need be said about FM, and it would be premature to say much about television. FM has disappointed its sponsors, and unless it results in a marked increase in serious broadcasts to large numbers of listeners, is unlikely to make a significant contribution to government public relations.

Television, on the other hand, is a public relations medium of great potential importance, and Washington information divisions with an eye to the future have been watching its development with interest. Among the pioneers, as so often before, was the Department of Agriculture, whose Radio Service began in 1948 a study into the ways in which television could be used for agricultural information. Its hopes were high. "Video is expected to offer extension workers the greatest medium they have ever had for demonstrating new farm techniques to large groups under convenient circumstances—in their own homes." [19] It is too early to foresee the future of television in government information. It will depend on a number of unpredictable factors, including the long-term economics of television, the sense of public responsibility of television stations, and the attitude of Congress to expenditure on the use of television for government information purposes.

The progress of television will also have as yet unforeseeable consequences upon the use of the motion picture in public relations. "Of all his public relations tools," said Harlow and Black, "the public relations worker will find the film the most adaptable to every need . . . The public relations worker need have only the slightest knowledge of the laws of psychology to realize the tremendous advantage the film has over other media in presenting a message. It stimulates and holds

[19] U.S. Department of Agriculture, Office of Information, *Annual Report for 1947-8.*

attention; creates interest through real-life situations; facilitates retention, recall, and recognition; and painlessly provides a mental 'set' as the preliminary background of action or behavior. In short, through the film, the public relations worker has at his command all the vast power inherent in audio-visual education, by which even the most intricate subjects may be taught more conveniently, grasped more readily, and retained more easily." [20]

This is too exuberant. The film has serious drawbacks as a public relations medium. It is relatively expensive. The pace cannot be regulated to the capacities of different individuals. The movie is best suited for putting over simple messages or for giving reality to lessons which are being taught by other methods. For most purposes it needs to be supplemented by preparatory campaigns through other media. For some, the slide film with a lecture is cheaper and more effective. As was said in the bulletin of the Southern Educational Film Production Service, it is necessary to change "this habit of passive reverie . . . into active realization. For years, county agricultural agents in the South have found the advertisements of 'free movies' a sure way to collect a crowd. . . . When the lights go on again, they vow they've enjoyed the picture. But it takes a skillful discussion leader to salvage from such a showing any recognition that there is a connection between the scenes on the screen and the ones most of his audience will see beyond their RFD mail boxes when they go back home." [21]

To say that the usefulness of the film as a medium of public relations has been exaggerated is not to deny its value when used with intelligence and discrimination. It has a high popular appeal. It is preeminently suited to audiences which will not read printed material. In the commercial theaters ready-made audiences of many millions a week offer a tempting if difficult target for the ambitious public relations man.

If the radio has disappointed the enthusiasts who saw a great opportunity for mass education in citizenship, the same is truer

[20] Harlow and Black, 309.

[21] *Southern Film News* (Southern Educational Film Production Service, Athens, Ga.), 2 (2), February 1948, 4.

of the film. The motion picture industry has been fettered neither by any express legal obligation to conduct itself in the public interest nor by any strong expectation that it would do so. Yet it has not altogether neglected the responsibility which, in the view of the Commission on Freedom of the Press, rests upon it to help in explaining government policies to the people.

In both the World Wars it cooperated extensively and systematically. In the first war films on war themes were produced and distributed for the Committee on Public Information, and theaters were made available for talks by the famous Four Minute Men. In the second war there was organized cooperation through the War Activities Committee. It is less generally known that this cooperation did not wholly end with the war. It continued through the Motion Picture Industry Coordinating Committee which the industry set up at the invitation of the President in 1946 and the small Motion Picture Liaison Division in the Executive Office of the President. That government agencies did not in fact ask for much help from the industry—the number of requests does not appear to have exceeded half a dozen in 1947—may be less important in the long run than that the principle of cooperation was accepted in peacetime.

How well the industry could rise to the occasion was shown by the experience of the food conservation campaign. "To make a movie of any length," reported the Luckman Committee, "naturally would have taken too much time for a campaign of this immediate nature, but with short documentary films, news-reel spots, and messages by stars, it was possible for the industry to add its great voice to the chorus of appeals." The main contribution was a documentary, "drawing a heart-stabbing contrast between scenes of harvest in the U.S. and hunger in Europe," which "concluded with a brief, moving appeal by Charles Luckman." [22]

This was exceptional. The help which the motion picture industry has given in government information has been almost entirely incidental to its ordinary commercial activities. It may

[22] *op. cit.*

not be less welcome or less valuable on this account. The expectation of profits is presumptive evidence of popular appeal, and, for the sake of ensuring accuracy as well as because of the publicity, federal agencies are anxious to help commercial producers who are interested in themes involving government activities.

For the more spectacular aspects of government—the training of the armed forces or the public appearances of the President—newsreels and magazines are highly effective media.

But some of the most valuable publicity is obtained as a by-product of feature films in whose purposes public information has an entirely subordinate part. The armed forces are probably the chief beneficiary, with the FBI a strong runner-up. Good examples of what can be done in a similar context are two films which were produced with Treasury Department cooperation in 1947. *T-Men* (Reliance Films) was a fictional film which told how Treasury agents broke up a narcotics gang. The other was a March of Time documentary which illustrated the different facets of the work of the "T-men," and should have left little doubt in the minds of the audience that crime against Treasury-administered laws did not pay.

Even so, the share of the motion picture industry in federal public relations is inconsiderable. It may at first glance seem surprising that the use which government agencies themselves make of films is also slight. The main reasons are the cost and the known attitude of Congress. There was a short period of high hopes in the 1930's when government films like *The River* and *The Plow That Broke the Plains* crashed into the commercial theaters, and the name of Pare Lorenz enjoyed an international reputation. It did not last. The war brought about important developments in the use of films as an aid to training, and since the war the military departments and other agencies have built upon the wartime experience. No corresponding advances have occurred in the use of films for government information.

Rather the contrary. McCamy said that of 456 government movies available in 1937 perhaps less than half could be regarded as "publicity in the sense of telling about the work, program or services of government." [23] Of 1,330 films listed in the *Guide to United States Government Motion Pictures* which the Library of Congress published in 1947,[24] the great majority were intended for training—on themes such as "blanking sheet metal on the squaring shear" (U.S. Office of Education) and "aviation free gunnery instructors' practice with 3A trainers" (Navy Department). Some prewar films were still in circulation, and of 300 at most which could be described as "publicity" in McCamy's sense, over 100 were historical records of the armed forces. Of the rest it is only by a stretch that many could be brought within McCamy's category—films dealing, for example, with the storage of garden crops, the habits and control of rats, methods of shell-fishing, and the manufacture of lime. There was no question in films such as these of exploiting "the tremendous advantage" which according to Harlow and Black the movie has over other media.

The only agency in which the prewar tradition was even flickering at the time of my investigation was indeed the Department of Agriculture. It was also unique among civilian agencies in having its own fully equipped Motion Picture Service; other agencies shared these facilities but used them almost exclusively for instructional films.

The motion picture activities of the Department of Agriculture are more interesting as an illustration of what might be done than of what had been done over the government as a whole. In 1946–1947 the Motion Picture Service produced seven films for the Department and collaborated in the production of eight for bureaus of the Department. It cooperated with state extension services on four more—*Men Who Grow Cotton,* jointly with ten cotton states; *Balanced Farming,* with Missouri; *Farming for the Future,* on land improvement, with Massachusetts; and a film on pastures, with Florida. *A Message of Famine* was a plea to save wheat, fats, and oils. *The Crop That Never Fails* (which won a medal awarded by the

[23] McCamy, *Government Publicity,* 85.
[24] *Guide to United States Government Motion Pictures* (Library of Congress, Motion Picture Division, processed, 1947), Vol. I, No. 1. The appropriation for this project was not renewed in 1948.

Festival Mondial du Film et des Beaux Arts de Belgique) was a savings drive picture, produced in cooperation with the Treasury Department on the theme "A financial reserve is one of the five links in the chain of good farming."

These are examples of the use of films to persuade people to cooperate in government policies by reinforcing simple messages which are also being publicized through other media. *The Golden Secret* told a soil conservation message by means of cartoons. It was "a fairy story about the golden top soil being washed away and what the son of the king's chief huntsman did to stop it and how the king rewarded him with the gift of the best farm in all the realm." A twenty-minute film, *Battling Brucellosis*, on the other hand, used a conventional technique for practical instruction. *Men Who Grow Cotton* was designed for the broader purpose of giving Southern audiences a background against which they could better understand how they fitted into the economy of the United States and the world. As is shown by the synopsis, it was intended to make people think rather than do anything specific: "Gaiety of the cotton carnival; cotton's contribution to the national economy; ups and downs of life in the cotton belt; higher yields; one-variety communities; diversification and mechanization; increasing foreign competition; flame cultivators and mechanical pickers; Southern industrial expansion; new uses."

The ten films produced in 1947–1948 were more specialized. Three dealt with forest fire prevention and control; four with the control of white pine blister rust; one with personnel management as a career in the Department; one with the work of the Bureau of Home Nutrition and Home Economics. All were short, inexpensive, and unambitious.

Cooperation with non-federal agencies has in part been a by-product of the restricted use which departments are able to make of informational films. It also reflects the tendency to work where possible through others. It has proved a fruitful expedient, without producing spectacular results.

The Mines Bureau pioneered; it has for many years collaborated with the mining industry in producing instructional and informational films. The Department of Agriculture had a big response from the states to its experiment with cooperatively produced pictures. Other agencies have made use of the same approach. In 1947, for example, the Children's Bureau collaborated with state governments in films about the detection and treatment of rheumatic fever and the emergency care of premature babies. An animated cartoon, *Winkie the Watchman,* was produced by the Tennessee Department of Health with the cooperation of the Public Health Service as part of a campaign to teach children to seek regular care for their teeth. The TVA and nine Southern states combined in 1947 to form the Southern Educational Film Production Service.

It is one thing to produce films. It is useless unless they can be distributed. Like other producers of documentary films, government departments have been handicapped by the lack of channels of distribution. With rare exceptions—mainly for films of special local interest—the commercial theaters are closed to documentaries unless they have a high topical interest or entertainment value. "Here," said Gloria Waldron in 1949, speaking of "information or documentary" films in general, "is the no-man's land between producer and consumer, for the most part a void yet to be filled by the public library or some other agency." [25]

It is usually easier, however, for official than for most unofficial agencies to supplement the normal channels with resources of their own. In some instances the audiences are more or less ready-made, as with films addressed to the armed forces and even many which are intended for use in agricultural programs. In 1947–1948 the Department of Agriculture was using 76 film libraries in state universities and extension services, its own field offices, and occasionally other film libraries; it had mobile projectors for the sparsely populated areas. During the year, 2,992 prints of Department of Agriculture films were sold, and 162,032 showings were reported: nearly 13½ million attendances were recorded, but the Department thought that 27 million would be a conserva-

[25] Gloria Waldron, *The Information Film* (Columbia University Press, 1949), 74.

tive estimate of the number who actually attended. The cost to public funds was reckoned to be a dollar for every thousand persons. In 1946–1947 Bureau of Mines films were shown more than 110,000 times to over 8 million people in schools, colleges, scientific societies, vocational training classes, the armed forces, and business and civic organizations.[26]

These figures are large. It may help the perspective to compare them with the 109,000 audiences and over 17 million people who saw Bell Telephone System films in 1947.[27] This was at a time when the estimated weekly attendance at commerical theaters was of the order of 80 million. Measured in hours of showing, the disproportion was of course considerably greater.

So we come back to the commercial theater. Films will continue to play a subordinate place in government information unless the motion picture industry comes to act upon that fuller conception of its obligations which was urged upon it by the Commission on Freedom of the Press:

"Obliged to surmount great technical obstacles and at the same time to establish itself on a profit-making basis, the motion picture industry has not yet developed its full possibilities. [The first is] to help the public to understand the issues that confront them as citizens of the United States and of the world. . . . The Commission would emphasize the fact that the public service or educational function of the movies, so brilliantly demonstrated during the recent war, faces new opportunities and responsibilities in the years ahead. It is imperative that the motion picture industry rise to the occasion. . . . By its own action, [it] should place increasing stress on its role as a civic and informational agency conscious of the evolving character of many political and social problems. The industry as a responsible member of the body politic cannot shirk its obligation to promote, so far as possible, an intelligent understanding of

[26] U.S. Department of Agriculture, Office of Information, *Annual Report for 1947–48*, and Department of the Interior, Bureau of Mines, press release, August 6, 1947.

[27] Eugene A. Bond, address to American Public Relations Association, Washington, D.C., May 26, 1948.

domestic and international affairs. . . . This service to good citizenship is often good business as well. At all events, in a free society like ours, it is a duty." [28]

This is not the same as saying that the industry is under an obligation to distribute government-produced films or to produce films with the specific object of furthering government information programs. The obligation is less precise, and it is not confined to the education and information of the public about matters of government. What is asked is that, like the radio, the industry should recognize that it has a duty to operate in the wider interest, and that as part of this duty it should help to inform the ordinary man about all the subjects which are his concern as a citizen of the American democracy. He should know what the Department of Agriculture is doing and should be made aware of his responsibilities for national savings and road safety. But he should also know about the National Association of Manufacturers and the CIO, about Harvard University and the Methodist Church, about the International Bank and the Association for the Advancement of Colored People.

Perhaps the best way of putting it is that as trustees for two of the great mass media the radio and motion picture industries should set before them *mutatis mutandis* the same broad objectives that have guided the best representatives of the press itself. It may be taken for granted that the movie at least will never be comparable in importance to the newspaper as an instrument of public information. The difference in their potentialities may, however, be less than past experience would suggest. Hollywood has from time to time paid lip service to ideas of developing the motion picture as a great medium of education in citizenship. Except during the two wars and then only to a limited extent, it has never seriously tried to translate the words into deeds. Yet, on the evidence of one of its chief spokesmen, Eric Johnston, writing in 1946, the scope is vast: "The motion picture is one of the most potent instruments ever devised for the dissemination of ideas, information and

[28] Inglis, v–vi.

mutual understanding between peoples. The motion picture no longer is looked upon solely as a device for mass entertainment." [29]

The continuance after the war of arrangements for cooperation between the motion picture industry and federal agencies did not mean very much in practice. It may, however, be of great long-term significance if it is evidence that the industry recognizes that it has some responsibility for helping the federal government to discharge its duties of public information and persuasion. A precedent has been set which would make it much easier for large-scale cooperation to develop should a dramatic change occur either in the outlook of the film magnates or in their relationship with the government. The honeymoon of federal radio activities during the 1930's might never have occurred but for the antagonism between the press and the radio which led the latter into temporary partnership with the administration. The remarkable partnership between American advertisers and the federal government was in part at any rate a response to public criticism which advertising leaders saw as a potentially serious threat to their interests.

It is paradoxical that alone of those concerned with mass communications advertisers should have made arrangements with the federal government which correspond fairly closely to the relationship which the Commission on Freedom of the Press envisaged for the mass media in general. At least it could hardly have been foreseen.

Advertising for purely administrative reasons is as old as administration. In modern conditions there are many routine matters which are not news but which must be brought to the notice of the public by means of advertisements—the disposal of government property, contracts, court decisions, tax defaulters. According to the *Congressional Directory* for 1901, the contract division of the Post Office Department prepared advertisements, and War Department and Army advertising was the responsibility of the chief clerk of the War Department.

[29] *ibid.*, 5.

The Bureau of the Public Debt and the Commissioners of the District of Columbia are examples of federal agencies which have been expressly authorized to advertise for routine administrative purposes. The outstanding contemporary example was the War Assets Administration. To carry out one of the greatest sales jobs in history it had to advertise extensively. In 1946–1947 it spent $16 million on advertising. It topped the list for newspaper advertising, which accounted for $8.7 million; Lucky Strike, in second place, was well behind. The expenditure on direct mail advertising exceeded $6 million.[30]

This kind of advertising raises few of the issues which have made Congress unsympathetic to the use of advertising for general publicity on behalf of government. That Congress should be unfriendly to the latter will cause no surprise. Advertising is associated with high-pressure commercial propaganda which is not always scrupulous in its methods, and with techniques of persuasion which rely not on argument but on exploiting the emotions. At the same time, advertisers have probably been more successful than anybody else in gearing their messages to the capacities of mass audiences, including the semi-literate and apathetic minority who present the publicist with his least tractable problem. Advertising may, therefore, make an important contribution to the popularization of an information program.

The nature of this contribution was described in 1947 by Drew Dudley, who had been in charge of government advertising in the Office of War Information: "It is the modern information technique. It is the new way. It is high-speed, geared to catch the eyes of those who read and run; and this includes almost all of us. It is peculiarly American. . . . It has the advantage of simplifying the Government's programs and making them understandable in A-B-C terminology to the great mass of American people." As had been done in the economic stabilization program, it was possible to translate high-flown, abstruse matter "into easy-to-read ads which explained the problem in the language of the street. Typical head-

[30] *St. Louis Post Dispatch*, May 8, 1947: and War Assets Administration, *The Task Ahead, Quarterly Report to the Congress*, Third Quarter, 1947, 29.

lines in the series ran like this: 'The dough you blow will bring us woe.' " [31]

The advantages of advertising as a technique for catching the eyes of all who read and run have never commended themselves to Congress as a strong reason for authorizing public expenditure upon it. Except in special circumstances, such as recruiting publicity after the Second World War, the Executive has had to depend upon the good offices of advertising interests when it wanted to use advertising as a publicity medium.

In the first war advertisers made a contribution to government publicity which on an incomplete estimate was worth $1,594,814, excluding outdoor advertising and window displays.[32]

Between the wars help was occasionally received in programs the purpose of which coincided with the interests of the advertiser. President Roosevelt acknowledged the assistance of the "advertising fraternity" in explaining his economic program to the nation.[33] The building trade advertised in support of the efforts of the Federal Housing Administration to stimulate private building. In 1936 the FHA spent $94,855 on supplying building interests with mats and other copy for newspaper advertising. It also enlisted the cooperation of sponsors for radio advertising. The following is an example of its "spot" announcements. "When Jack Frost warms his fingers at your window he leaves a fine, feathery piece of art work in return for the heat he borrows. Frost pictures on the windows may amuse the children, but practical grown-ups aren't likely to think they're worth the price of extra fuel. And smart folks can out-trick this stealthy thief-in-the-night with storm windows—installed on the FHA Pay-by-the-Month Plan for fixing up your home." [34]

[31] Drew Dudley, "Molding Public Opinion through Advertising," *Annals* of the American Academy of Political and Social Science, vol. 250, March 1947, 108.

[32] James R. Mock and Cedric Larson, *Words That Won the War* (Princeton University Press, 1939), 100.

[33] Pollard, 782.

[34] Sayre, 64.

Until 1942 the help received from advertisers was sporadic, *ad hoc,* and insubstantial. The new feature since 1942 has been the organized participation of advertising agencies and advertising media in campaigns on public service themes proposed by governmental and other agencies—themes of no immediate financial interest to themselves such as national savings, the prevention of forest fires, the improvement of teachers' conditions, and better inter-racial relations.

This is the sequel to a memorable meeting of the Association of National Advertisers and the American Association of Advertising Agencies at Hot Springs in November 1941.[35] One object of the meeting was to consider measures to meet the threat to advertising interests from popular distrust and governmental animosity. Advertising men blamed the federal government for many of their troubles, and they feared that worse was still to come. The majority were in a belligerent mood. A small group, however, took a different view of the responsibilities of advertisers in the face of almost certain war. It was due to these that at the last minute William Batt and Leon Henderson were invited to address the conference. Batt and Henderson spoke frankly about the gravity of the situation, and at the same time allayed the apprehensions of their audiences about the intentions of the administration. The upshot was that, instead of making plans to attack the government, the conference decided that a scheme for helping it should be prepared.

A month later the United States was at war. As a consequence of the Hot Springs meeting, a group of prominent advertising men, on behalf of advertising interests as a whole, at once offered their services in the home information program of the government. Donald Nelson and other leading officials

[35] I was fortunate in being able to talk with a considerable number of people with first hand experience of the Advertising Council at different stages in its career, and thanks to Mr. James W. Young and Mr. Charles G. Mortimer, Jr., chairman of the Council, I was privileged to be present at a meeting of the Board. Mr. Theodore S. Repplier, president, Mr. Allan Wilson, and other members of the staff of the Council gave me much help. The account of advertising in government publicity in this chapter follows closely an article of mine, "Public Service Advertising: the Advertising Council," in *Public Opinion Quarterly,* 12 (2), Summer 1948, 209–20.

welcomed the offer, and in March 1942 the War Advertising Council was set up. Fully representative of the main advertising interests, it made every kind of advertising facility available without cost, and became a major instrument of government information policy. In close collaboration with the Office of War Information, the War Advertising Council was responsible for over a hundred campaigns, employing advertising time and space to an estimated value of a billion dollars.

The achievement was creditable but not particularly remarkable. It was war. There were similar arrangements with the motion picture and other interests. The cynical could point to the incentive to buy public favor on the cheap which the excess profits tax provided; to the shortages which reduced the need for commerical advertising; to the advantages of a method which kept an advertiser before the public as a patriotic citizen who was doing his bit for his country.

The remarkable circumstance was that, alone of the domestic information programs of the war, this survived into peace with every appearance of becoming permanent. It was chiefly due to the vision of the few men who had given most of the dynamic to the War Advertising Council. The proposal to continue the Council was naturally welcome to the administration. While the war was still on, President Roosevelt had said in 1945: "After the war, there will be many critical national problems requiring the understanding and cooperation of every American. It is vitally important that the partnership between business and government, which has so successfully brought information to the people in wartime, continue into the postwar period." [36]

The other partner was the more likely to withdraw. Common sense opposed the continuance in peacetime of philanthropy either to the taxpayer or to a government which many businessmen thought overgrown and muddleheaded, if not worse. The OWI and other war agencies were being wound up. Some dismissed the advocates of continuance as "boy

[36] Quoted by Paul B. West, president, Association of National Advertisers, in an address, "When Advertising Comes Marching Home," Washington, D.C., February 27, 1945.

scouts." Others suspected New Deal influence. Liberals thought that such eccentricity masked some plot of Big Business.

Those on whose support the survival of the Council depended had to be reassured. Some important changes were made. The Council broadened its scope to include public service campaigns initiated by other than government agencies. This had the incidental advantage of relieving advertisers of the invidious task of sifting the many appeals which they received for help in worthy causes. Safeguards were provided to ensure that Council projects were "non-partisan, non-controversial, and in the interest of *all* the people." One of two conditions had to be satisfied. Either the purpose must accord with national policy as established by Act of Congress, or it had to be approved by a three-fourths vote of the Council's public policy committee. Pains were taken to make the committee authoritative and representative. Public figures such as Evans Clark, James B. Conant, Helen Hall, Paul G. Hoffman, Herbert H. Lehman, Eugene Meyer, Reinhold Niebuhr, and Elmo Roper have sat alongside representatives of business and organized labor, including both the AFL and the CIO.

The appeal to the better instincts of businessmen was reinforced by arguments addressed to their self-interest. The Council urged that "the best public relations advertising is public service advertising." "What helps People helps Business." Charles G. Mortimer, Jr., of General Foods, the chairman of the Advertising Council, was quite explicit in a speech to businessmen in 1947:

"If I have given the impression that when you give a page of space or five minutes of radio time to a Council campaign you are merely contributing to the national welfare, let me correct it now. True, you are casting your bread upon the waters —but it will return to you well buttered. You are acting in your own enlightened self-interest. For when public service advertising appears over your company name, you are giving evidence with deeds instead of words that your business is conscious of its social responsibilities. . . . You are by your actions refuting those enemies of business who are so fond of claiming that the heart of business is located in its pocketbook." [37]

So the new chapter began. Considerably less was done than during the war, but more than might have been expected. In 1946–1947 the Advertising Council provided the federal government with time and space of an estimated value of $80 million, and the equivalent of $20 million more for nongovernmental campaigns. In 1947 practically every national spot radio advertiser had agreed to broadcast a Council public service message at least once every six weeks; and the estimated number of "listener impressions" during the year exceeded 14 billion. The campaigns receiving most support were, in that order: Stop Accidents, Savings Bonds, Student Nurses, Crisis in Schools, and American Red Cross. The National Association of Broadcasters supplied local stations with material which they could broadcast in their own time. Newspapers and advertisers ordered over 220,000 mats for newspaper advertisements from the Council and client organizations; over 100,000 were for use in the Army Prestige campaign, and 72,000 dealt with savings bonds. More than a thousand national magazines with a circulation of 180 million gave the Council a page a month, which was devoted to savings. Car card, poster and other advertisers also helped; almost a million car cards were displayed.

To the official and unofficial organizations which they benefited, these campaigns cost only the actual out-of-pocket expenses of preparing the publicity material, and not always that. Otherwise the normal relationship between client and advertising agency was in general preserved. A member of the Council's own staff acted as "expeditor," but the main responsibility for the campaign rested with the advertising manager or agent who was appointed as coordinator, and the advertising agency or agencies which constituted the task force. The major difference from the ordinary commercial campaign is of course that instead of being able to buy time and space where they are likely to be most advantageous the task force is dependent upon the facilities which advertisers and owners of media are pre-

[37] Address by Charles G. Mortimer, Jr. at Washington, D.C., October 27, 1947.

pared to give. There are no budgetary anxieties to set an upper limit to the scale of the campaign, but the weight given to the different media is arbitrary, and the volume of support varies with the appeal which the particular campaign makes to the donors of help. During the early postwar period most of the support came from national advertisers and the advertising agencies which worked for them, and the radio was the medium which played the most important part in Council campaigns. That this should be so is easy to understand. National advertisers with their superior resources and wider outlook are more likely than smaller advertisers to make use of public relations advertising; and, where, as in radio, commercial and public service messages can be combined on the same occasion, the opportunity of making the best of both worlds has obvious attractions to the businessman whose enthusiasm for the public interest is tempered by a strong sense of duty toward his stockholders. The *Saturday Review of Literature* published in 1947 a cartoon by Doris Matthews with a text which only slightly exaggerated this eminently practical point of view:

"Herbert's, the clothing store for better prices and greater savings, where wise shoppers go for double-their-money value, the store preferred by millions of happy buyers, FOREGOES ITS COMMERCIAL to bring you an important public announcement—Drive carefully!" [38]

It is hard to appraise the achievement of the Advertising Council. There is no yardstick by which it can easily be measured. Calculations of the dollar equivalent of the facilities provided necessarily lack precision. The result depends for one thing on whether the object is to measure the cost to the donors or what the cost would be to the beneficiaries if they had to pay commercial rates. And there are other complications. Commercials and public service messages may occur in the same program. An artist may "plug" a public service theme. Space and time may be given to public service advertising because they cannot be disposed of commercially. And some advertisers stand to gain from particular campaigns, as insurance companies do from the reduction of accidents, soap manufacturers

[38] *Saturday Review of Literature*, 31 (4), January 24, 1947, 21.

from fat salvage, and textbook publishers from improved conditions in schools.

It is enough for the present purpose that advertising has made a really substantial contribution to certain government information campaigns, mainly through the agency of the Advertising Council, but also less systematically as a result of the participation of individual advertisers in the savings, recruiting and other campaigns. If the Council's own estimate of $80 million as the rough equivalent in dollars of the contribution made to government publicity in 1946–1947 is compared with national advertising expenditure of the order of $4,000 million, it may seem small. Set against what Congress would have been likely to appropriate for government advertising on the same themes, it is large. The War Assets Administration, with its formidable sales program, spent $16 million on advertising in the same year. Forty-five states were spending something of the order of $5 million on advertising their amenities in 1947–1948.[39]

The help of the Advertising Council has covered a wide range. Of the fourteen campaigns which were conducted at the instance of the federal government in 1947, the simpler were straightforward publicity drives with objects such as the sale of bonds, forest fire prevention, soil conservation, Army and Navy recruiting. Others set out to modify everyday behavior —as with food conservation and fat salvage; and to make people exert themselves as citizens—as with the American Heritage and Crisis in Schools campaigns.

How far the campaigns were effective must in the present stage of knowledge remain largely a matter of opinion. It remains to be proved whether, as was claimed by James W. Young, Chairman of the Advertising Council in 1946–1947, "the channels of advertising communication" are "the greatest aggregate means of mass education and persuasion the world has ever seen." [40] It is an open question whether the successes of advertising in selling products can be repeated when it comes

[39] *Advertising by the States* (Chicago, Council of State Governments, 1948).

[40] West, *op. cit.*

to changing ideas and habits and disseminating information. To make the experiment can be only praiseworthy.

As a matter of constitutional theory, it may seem anomalous that advertising on behalf of government should be conducted through an unofficial body not subject to government control, and that the favor of private individuals, rather than administrative need, should determine its volume and its distribution. It involves some abrogation of official responsibility for activities which are necessary to efficient administration. It means that a group of private citizens, unknown to the Constitution, assume authority to judge whether the proposals of the Executive are non-partisan and non-controversial.

The partnership of the Advertising Council with the Executive is not least remarkable because most of the help does not come from owners of advertising media but from a small group of business firms which hire those media. It is a partnership between certain sections of business and government in which the contribution of the media, though important, is secondary. As such it is an aspect of big business policy, but it is relevant to a consideration of the proper relations between the media and the Executive because it expresses itself through the media and those who command the use of them.

If the system is a constitutional anomaly, it is not necessarily the worse on that account. The main argument in its favor is that there would otherwise be no system and very much less public service advertising. Empirically, the architects of the Advertising Council found a way round two of the strongest Congressional objections to government publicity—its cost, and the danger that it might be partisan.

The system has administrative advantages as well. It relieves the government agency of the potentially dangerous task of choosing between different claimants upon advertising allocations. The machinery of the Advertising Council is flexible and adaptable to an extent which is uncharacteristic of official agencies. It is not hampered by the necessarily meticulous supervision to which official agencies are subject. The speed with which it was able to respond to an emergency was shown by a campaign which was undertaken during the shortage of fuel oil in 1948. What may be called its artistic licence is probably also greater than would be possible with an official body. It may be doubted whether comedians such as Jack Benny, Bing Crosby, and Bob Hope would have been used in the forest fire prevention campaign if it had been managed directly by the Forest Service. It might not have been so easy to introduce and exploit "Smokey," the cartoon bear who was created for the campaign by Albert Stahle, the well-known magazine illustrator.

The Advertising Council is interesting not only as an administrative expedient but for the attitude it reflects. It is possible to be amused at the sometimes uncritical enthusiasm of its exponents. It is possible to be cynical about the motives of some of its supporters. It would be naïve to suppose that advertisers as a class have become disinterested idealists. According to personal view, the development of public service advertising may be looked upon as a more or less skillful but negative reaction to collectivist tendencies, or as a positive step toward a new conception of private business as a form of public trusteeship. Was the continuance of the Advertising Council after the war —as President Truman suggested in a message on its fifth birthday—"evidence of a new recognition by business of its social responsibilities"? [41] Was it, as was claimed in 1947 by its chairman, Charles G. Mortimer, Jr., "evidence of a quiet revolution which has taken place in business thinking"? [42]

The future of the Advertising Council will be decided less by the value of its contribution to government public relations than by economic conditions and trends in business thinking. Even, however, if it should not survive, it will continue to be of permanent interest as an experiment in the kind of partnership which, if the Commission on Freedom of the Press was right, should exist between the federal government and the mass media. Its story deserves the study of all who are exercised by the problem of harnessing the communication industries to the needs of public information without fettering their independence.

[41] Quoted in *Thanks to Business* (Advertising Council, 1947).
[42] Mortimer, *op. cit.*

PART III

PUBLIC RELATIONS AND AMERICAN DEMOCRACY

◇◇

CHAPTER 8

"WHAT'S WRONG WITH PUBLIC RELATIONS?"

◇◇

W HAT are some of the general reflections which are suggested by the case study of federal government public
relations in Part II, and what light do they throw on the place
of the public relations group in the American democracy?

(1) There is a widespread suspicion of "public relations"
which is a handicap to its orderly development as a function of
management.

(2) Public relations is often equated with propaganda.

(3) Federal public relations is conducted on two planes,
and the distinction, though sometimes blurred in practice, is
important. The first is the political, and is the province of the
political chief and his associates. They engage in public relations activities to maintain, consolidate, and extend their political influence, and to shape opinion as a support for present and
future policies. The second plane is the administrative. This is
the province of official information services. Public relations is
indispensable to the efficient administration of many programs,
which cannot be carried out unless the public are adequately informed and, in some cases, persuaded to cooperate. It is the
duty of responsible organs of government to report to the
people: to do so effectively involves popularizing the reports,
and the participation of specialists in their presentation.

(4) Federal information divisions are almost exclusively
confined to communication; interpretation of the public to the
administrator is a secondary and imperfectly developed func-

tion. And they are usually under the direction of communication specialists, who—much more often than not—are former newspapermen.

(5) Federal public relations activities are in the main conducted through other people, notably the mass media, but also other Federal employees and public and voluntary agencies.

(6) The techniques which are in use are lacking in precision, and poorly adapted to the less literate sections of the population. Little is done to measure results.

For all the apparent differences between governmental and non-governmental public relations activities, and despite the comparative isolation of federal information staffs from their fellow practitioners, the state of affairs in Washington is broadly representative of the position generally. The chief reasons are no doubt that the administrative needs which lead to the evolution of specialist public relations are broadly similar; the social climate in which the specialists operate is more or less the same; and the same kind of people in the face of problems of the same kind deal with them in much the same way. The most significant difference, as we shall see in the next chapter, is perhaps that the public relations specialists of the federal government have been subjected to strong external checks from which the public relations practitioners of non-governmental organizations have been free. But the experience at Washington provides some valuable pointers in appraising the contribution of the public relations group as a whole to society.

"The false impressions created by the rash of articles appearing under some variation of the title, What's Wrong with Public Relations?," wrote Glenn Griswold, editor of *Public Relations News*, in 1946, "are not minimized by the fact that the carping almost always comes from the pens of tyros in the business. So it's about time for competent critics to tell the world what's *right* with public relations." [1] He was obviously referring to the much discussed article by Millard Faught which *Tide* magazine had published under this title earlier in the year. [2] No doubt unintentionally, he was somewhat unkind

[1] Glenn Griswold, *Printer's Ink*, September 13, 1946.
[2] Faught, *op. cit.*

to the leading advocates of public relations who had devoted much ink to telling the world that they knew the answer to some of its gravest problems.

The chief interest of Griswold's remarks is not, however, that he drew attention to any lack of energetic advocacy for themselves and their craft on the part of public relations leaders; it is hard to take seriously the chidings which they occasionally exchange for alleged excesses of modesty. Nor is it that one of their chief spokesmen chose to rebuke some of the tyros in the business. It is that, like the interest excited by Faught's and similar articles, it illustrates the consciousness that all is not well with the public relations of public relations. That this is fully realized was made clear to me in most of the interviews I had with important practitioners, and the subject came up at two conferences which I attended. The annual convention of the American Public Relations Association, held in May 1948, adopted a proposal that there should be a campaign to promote public relations in general and the association in particular. At the national conference of Business Public Relations Executives in the same year, Holcombe Parkes told his audience that as a group, however modest they might be, they must stop hiding "their light under a bushel basket," and must "learn how better to use the tools of public relations—all of the arts of persuasion and presentation—to sell public relations itself." [3]

The fact is that public relations practitioners have never enjoyed good public relations. "The name," said a British writer, Francis Williams, public relations adviser to the Prime Minister from 1945 to 1947, "has, perhaps unfairly, a dubious flavour. It conveys an impression of biased advocacy, special pleading, and a slightly ingenious effort to put an ethical gloss on a sales campaign." [4] As the titles "press agentry" and "publicity" depreciated in esteem, "public relations" took their place. A bill to make press agentry an offense in 1913 was a gesture indicative of its low repute at the time. The newspapers

[3] *Business Public Relations Executives*, 44.

[4] Francis Williams, *Press, Parliament, and People* (London, Heinemann, 1946), 130.

have often been openly hostile and never really friendly. The "father of public relations" was known to some as "Poison Ivy" Lee; other unfriendly descriptions included "minnesinger to millionaires" and "little brother to the rich." Federal agencies dare not use the name because of its connotations for Congress. The March of Time film, *Public Relations—This Means You,* which was released in 1947, was originally to be called *The Publicity Racket.*[5]

Why is it that the professed experts in creating healthy public relations for others have been unable to heal themselves? Why is it that, as those who make the experiment will find out, a common reaction when public relations is mentioned to informed Americans (most people do not know what it means) is a shrug and a deprecatory remark, or, if neither of these, a smile? Why is there still so much consumer resistance even in business, where, seemingly, public relations is firmly established, and why do some managements "shy away from the term 'public relations' and put it under such labels as department of information, education and training, et cetera"? [6] How can these circumstances be reconciled with the remarkable progress which has been made in so many directions?

One answer, which public relations practitioners themselves favor, is that their indifferent reputation is due to the incompetence and dishonesty of a minority of their number—to "the lunatic fringe of the profession, the headline wheedlers, the something-for-nothing boys," to "the antics of the quacks and charlatans who cling to the fringe of our profession," to "the snide, weasel-minded, smart, conscienceless lads," who can make "a chiseling steel firm . . . seem to be the liberal lover of labor, blind widows, and infantile paralysis victims." [7]

[5] Quoted with permission from *Public Relations News* (52, Vanderbilt Avenue, New York 17, N.Y.), January 26, 1948.

[6] Griswolds, *Your Public Relations,* 80.

[7] Edward B. Lyman, assistant to the president, Fordham University, and president, American Public Relations Association, in *Anvil* (American Public Relations Association), 1 (2), 1949; John P. Syme, vice president, Johns-Manville Corporation, *Business Public Relations Executives,* 115; and review of Charles Yale Harrison, *Nobody's Fool,* in *Washington Post,* September 19, 1948.

This is one of the chief grounds advanced for professionalization. In 1947, Harlow and Black wrote: "Professionalization is
vital. Counselors and consultants will in all probability seek
[it] as protection against the destructive attacks against the
profession because of incompetent and unscrupulous men and
women who have entered the field." [8]

There is something in the argument. As an explanation of
the persistently poor reputation of the group it is, however,
neither probable nor in accordance with the facts. Other professions carry lunatic and even dishonorable fringes without
suffering much loss of esteem; and the truth is that public distrust arises less from tyros and quacks on the fringe than from
the more widely publicized activities of some of the leading
figures.

Any attempt to improve the public relations of public relations starts with a serious handicap in the dislike which, as we
have seen, most people have of being manipulated. They like
it all the less when the manipulator is unknown to them, when
they may be uncertain whether they are the object of his attentions, when they are ignorant of the interests for whom he
is acting, and when they suspect that as a hired man he may
have compromised his sincerity. Public relations practitioners
cannot escape their share of the unpopularity attracted to themselves by lobbyists, political bosses, advertisers, and other artists in manipulation. It is doubtful if it will ever be entirely
eradicated. The most that in the short term they can hope to
do is to mitigate it.

Having said this by way of general introduction, let us
try, albeit crudely and without undue recourse to psychology,
to analyze the reasons for the evident maladjustment in the
relations between the group as a whole and some at least of its
"publics."

There are, firstly, its professional associates and rivals. It is
unnecessary to probe deep to explain the strained relations with
these. The traditional suspicion of "publicity" among the
newspapers is partly due to professional *amour propre;* they
are afraid of being used as unsuspecting tools by the astute

[8] Harlow and Black, 381.

agents of groups and individuals who wish to color or to fabricate news. "Spike anything that even vaguely smells of publicity," a subeditor told a British journalist a quarter of a century ago.[9] The attitude of the press is due partly to the natural tension which exists between any group and those of its members who have turned their training and experience to more profitable uses outside. It springs partly from the old fear that free publicity is an alternative to paid space in the advertisement columns.

Similarly with the advertising men, the personnel experts, the labor relations counsel, and other specialists whose own positions are jeopardized. It is natural that they should be irritated by the pretensions of their public relations colleagues. The advertising men feel particularly sore, because they are the most closely affected. As it seems to them, their new rivals have lifted themselves up largely on the strength of the achievements of advertising, and now have the effrontery to assert their superiority.

All of this is part of the give and take between the different specialists who constitute the bureaucracy of modern management, whether in business, government, the universities, or elsewhere. There is not much for the public relations group to do about it. No doubt they would be wise to moderate their pretensions and aim only at goals which are reasonably attainable; to avoid needless offense by not treading without good cause on the susceptibilities of their colleagues; and to be careful not to bring themselves into ridicule by opening their mouths too wide. No doubt they should rely as much as they can upon solid achievements and their proved contribution to successful administration. But they would be foolish if they trusted entirely to others for proper recognition of their merits and did not press their own claims to a higher status. To press these claims is bound to lead to friction with their competitors.

Can public relations practitioners do more about their reputation with the other "publics" whose attitudes are important for their future? They must satisfy those who hire them. They

[9] Hugh Ross Williamson, "Publicity for the Church," *World Dominion and the World Today* (London), 25 (3), June 1948, 151.

must attract new clients and employers. Their work will be more effective if they are acceptable to their audiences. They need the good will of the "general" public upon whom they depend for eventual recognition of their professional status. More precisely, they need the good will of the relatively small sections of the general public which are likely to have any opinion about them at all—businessmen, legislators, officials, labor leaders, newspapermen, university administrators and teachers, publicists—those who may themselves make use of public relations or are professionally interested in its operations.

There are three main reasons why public relations has a mixed reputation with people like these: (1) Public relations practitioners are identified with unworthy causes. (2) They are thought to use dishonest and other undesirable methods. (3) Some of their claims are believed to be "eyewash."

The first belief goes back to the days of press agentry. As public relations leaders have often pointed out, their reputation has suffered from the "stunts" which have been associated with the promotion of stage and screen stars and some commercial enterprises. These have emphasized in the public mind what it is fair to say are the least significant aspects of public relations, have confirmed the impression that it is "ballyhoo," and have attracted to it some of the stigma which attaches to the more sensational forms of advertising.

It is more serious that public relations has shared in the inherent unpopularity of lobbying and "fixing" throughout the ages. The era of "whitewashing"—still not wholly past—has also left its mark, and there has been a succession of unfortunate incidents ranging from the inevitable cases of open criminality to revelations that public relations counsel had been hired to promote causes which most Americans would regard as antisocial. A Congressional committee disclosed, for example, that the German Dye Trust had hired Ivy Lee's own firm in 1934 to help to correct American reactions to events in Germany. Another important organization represented the "tyrant," President Machado of Cuba.[10] Nor did the alleged mis-

[10] George Seldes, *Lords of the Press* (New York, Julian Messner, 1938), 312.

use of public relations by the New Deal administration help to allay the mistrust.

Probably, however, nothing has been more responsible for the bad public relations of the whole group than its identification by many people with the section of the community which, as it happens, it has been most anxious to woo—big business. There are substantial reasons for cultivating the connection, and it is an important asset in many influential quarters. Yet big business has been decidedly unpopular, even among lesser businessmen; how to make it more popular was one of the chief items before the Annual Conference of the Business Public Relations Executives in 1948. "The most important problem business faces today," said *Fortune* magazine in 1949, "is the fact that business isn't out of the doghouse yet." [11] Its unpopularity has naturally reflected upon public relations practitioners, the more particularly because they have so often gone out of their way to protest their personal loyalty to the big business cause. It is immaterial for the present purpose whether the unpopularity is justified.

Among liberals and other critics of big business, public relations has come to be regarded as an instrument by which the people are fooled in the interests of a small and unscrupulous minority. In one of its earlier guises, this attitude is illustrated by an article which the *New Republic* published in 1926 under the title, "The Confessions of a Shirt Stuffer." It told how Crackum Q. Bunkus, the industrial magnate, was built up into "a combination of statesman, orator, humorist, philanthropist, and industrial saint." [12] A more sophisticated and agreeably pungent version of the same thought came in the next decade from Professor T. V. Smith, then of the University of Chicago, and was quoted with approval by the arch-iconoclast, George Seldes. Professor Smith described the public relations counsel as a "plutogogue": "Plutogogue is the voice of the wealthy when they can no longer speak for themselves, the successor

[11] *Fortune*, 39 (5), May 1949, 67.
[12] Quoted in *Readings in Public Opinion*, ed. W. Brooke Graves (New York, D. Appleton, 1928), 584 *seq*.

of the plutocrat of other days. He is not Allah, but Allah's public relations counsel. These men perform wonders in ectoplasmic surgery, lifting fallen faces, enlivening sullen eyes, and, in emergencies, grafting entirely new reputations upon financial satyrs who need only to be known in order to be rightfully despised.[13]

Essentially the same view was expressed more philosophically by Robert A. Brady in *Business as a System of Power* (1943). He regarded public relations as one of the weapons used by business in meeting the challenge to the survival of capitalism, and he drew largely for evidence upon the revelations of the La Follette Committee about the activities of the National Association of Manufacturers. It was stated more gently by Bruce Lannes Smith: "The rich whose foci of attention have thus been narrowed have seldom been able to justify their privileges successfully to the poor. That function is performed in their behalf by communication specialists from the middle income classes: by public relations counsels, attorneys, editors, publicity men, clergymen, journalists, schoolteachers —and notably by politicians." [14]

Public relations practitioners are thus not alone in facing the charge that they are hirelings of the wealthy. Nothing else could be expected than that they should be particularly associated with the dominant economic group. Perhaps they have had an undue share of the odium which—rightly or wrongly— those who dislike the dominance of big business attach to its entourage. For obvious reasons the identification has been closer than in the case, for example, of teachers or even of politicians. Yet to condemn public relations because it has been used to further supposedly unworthy causes involves a misconception. It is to confuse the tool with the purpose for which the tool is used. It is like condemning the internal combustion engine because men have employed it in war. Nor is the issue whether the particular cause is good or bad; that is a matter on which opinions may legitimately differ, and it is arguable that a pro-

[13] Seldes, 303–04.
[14] Smith, Lasswell, and Casey, 53.

fessional approach implies neutrality about the purpose of a campaign, provided that it does not offend against common ethics or the law of the land.

The fact remains that it has been disadvantageous to public relations practitioners that they should have been so prominently associated with one sectional interest. This would be a drawback in any event, whatever the particular section happened to be, in view of their aspiration to be recognized as a profession serving all sections of the community. It is the more so because of the unpopularity of organized business. The identification has been enhanced by the preoccupation of most public relations literature with business problems, the predominance of business corporations and organizations among the clients and employers of the leading men, and the almost exclusively business character of the membership of the chief professional body, the National Association of Public Relations Counsel, and now the Public Relations Society of America. There are, however, some signs that a broader approach is developing. Recent books on public relations are increasingly catholic in scope; and public relations has been making if anything more rapid progress in education, labor, and other spheres than in business itself.

All of this is important. The best corrective to the impression that public relations is a tool of big business is probably to emphasize the contribution which it is making to the furtherance of objects about which there is no controversy. In explaining what was right with public relations, Glenn Griswold went some way in this direction, so far indeed as to make the statement—which he would have found it hard to document—that "the most convincing mass demonstration of the effectiveness of public relations is in education, religion, and organized charity." Whereas formerly they had depended on a few rich people for financial support, these sources were drying up, and they had turned to public relations to finance themselves from the millions of little people. The claim was exaggerated. The approach was well advised.

The second belief—that public relations practitioners use dishonest and other undesirable methods—cannot be so easily disposed of. It raises some fundamental questions, and it is not enough to admit that malpractices exist but to attribute them to the undesirable fringe of quacks and charlatans. This may be true of obvious chicanery, financial laxity, the canvassing of other people's clients, and similar gross lapses from professional standards. It leaves unanswered the main suspicion—which is in effect that deception and distortion are inherent in public relations practice. "The people," said Herbert Brucker, "sense that much in modern publicity is synthetic. [The public] resents ghost-thinking even more than ghost-writing." [15]

The textbooks are lacking in the consideration which is given to a subject which goes to the root of the claim to professional recognition. They observe a discreet silence on the basic problem with which the existence of public relations practitioners as a group of paid propagandists presents society. There is plenty of discussion of ethics, but it is mostly superficial. That the writers are not unaware of the more fundamental question is, however, shown by their frequent protestations of the importance of scrupulous adherence to the truth. "Do not misrepresent, do not lie, do not exaggerate, do not mislead," said Shepard Henkin in his book on public relations as a career, "Tell only the truth." [16]

Every self-respecting public relations campaign is "educational" or "informational," and confined exclusively to the "facts." The Code of Practice of the National Association of Public Relations Counsel placed "distortion of facts and statements of half-truths" first among the "questionable or misleading . . . methods that misrepresent the aims of the profession or retard the steady development of public confidence in the integrity of its function," and which its members were enjoined to guard against "most sedulously." Second it placed "concealment, by means of subtle and questionable devices, of the true nature and purposes of any cause for which publicity is sought." Other objectionable practices were the offer of favors to secure publicity and attempts to introduce special plead-

[15] Herbert Brucker, *Freedom of Information* (New York, Macmillan, 1949), 146.
[16] Henkin, 71.

ing for controversial causes into non-partisan publications such as school textbooks, under the guise of fact-writing.

The reader can judge from his own experience and from the examples which have been given in this book how far public relations in practice has attained the standards recommended by the National Association. The more interesting question is, however, not whether they have been attained but whether they are attainable. Is it possible to "tell only the truth," and never "exaggerate" or "mislead"? Is it possible to eschew entirely "distortion of facts and statement of half-truths," and never to conceal the true nature and purposes of the cause for which publicity is sought? Is it possible to do so and survive in public relations practice?

It may help to clarify the issue if, bearing the Association's Code in mind, we look as dispassionately as possible at what was said by the organizers and the critics respectively of two major and much criticized postwar campaigns: those of the National Association of Manufacturers and of organized labor.

The purpose of business under the leadership of the NAM was the simple one of conveying economic "facts" to the public. It was the thought of the sponsors of the conference of Business Public Relations Executives, said Franklyn Waltman, director of public relations, Sun Oil Company, that "this job of educating the public regarding the economic facts of life had to be done by the business enterprises of America, each speaking frankly and candidly." [17] At the same conference Dr. Claude Robinson, president of the Opinion Research Corporation, spoke of the use of advertising to tell the profits story, and said that the "movement to increase the flow of economic information" was gaining headway; he gave as a recipe for its success "showmanship, simplicity, and honesty." [18]

It will be no surprise that what seemed plain facts to the NAM looked distinctly colored when seen through the spectacles of its critics. Their reaction to the way the profit story was told was crystallized in an article by Nathan Robertson in the *Progressive* (January 1948), "How Big Business Kids the

[17] *Business Public Relations Executives*, 8.
[18] *ibid.*, 27.

Public. Deception and Double-Talk Invoked by the N.A.M. to Conceal the Profits Picture from the People." The article alleged that deliberate advantage was being taken of the public's misunderstanding of statistics to conceal the fantastic level of profits. A nationwide advertising campaign was telling the people that profits—in the sense of the profit margin on sales —averaged 4%, whereas the average American believed that "a fair profit for business to make" lay between 10% and 15%. But the true measure was the return on net worth or invested capital, and in the case of Armour and Co., for example, a profit margin of 2.0% on sales meant 15.7% on net worth.

That was one reaction. Another came from Senator Harley M. Kilgore. In a press statement released on December 23, 1947, he described the NAM's advertising campaign outlining twelve steps to halt inflation as "deceitful propaganda, ostensibly to halt inflation," but "designed instead to prevent enactment of President Truman's anti-inflation program." It resembled the "campaign of misrepresentation and downright deceit" which the Association successfully organized against price control in 1946 and which its public relations chief had described as a "difficult educational job—the job of presenting the economic truth about price control so effectively that the majority of the people would reverse their opinions . . . The N.A.M. used the technique of the Big Lie."

Labor's ostensible purpose was also to tell the "facts" to the people. How these "facts" seemed to management may be illustrated from a talk to the American Management Association in 1947 which was given by Rodney Chase, director of public and industrial relations of the Chase Brass & Copper Company, Waterbury, Connecticut. He warned his colleagues against the "distorted propaganda" which had implanted in the American working man such misconceptions as that "wages should be raised to keep up purchasing power, which in turn will bring prosperity," and that "practically all companies make enormous profits." "We must talk about what *is* so, despite the misinformation, the fallacies, the false premises and promises, that have been poured forth under the labels of 'liberalism' and 'new' economics. . . . Labor, we must remember, puts things on a personal, emotional basis. . . . It knows how to talk to groups of people very much better than management does. It is not hampered by trying to keep very strictly to the facts, to tell the complete story." [19]

Bert C. Goss, vice president of Hill & Knowlton, told the Steel Founders Society in October 1947 that the Taft-Hartley law had shown what labor's "huge propaganda machines" could do. "The false accusations about the 'slave labor law' and the rest were indeed effective"; and business must inform the nation of the "true facts about production, prices and working conditions." [20]

The charge in each case is the same: deliberate distortion of so-called "facts." It is familiar enough. It has been exchanged in public relations advertising about "socialized medicine"; it is leveled by the distillers against the "drys," and by the "drys" against the distillers. It is the favorite charge of one group of propagandists against another.

That does not make it less valid. There is no doubt that in a greater or less degree distortion and deception enter into many public relations campaigns. Sometimes this is unintentional; often it is deliberate. There are "statements of half-truths," and "the true purposes" are concealed "by means of subtle and questionable devices." Lying may be said to be an occupational disease of public relations practice, and "sedulous" care is necessary to escape it. The temptations to the unscrupulous are obvious, and it is easy for men of principle to rationalize lapses from high standards where the cause seems to them good or where others have set the example. According to *Fortune*, "no profession poses more ethical problems, even for its ablest people, than the practice of public relations." [21]

The indictment is serious, and it is all the more important not to get it out of focus. It is not peculiar to public relations or to newspaper publishers, politicians, and other propagandists.

[19] Rodney Chase, in American Management Association, *Developing Public and Industrial Relations Policy* (New York, American Management Association, 1947), 16 and 20.

[20] Bert C. Goss, *Using Public Relations to Increase Production*, an address before the Steel Founders Society, October 14, 1947 (privately printed).

[21] *Fortune*, May 1949, 196.

For these the temptations are above the ordinary, but they are great wherever the stakes in money or power or influence are high. There is certainly no reason to think that as far as personal integrity is concerned public relations practitioners generally are unrepresentative of the middle sections of American society, and there are large areas of public relations activity in business and elsewhere where the temptations are no greater than in other occupations.

In some respects, too, standards have risen as a result of the emergence of public relations specialists. The very suspicion that the truth may not be told sets a premium upon scrupulous accuracy about verifiable facts, and on many matters the public receives fuller and more reliable information than would otherwise have been the case. This is true in particular of information released to the press. It does not pay to mislead a newspaperman, whose good will is a valuable asset; it is more difficult to garble a story when it is on the record in the form of a press release; particularly on technical subjects, it helps the reporter to have the *ipsissima verba* of the source. The issue of the text of a speech is at least a guarantee against careless reporting.

The insistence of promoters of public relations campaigns that they deal only in "facts" will not be taken too seriously. Yet, as far as literal accuracy is concerned, there are already substantial sanctions against distortion. Professor N. S. B. Gras even suggested that the upshot of recent developments would be that "the ethical standards of large business concerns will be on a much higher plane than those of the citizenry. . . . Under the aegis of the public relations movement . . . the big business concern is going to be put into the kind of position in which the preacher and teacher find themselves—they must make good in conduct as well as in theory." Professor Gras was anxious about the consequences: "That such strict behavior will lead to an unfortunate rigidity in business is very likely." [22]

The issue is not the avoidance of open lying. It is the much more difficult one of protecting society against the subtler forms of distortion, which arise from the way in which facts are

[22] Gras, 28 and 30.

selected, interpreted, and presented, and from the use of rhetoric, emotional appeals, and other propagandist devices to delude the audience. This problem is by no means confined to public relations, and it will not be solved by raising public relations standards alone. There is no problem, however, more important for all who are anxious to advance the professionalization of public relations. There is none which is more difficult.

No attempt will be made here to deal comprehensively with this vast and thorny subject, but it may be useful to pose some of the questions which require consideration. If this does no more, it will at least show that it is vain to look for a clear-cut solution.

It is even doubtful whether unqualified condemnation of distortion and deception is justifiable. It is still harder to decide in what circumstances rational argument may legitimately be replaced or reinforced by appeals to the emotions. It is hardest of all to say how far public relations practitioners should compromise the highest ethical principles in deference to the realities of an imperfect world.

The commonest form of distortion is the suppression of information unfavorable to the source. Few would say that this is never permissible. That some latitude must be allowed is clear; nobody is going to hire a public relations counsel to blacken his reputation, any more than he would hire a lawyer to secure his own conviction. Even in the federal government, where the checks on abuse are probably stronger than anywhere else, every delinquency will not be published as well as every achievement. There may be circumstances in which it is good policy to anticipate criticism by disclosing a mistake, but no organization can be expected to wash all its dirty linen in public. It would not be healthy that it should; and, if it did, the picture would be much more distorted than as a result of the most extravagant outpouring of favorable publicity. The latter will be discounted, and the admissions exaggerated. Nor should the public relations practitioner be asked to accept on behalf of his client a higher standard of conduct than would be asked of him as a private individual. The analogy which is often drawn with the legal profession is apt in this connection, but it is subject to the important reservation that, whereas a trained judge presides over the court which the lawyer addresses, "the court of public opinion" in which the public relations counsel is fond of saying that he pleads is not similarly equipped to sift the false from the true. There is thus a special responsibility upon those who plead in "the court of public opinion." It does not go so far as to oblige them to inculpate their clients.

There may be occasions on which departure from the literal truth and even deception are innocent and legitimate. I was told of a chain of gas stations which had tried various methods of improving the standards of cleanliness of its employees. At last they found the solution; they put up notices: "The cleanest gas stations in the United States"—and the employees responded to the challenge. What of the famous exploit which made a financial success of the painting *September Morn?* This involved the deception of the public in general and Anthony Comstock of the Anti-Vice Society in particular. A simple device was used to deceive Comstock into organizing a campaign against the supposed immorality of the picture. He was struck by the young people who clustered around the window in which it was being shown, and he attributed their interest to sexual curiosity. He did not know that they had been paid to stand there.

In what circumstances is it legitimate to play upon people's emotions? As Robert K. Merton asked, does the excellence of the object justify stimulating the anxieties and exploiting the frustrations of the audience? It may be right to use fear to persuade people to be immunized against diphtheria. Is it right to provoke hatred of Communists or capitalists? There is no question of excluding appeals to the emotions; they are basic to effective mass communication. The problem is where to draw the line.

Probably the most that can be said in answer to these and other questions like them is that neither distortion, deception, nor appeals to the emotions should be used where they might have socially harmful consequences.

It is one thing to appeal to self-respect, pride of home, neighborliness, loyalty, love of family, and other motives which contemporary American society accepts as worthy. It is another to stimulate fear, aggression, hatred, anxiety, inferiority feelings, and other emotions which are disruptive to the individual and to the community. Should this never be done? Well, hardly ever. Perhaps a public health authority would be right to promote fear if it seemed to be the only method of combating an epidemic of bubonic plague. It is arguable that in time of war it is right to provoke hatred of the enemy. It is arguable, in other words, that the end sometimes justifies the means. But that argument can be left to the moral philosophers; it is a dangerous doctrine, and its apparent acceptance by some public relations practitioners has contributed to the suspicion of the group as a whole.

These observations may seem platitudinous. So they are. They may help, however, to show how hard it is to set objective standards of ethics and good taste for public relations practice, how important it is that proper standards should be observed, and how difficult it will be to enforce them. Tenuous though it may be, the chief hope is probably that, as with factual accuracy, restraint will be found to be more advantageous than licence. There are some public relations activities in which this is already true—public schools and libraries are examples of institutions which generally speaking have more to lose than to gain from the grosser distortions of the truth and the more extreme forms of emotional appeal. The same applies over a wide range of business. Where profit and power are the goals, scruples will easily, however, be submerged in facile rationalizations. It is not unduly cynical to say that one of the reasons for the relatively high standards of federal information offices is that such methods would pay poor dividends in public administration and would speedily invite the condemnation of Congress and the press.

Lastly, there is the belief that much of public relations is "eyewash," that some of the claims on its behalf cannot be substantiated, that its practitioners are trying to lift themselves by their boot straps to a status they do not deserve.

In the article already quoted, one of their own number, Millard Faught, had some hard things to say on this subject. The approximate formula for most brands of public relations on the market was "one part fact and two parts imagination, dissolved in a solution of banana oil and spirits. Occasionally a brand shows up where the factual concentration is much higher; but the market also abounds in cut-rate brands which resemble highly diluted solutions of factual DDT in mild eyewash. There are still other brands of public relations which are more like faith healing than patent medicines."

Roger William Riis enjoyed himself in the *New Leader* (May 17, 1947): "[Public relations] has drawn to its ranks a disproportionate number of those who delight in selling illusion. . . . If [the public relations man] has bacon to sell, he 'makes use of the conditioned reflex; he does not mention bacon at all, he manages a kind of vogue for heartier breakfasts.' . . . Within its inner sanctums, public relations has reached heights of mumbo-jumbo hard to believe. . . . One firm in the business once advertised its service in public relations with a parenthesis: 'Same thing as publicity, but it costs you more.' . . . The more the public relations man talks about the client's sales and the less he talks about Freudian motivations, the better. . . . Talk with public relations men whose names are not familiar to you. Maybe they get the good publicity for their clients rather than for themselves."

Neither Faught nor Riis denied that there were sound practitioners of what seemed to them true public relations, or that this could validly be distinguished from publicity. The immediate interest of their remarks is that they reflect the widespread mistrust of "public relations" as a dubious mixture of the old-fashioned publicity with a sales paraphernalia of psychological jargon, expensive offices, pseudo-science, and high fees.

The main charge, which many public relations leaders would endorse, is that, as Faught said, "publicity is the main (and in most cases the only) service that the new expert has to offer"; businessmen were prepared to pay more for publicity "under the heading of public relations." He went on to lament that "in spite of their travails during a decade in the doghouse still too few businessmen seem to realize that public relations is something *more* than mere publicity."

Perhaps they can hardly be blamed. No less an authority than Edward L. Bernays advertised that "it is difficult for . . . a layman to differentiate among the publicity man, the press agent and the counsel on public relations." The distinction is evidently esoteric, because the advice which Mr. Bernays gave was that the layman could not do so unaided. Instead he should evaluate personal references, consult a bank or credit organization, consult with officials of major communication media, and ask for and study the biographies of the principals. "Years of apprenticeship and experience are needed to provide sound public relations advice." [23] Nor would the layman do much better if he took a course in the public relations textbooks. As was said by the reviewer of one of them: "Strictly speaking, there have as yet been no books published on *public relations*, though many have been written about publicity under the title of public relations. This is natural, for not only is the belief widespread *outside* of the profession that public relations is very little more than publicity, but it is shared generally by the average public relations counsel in the field." [24]

Broadly, three reasons—not altogether separable—are advanced for the claim that public relations is more than publicity:

(1) The public relations practitioner is or should be a practising social scientist, able to give advice to management extending beyond mere communication to the public. "Public relations work is applied social science," [25] according to Karl E. Ettinger, editor of the *Public Relations Directory and Yearbook*. "The broad underlying skill which the public relations man must exercise," concluded a panel arranged by *Tide* magazine, "is that of integrating the social sciences practically." [26]

[23] Advertisement in *New Republic, op. cit.*
[24] David M. Cox, *Public Opinion Quarterly*, 12 (2), Summer 1948, 341.
[25] Karl E. Ettinger, "Sorcerer's Apprentice," *Public Relations Journal*, 5 (9), September 1949, 14.
[26] View taken by panel on the public relations of business organized by *Tide* magazine, *Tide*, 20 (19), May 10, 1946, 21.

(2) The public relations practitioner is engaged in "human relations."

(3) He interprets, or should interpret, the public interest to his client or employer.

The claim that public relations practitioners are applied social scientists has already been discussed and in large measure dismissed. It was dismissed firstly because with few exceptions they lack the qualifications of training and experience for such a role, and secondly because in the vast majority of instances they are hired only to act as the communication specialists which their qualifications fit them to be. Like newspapermen, ministers of religion, welfare workers, and others who have to deal with the public, they will presumably, though not necessarily, be the better at their job if they have a good grounding in sociology, economics, social psychology, and similar disciplines, which provide what Boston University called in 1949 "the social science background so essential to the understanding of basic problems in public relations." [27] They "should understand what is going on in contemporary society," said the *Tide* panel, and "be able to integrate a number of skills and sciences and bodies of knowledge." [28] So should a great many other people. Even now there are exceptional men whose personality, training, and experience enable them to give advice on public relations in the broader sense of the adaptation of an institution's policies to social trends. As we have seen, however, they are the aberration, not the mass of their colleagues.

It is doubtful whether the social sciences are well enough advanced to provide the specific practical guidance which the man of affairs ordinarily needs; certainly he remains to be persuaded that they are. As Professor Doob found in the Office of War Information, social scientists at the present stage are likely to find "their research and scientific wisdom not eagerly accepted, wisely interpreted, or sensibly followed by policymakers," and those of them who want to be useful have to learn "to function in a situation teeming with problems in social science, but lacking the data of social science." Professor

[27] Boston University School of Public Relations brochure, 1949.
[28] *Tide* panel, 21.

Doob found that "this required a kind of plasticity which had no relationship whatsoever to social science," and that social science meant little to the public relations men among his OWI colleagues.[29]

In such circumstances, intuition, insight, detachment, and a capacity for synthesis are likely to be more valuable to a general adviser on management than the techniques or the findings of social science research. There is no more reason, however, why these qualities should be found in an expert in communication than in any other expert; and it seems likely that the small minority who practice public relations in the cosmic manner will develop on entirely different lines from the majority of those whose name they share. They have a broad role covering most if not all of the operations of the institutions they are advising. This requires no specialist knowledge of communication techniques, and their natural course of development would be to merge with the management counsel, the efficiency experts, and other management advisers to whom they are more closely akin. It only causes confusion to pretend that the majority of present-day practitioners are qualified or will ever be qualified for this broader function.

A claim which is growing in favor is that public relations is "human relations." It is natural that it should be made. It harnesses public relations to a star which is obviously going to rise high. "In industrial human relations," Henry Ford II said in 1946, "we have a new and relatively unexplored frontier. And beyond this frontier lie opportunities greater than perhaps any of us can imagine." [30]

"Watch Out, Industry: Human Problems Ahead," advertised Edward L. Bernays in 1946. "The social sciences can serve industry's human relationships in the same way that physical sciences serve industry's technological progress." [31] "Human Relations Is Our Job" was the theme of the annual

[29] Doob, *American Political Science Review*, August 1947, *op. cit.*, 649 and 667.

[30] Speech to Society of Automotive Engineers, January 9, 1946.

[31] Advertisement in *New Republic, op. cit.*

convention of the American Public Relations Association in 1947. With more enthusiasm than clarity, its program described the cheerful prospect ahead:

"On all sides there is evidence of what a driving influence can accomplish. The mounting Sun is setting the inevitable forces of Nature at work. For centuries, these stirrings have been followed invariably by fruition. . . . Through human relations . . . advances now undreamed can be made."

"Public Relations," according to Boston University in 1949, "represents an all-embracing conception of human relationships." Its School of Public Relations, according to Raymond W. Miller, was a step in the field of "education for human engineering" which "may well rank as one of the greatest contributions that New England has made to the progress of America." [32]

To equate public relations with "human relations" is an example of what the propaganda analysts call a "glittering generality"—and probably of other propagandist devices. It is perfectly true that public relations activities are concerned with human relations, but in a much less precise sense than education, labor relations, personnel management, social welfare work, not to mention politics and religion. "What," asked the magazine *Your Human Relations* in 1948, "is this thing called 'human relations'?" "The public relations man," it shrewdly answered, "knows that it IS Public Relations," "the successful salesman calls it 'horse sense,' " "the practical clergyman is sure it is 'religion,' " and so on through a long list.[33]

In fact, "human relations" is a catchword of the moment, and many groups are cashing in. Public relations leaders cannot be blamed for doing so, except when they suggest that human relations is their particular province. After all, it was Ivy Lee's own technique to present business corporations in human terms, and it has long been recognized that—as was said

---

[32] Boston University *Bulletin*, 38 (12), March 25, 1949: and Miller, *Humanizing the Corporate Person* (Boston University School of Public Relations, 1947), 1.

[33] *Your Human Relations*, 1 (1), January 1948.

in 1926—"publicity implies not only explaining business and justifying business, but humanizing business." [34] It is all to the good that the heads of large organizations should not be allowed to lose sight of the human element; it is important that they should apply the remarkable discoveries which have already been made in the field of human relations, and should encourage further research into the many problems which are only beginning to be solved. It is desirable to remind them of the contribution which public relations can make to good human relations, but its exponents should be careful not to overplay the card.

The third major claim is that public relations is a method by which policy is equated with the public interest. Schools like that at Boston, said Denny Griswold, will teach "leadership in the public interest." [35] Business, said Millard Faught of the contribution which public relations should be making, was never in greater need of "some really high caliber public statesmanship." [36] Thurman Arnold said in 1946 that the public relations man should be the "statesman of business," and in the same discussion a New York management counsel, Joseph M. Goldsen, said that he should interpet the public interest.[37] The same thought underlies the prevalent public conscience theory. "It is in the creation of a public conscience," according to Bernays in 1923, "that the counsel on public relations is destined, I believe, to fulfill his highest usefulness to the society in which he lives." [38] Public relations directors, urged another management counsel, Leo Nejelski, in 1946, must be "the social conscience of their companies to a greater extent than any other persons in management." [39]

Some of the difficulties of this view have already been discussed. It begs more questions than it answers.

Where the public interest lies in given circumstances is a

[34] Glenn C. Quiett and Ralph D. Casey, *Principles of Publicity* (New York, D. Appleton, 1926), 175.
[35] Denny Griswold, 5.
[36] Faught, 20.
[37] *Tide* panel, 20 and 22.
[38] Bernays, *Crystallizing Public Opinion*, 218.
[39] *Tide* panel, 21.

matter of opinion and judgment. There is no reason for supposing that the view of the public interest taken by the public relations specialist will be superior to that of the top executive; the contrary is to be strongly presumed. Even allowing that the communication process is two way, it remains to be proved that the public interest will necessarily be discovered in the course of it; it is prima facie unlikely. Only an innocent would suppose that where public and private interests seemed to clash, the public interest would as a matter of course be preferred. The theory is entirely inapplicable to government, where in the last resort only elected representatives can decide what is in the public interest; its inadequacy in this context is in itself enough to cast doubt upon its validity as a generalization about the public relations function.

We saw earlier that it is unrealistic for public relations practitioners to claim that as a group they are better qualified to judge the public interest than their employers or other executives. It is naïve to suppose that the National Association of Manufacturers would hire a public relations counsel to advise whether the public interest demanded that it should campaign for lower profits, or that the CIO would look to him for advice on its policy toward wages. He might be listened to if he said that he did not think a proposed campaign would succeed. He would quickly find the door if he questioned whether it was in the public interest.

These are some of the causes of the widespread distrust of public relations. They are not all of equal weight, and their significance should not be exaggerated. It is of secondary importance that some practitioners shroud themselves in mystery and try to palm off eyewash as a cure-all, and that "some men whose names are bywords in public relations" "are cold as a mackerel just out of the deep freeze." [40] These deficiencies are characteristic of a minority, which, however, includes some of the leaders. It is true that the group as a whole is trying to lift itself to a status to which its qualifications do not entitle

[40] Rex F. Harlow, "A Plain Lesson We Should Heed," *Public Relations Journal*, 5 (3), March 1949, 7, quoting a letter from a "nationally known public relations counselor."

more than a small proportion of its number. But this is no ground for serious criticism. It is evidence of vitality and am-bition, and the higher the sights the greater the incentive to improved performance; there is no lack of correctives to exag-gerated pretensions. Public relations practitioners are not unique in their fondness for mumbo jumbo and their lack of a clear conception of where they are going; nor even in facing charges of deception and distortion. Full allowance must be made for the rhetorical excesses and other normal accompani-ments of youthful enthusiasm.

It is also important that none of these factors should be un-derestimated. Separately it is easy to belittle them, but taken together they afford a solid foundation for the bad public rela-tions of a group who above all others should value good public relations. To achieve it is a challenge to their self-respect.

That is one answer to those who may argue that it is of little account that public relations is of poor repute, provided that those who hire its practitioners are satisfied; it is obviously on the upgrade, and there is no sign that its progress is being se-riously retarded. There are other reasons for thinking that this argument is unsound. The general reputation of the group is bound to affect prospective employers; this is a proposition which public relations men should be the last to question. In public administration, in education, often even in business, public relations directors are conscious of the psychological barriers which impede their acceptance as equals by colleagues whose professional standing is more assured, and sometimes handicap them in the impact which they make upon their "pub-lics." A good reputation will not only speed the advance toward professional recognition and soothe anxious consciences, but will make it easier to do effective work.

These things are important, but it is none the less true that in the long run the future of public relations depends on giving satisfaction to the "public" which pays the bill—to the business executives, the officials, the legislators, the university presi-dents, the labor leaders, all with whom it rests to decide when and whom to hire and fire. It is also true that in the last resort these hardheaded men and women will not be swayed by sentiment; they operate at a more primitive and realistic level. What will interest them is not whether public relations practitioners are nice people who are liked by all, but whether there is a payoff in dollars and cents which looks persuasive in the cold light of the annual budget.

On the whole, public relations exponents have been shy of this awkward subject, and they have been able to transmit their own faith to others. Conditions during and since the war have made it comparatively easy to do so. This happy state of affairs will not continue indefinitely, though it does not follow that a depression would be disadvantageous to the public relations group; it might well increase the need for their services. In 1948, Joseph E. Boyle of J. Walter Thompson Co. said: "The biggest problem facing public relations USA today is the problem of convincing business management and other sponsors of public relations of the value of our work. . . . Unless we can prove *results*, unless we can prove reasonably to management that good public relations pays good dividends, then public relations will never attain the stature it rightfully should in our system of business and enterprise . . . The end result of all our public relations work should be larger returns and dividends for employees, management and stockholders alike." [41]

This is the challenge. What is the reply?

Up to a point there is no need to say very much. In so far as a public relations department represents the differentiation of management functions which would otherwise be performed by non-specialists, the issue is simple. It may not involve increased expenditure; it may be more economical. A university president should not have to attend to every press release or supervise in detail the production of an alumni magazine. A corporation must report to its stockholders; it may be cheaper and more convenient that a specialist should edit the report. It is the duty of a public authority to report to the people; the only question should be how to do it most economically and effectively. It would be impossible as well as absurd for the

[41] Press release of speech to American Public Relations Association, Washington, D.C., May 25, 1948.

President of the United States to conduct all his own press relations.

The area where proof is unnecessary ends very soon, but no deficiency in the literature of public relations is more conspicuous than the lack of scientific evidence to substantiate the claims on behalf of the "science of public relations." It is in singular contrast with the proliferation of scientific and pseudo-scientific methods which are used in measuring the effectiveness of advertising.

Admittedly, the task is more difficult than for advertising. There will always be a large area of uncertainty. There are some campaigns which are closely akin to advertising where assessment of results is fairly straightforward; if the object is to promote iceman's ice or bowling, they will express themselves in sales. Some argue—and others vehemently deny—that sales, or at any rate profits, are the ultimate purpose of all the public relations activities of business, but there are many business campaigns in which the effect on sales or profits is hard to trace. There is no question of a financial yardstick for measuring the effect of the public relations of governments, and other non-profit-making organizations. In many cases all that can be asked for is better evidence that public relations practitioners are securing at the minimum cost the purposes for which large sums of money are being spent.

Even this is not easy. Before the recent developments in opinion research, proof was extremely hard to obtain except in the simplest instances. Increasing use is now being made of the new tool to provide the material for planning public relations campaigns and to a lesser extent to measure the results. That it is not being used more is not wholly the fault of public relations practitioners. Opinion research is expensive, the area to be covered is vast, and existing techniques will not answer all the questions. Yet the problem is urgent. The price of hit-and-miss methods is high. Millions of dollars are wasted every year on publicity which will never pay dividends, either because the goal is unattainable or the publicity misdirected. It is in the interests neither of the community nor of the public relations group that this state of affairs should continue.

Theoretically, there are three questions which call for an answer.

1. Is the purpose worth achieving at the estimated cost?
2. Can the program achieve its purpose?
3. Will the program achieve its purpose in the most efficient and least costly way?

Ordinarily, the public relations practitioner does not have to answer the first question. The Thomas Paine Memorial Committee had to decide for itself whether it was worth spending a thousand dollars to get Paine into the Hall of Fame. The National Association of Manufacturers must decide whether collectivism would be disastrous to its interests. Congress must decide whether public money should be spent on agricultural information. There is, however, one exception to this convenient generalization, in which the onus of proof rests on the advocate of public relations. It is for him to substantiate the basic public relations dogma that a good reputation is a valuable asset and will pay dividends in the long run, whether by facilitating sales or in other ways such as fewer industrial disputes, reducing the risk of trouble with public authorities, or bringing in charitable contributions.

The argument is plausible, but the conclusion is not self-evident; it still awaits scientific proof. The days are not yet past when a businessman can damn the public and make a fortune. How far are purchasers influenced by the reputation of a manufacturer, as distinct from the reputation of his wares? Is it true that "the public is almost as much interested in the integrity of the company and the craftsmanship that goes into its wares, as in the quality and price of the products?" [42] It is not even self-evident that a good reputation with employees contributes to increased productivity and is a guarantee against labor trouble.

Glenn Griswold chose the Studebaker Corporation as an example of effective public relations in industry. He credited its freedom from strikes to a good public relations policy over many years. It may equally well have been due to other causes. Elton Mayo and others have shown how complicated

[42] Griswolds, *Your Public Relations*, 11.

are the factors which enter into industrial morale. General
Motors, also distinguished by an outstanding public relations program, did not share the same immunity from strikes.
What is the value of a good reputation with the general public?
After a plant tour, a minister said: "The tour tends to show that
corporations are not the soulless monsters we are sometimes
led to believe." [43] This was cited as evidence of the usefulness
of plant tours as a public relations method. What is the value
in dollars and cents to a particular corporation of a "tendency"
to think better of business corporations in general? What is a
"good reputation"? How much does it really matter whether
5% or 50% of the public think well of General Motors, or
have any opinion about it at all?

These and similar questions await conclusive answers. There
are obviously some circumstances in which a good reputation is
of practical value, but very often the argument rests upon the
reasonable but unproved assumption that of itself public good
will produces material returns as well as dividends in incon-
vertible currencies such as the affection of employees and the
respect of the community.

The second point is whether a public relations program can
achieve its purpose. The conventional textbook answer is that
it will not do so unless it "deserves" public support. That is
not, however, sufficiently precise to be of much use as a guide;
nor is it necessarily true.

It is easy to find examples in which the results of campaigns
with specific practical objects have been spectacular. Some, such
as the campaign to promote bowling, have already been mentioned. Public relations advertising may be given the immediate credit for solving the crisis which faced the Maritime
Commission in December 1944. There was a grave shortage
of merchant seamen and a strong risk that the convoys would
be held up. The Commission appealed to the War Advertising
Council, and an intensive advertising campaign was begun. "In
the Great Lakes area alone, 450 seasoned sailors packed their
bags and headed for Coast ports. For the first time . . . all

[43] *Tide,* 22 (27), July 2. 1948, 17.

convoys in December and early January sailed on time." [44]
There is plenty of evidence of the effectiveness of isolated instances of publicity. Kate Smith's marathon bond drive is an
example. William C. Ackerman quoted another, not the less
illuminating because the occasion was so trivial. A twenty
second radio announcement in 1943 asked listeners to send a
penny to a Staten Island lady to help her to buy War Bonds
for her son in the Marines. One hundred and twelve sacks of
mail containing over 300,000 pennies reached the network. [45]

For the most part, however, the evidence is more slender,
and the more general and the more controversial the objectives, the stronger the doubts. It is admittedly difficult to isolate public relations from other factors which may have contributed to the desired result in a complex situation. Advertising would not have produced the merchant seamen if they had
not been predisposed to cooperate in winning the war. It was
partly an administrative device for telling them where they
were most needed. Glenn Griswold maintained that during the war the liquor industry averted prohibition, thanks to
an "intense and nationwide" public relations campaign: "While
local option made some progress, nothing remotely resembling
a national prohibition menace developed." [46] Perhaps he was
right, but he did not mention all the other circumstances which
made it unlikely that the experience of the first World War
would be repeated. Alfred McLung Lee would have been less
confident that liquor industry public relations was an important factor. His researches led him to the conclusion that the
effectiveness of the publicity projects of the "wets" and "drys"
"depends upon the extent to which they can and do make
plausible explanations of facts, experiences, needs, events, desires felt by their audiences." [47]

[44] Paul B. West, *op. cit.*
[45] William C. Ackerman, "The Dimensions of American Broadcasting,"
Public Opinion Quarterly, 9 (1), Spring 1945, 16.
[46] Glenn Griswold, *op. cit.*
[47] A. M. Lee, "Techniques of Social Reform: An Analysis of the New
Prohibition Drive," *American Sociological Review*, 9 (1), February 1944,
76.

The Forest Service estimated in 1948 that but for the forest fire prevention program, the number of man-caused fires would have increased from an average of 185,000 a year before the program was launched to about 243,000 in 1947. It based this on the increased use of the forests.[48] No doubt it was the best guess that could be made, but it was hardly scientific.

These examples will illustrate the substitutes for scientific proof which are current. There are also many cases in which campaigns have failed despite heavy expenditure on publicity and the employment of high-level public relations talent. There is growing disillusionment because of the poor results which are obtained from "educational" activities; thus, as we have seen, the Bureau of Agricultural Economics found that after years of intensive work by governmental and private agencies, only 4% of the homemakers surveyed had an adequate knowledge of nutrition, and more than half had none.[49]

The doubts are even stronger where the purpose is controversial. Presidents Roosevelt and Truman were re-elected though their opponents commanded considerably greater publicity resources. Heavy expenditure by the National Association of Manufacturers on "education" in answer to New Deal "misrepresentations" had little apparent effect until other circumstances swung opinion away from the Administration. Millions of dollars have been spent on the best public relations advice and extensive publicity in efforts to eradicate race prejudice. These efforts may have done some good, but they have been largely ineffectual, because publicity was expected to accomplish the impossible. There is evidence that it sometimes produces the opposite result of strengthening prejudice. In psychological language, the prejudice may be so well structured that to change it is almost equivalent to "splitting the superego." [50]

[48] *Editor and Publisher*, 81 (24), June 5, 1948, 21.
[49] supra, p. 137.
[50] Samuel H. Flowerman, "Mass Propaganda in the War Against Bigotry," *Journal of Abnormal and Social Psychology*, 42 (4), October 1947, 432. Flowerman dealt with the same theme in "The Use of Propaganda to Reduce Prejudice: A Refutation," *International Journal of Attitude and Opinion Research*, 3 (1), Spring 1949, 99–108.

Truly, as W. Howard Chase told the Business Public Relations Executives in 1948, information does not necessarily mean communication.[51] Still less does it always mean penetration. Mistakes will sometimes occur. Some campaigns will be more skillful than others. Nobody supposes that all will succeed. Obviously, where there are public relations experts on both sides of an argument, there must either be a stalemate or one must fail. The criticism is, however, that "information," "education," and other public relations devices continue to be used with little discrimination for purposes to which they are unsuited. This is not always the fault of the public relations adviser; it may be that his opinion has been disregarded. Often, however, he is chiefly to blame, and many public relations practitioners have a naïve and unscientific faith in publicity. As was pointed out by two students of the reasons why some information campaigns fail, a favorite remedy for failure is to increase the dose of publicity; but mere quantity will make little impression on the psychological barriers to the acceptance of information and ideas.

"Interested people acquire more information than the uninterested; people seek the sort of facts which are congenial to their existing attitudes; different groups interpret the same information differently. . . . [What is needed is] a proportionately greater attention to these [intangible] factors on the part of those who plan and carry out programs involving mass communication." [52]

It was well said. Blind shots into the darkness are costly to clients and employers. Much waste occurs because so little is known about the circumstances in which publicity is likely to be effective, the relative effectiveness of different methods, and the quantity of publicity which is required to produce a particular effect. The work which has been done on this subject by opinion research organizations and universities has only skimmed the surface; and though some important projects are

[51] *Business Public Relations Executives*, 69.
[52] Herbert H. Hyman and Paul B. Sheatsley, "Some Reasons Why Information Campaigns Fail," *Public Opinion Quarterly*, 11 (3), Fall 1947, 412, 422.

being undertaken, the subject is so complex that early results of great practical value must not be expected. The time may never come when, as was envisaged by Stuart C. Dodd, director of the Public Opinion Laboratory in the State of Washington, publicity can be planned in accordance with scientific laws. He suggested exploration of the hypothesis that Weber's law holds for people's attitudes:

"Weber's law states that constant increases in a person's sensation, by eye, ear, tongue, etc., require logarithmic increases in the stimulus. . . . If attitude changes require logarithmic increases of the stimuli causing them, can Weber's law predict a measurable change in public opinion from the measured effort (in units of man-hours, money, publicity space, etc.) of some public campaign?" [53]

At any rate, that is to look far into the future. But it is better to be visionary than pedestrian. Nothing is more "wrong with public relations" than the uncritical attitude of most of its practitioners—and most of those who foot the bill—toward the measurement of results and the refinement of methods of attaining them. It is true that before they can do much more they are dependent upon the outcome of further fundamental research; but, judging from public relations writings and speeches, from the discussions of research in public relations journals and conventions, and from the evidence of public relations in practice, they still have a considerable way to go before they will have caught up with the meager but not insignificant discoveries which have already been made.

[53] Stuart C. Dodd, "The Washington Public Opinion Laboratory," *Public Opinion Quarterly*, 12 (1), Spring 1948, 120.

◇◇◇

CHAPTER 9

PUBLIC RELATIONS AND AMERICAN DEMOCRACY

◇◇◇

LET us in conclusion return to "what is right with public re- lations"—to the social needs which are met by the development of public relations specialists.

It is not enough to say that the development was a natural response to the growth of the mass media. This does not explain why the response was natural, and does not allow for the other factors which contributed to the emergence of the group. It was also an aspect of the increasing differentiation which has characterized most social functions—management, public administration, industry, personal services—throughout the economy of every complex modern society. This in turn was due to increasing wealth, expanding markets, population growth, technological progress—indeed, to all the circumstances which produced the Industrial Revolution through which the world is still passing.

As is often pointed out, what is now called public relations has had counterparts throughout history. Princes and emperors had to communicate with their subjects, and could not disregard this impact upon the "publics" of the day. They needed means of keeping in touch with trends of opinion among those upon whose loyalty they depended, and they kept in touch by a variety of methods—spies, parliaments, through court gossip, sometimes by leaving their thrones and traveling incognito among the common people. So with the church, and in trade and industry. The Church of Rome had an efficient intelligence system, and was a pioneer in employing propaganda specialists. The small New England businessman of a century ago attended to his own public relations—in his everyday contacts with his customers and employees, and as he exchanged conversation on his way to and from work. He was his own director of public relations, just as he may have been his own accountant and engineer, and almost certainly was his own personnel manager.

There is nothing dramatic about this reason for the evolution of the public relations specialist. Because it is not dramatic, it tends to be overshadowed by more colorful theories. It is none the less of great importance, as an explanation both of the past and of the uneven development at present. It is still true of the majority of business people, as it is of the majority of other people who have "publics" to consider—clergymen, teachers, heads of social welfare agencies, mayors of small towns, for example—, that they conduct their own public relations. Some of them are highly successful.

Public relations is still much less differentiated than other branches of administration and management, such as law and accountancy. It is more a luxury than law and accountancy because it does not demand such expert knowledge that if need be the layman cannot ordinarily fend for himself. That is why, broadly speaking, only large organizations employ specialists for their public relations. There are many exceptions. Some institutions and some individuals are in greater need of expert help than others. There is every reason for thinking that the saturation point in the demand for public relations counsel and executives is far from having been reached. When it comes will depend on economic and other unpredictable circumstances, but there will never be a time when all who—in professional parlance—"need" good public relations will be able to hire expert advice or, for that matter, will want to do so.

The first reason for the emergence of public relations specialists is thus the general tendency to greater specialization; experts have been employed to carry out a hitherto undifferentiated management function. "Public relations," according to Boston University, is "an advanced function of administration arising out of increased social interdependence on the one hand and increased specialization of knowledge on the other." [1] For the same reason, specialization has appeared within the public relations group, and this process will continue. It is also one of the reasons for thinking that there is no future for the public relations director as a general adviser on all the relations between an institution and all its "publics."

It is necessary to look elsewhere for answers to the more interesting question of why, as has also happened, it has become increasingly important to communicate with the public, and—conversely—to take public attitudes into account. The answers are not neatly separable, but fall into three broad categories.

The first answer may seem paradoxical. It became more difficult to communicate with the public. In the language of the conference of Business Public Relations Executives, this may be called "bigness." It was comparatively easy for George Washington to communicate with the small minority who were politically articulate in 1776. It was easy for a small nineteenth century businessman to look after his own public relations. But government, business, labor, the universities, have grown bigger and still bigger. So has the public. The population has increased. Popular education has increased the proportion which is literate, and hence the audiences for the mass media. The public grew numerically, and it became growingly differentiated. Hence the conception of a number of "publics"—stockholders, employees, customers, dealers, plant communities, and the rest—which underlies modern public relations practice.

As the organizations increased in size and the "publics" along with them, they also became more remote, more impersonal, more incomprehensible. There emerged large bureaucracies; "soulless" corporations responsible to anonymous owners and directed by small groups of professional executives; labor unions whose leaders were unknown personally to the rank and file; giant universities in which most of the faculty hardly recognized the president. The media of communication also grew "bigger" and more intricately organized. Press

[1] Boston University *Bulletin*, 37 (16), June 23, 1948, 36.

agentry was bound to be an anachronism as the radio and the motion picture developed alongside the newspaper.

Secondly, it became more necessary to communicate with the public. This was due to several causes. It proved to be more efficient to be open than to be secretive. Employees worked better; dealers were more loyal; stockholders were more contented. It is good railroad management that passengers should be educated to orderly, decent, and considerate behavior on trains. It helps in the conduct of a university to have the understanding of students, parents, alumni, and local communities. In many government programs economy and efficiency will be secured only if those affected understand exactly what the program is for, how they will benefit, and how they can best cooperate. The spectacular progress of advertising and the experience of the first World War brought home the supposed effectiveness of propaganda. Simultaneously, advances in mass education and other changes made the public more responsive to "information," and more insistent upon being informed.

With all of this came new ideas about the responsibilities which business and other private interests owed to society, and as a corollary the necessity to justify themselves to society. Business public relations, said Leila A. Sussmann, expresses "an ideology of defense." [2] The new point of view was expressed by E. K. Hall, vice president of American Telephone & Telegraph, in the early days of the long and successful public relations program of the Bell Telephone System (1909):

"So we start out in our dealings with the public under a heavy handicap; they do not know us, they misunderstand us, they mistrust us, and there is a continued tendency to believe that our intentions toward them are not fair. . . . This general attitude of the public mind is, as I believe, not only a serious danger to the property of the business but it is in my judgment the only serious danger confronting the company, because the natural tendency of such hostility, founded as it is on misunderstanding, prejudice, and distrust is, under slight incentive, to crystallize at any time into adverse legislation." [3]

[2] Sussmann, 708.
[3] Long, 20–21.

The third answer is a variation of the second. Some of the alternatives to public relations as a method of giving effect to policy became offensive to general opinion and correspondingly less serviceable. Within the factory the more arbitrary methods of enforcing discipline and securing compliance with the will of management had to be modified in the face of organized labor unions, government intervention, and a changed public opinion. The La Follette Committee stigmatized the use by business of espionage, violence, and other methods which interfered with the civil liberties of labor. Lobbyists and pressure groups are making less use of bribery and similarly crude techniques. "Now, more than ever before," said the National Association of Manufacturers in 1937, "strikes are being won or lost in the newspapers and over the radio. The swing of public opinion has always been a major factor in labor disputes, but with the settlement of strikes being thrown more and more into the laps of public officials, the question of public opinion becomes of greater importance." [4]

Add to these factors the mass media, and the circle is complete. The mere existence of the mass media did not create the specialist in public relations. He developed because of the demands of other people upon the media, and the latter became indispensable to all who had messages to communicate to large groups. It was more and more necessary to employ experts who were familiar with the media. The dependence on experts increased as the newspaper industry grew bigger and more complex, as other vast industries and new skills appeared with the progress of radio and motion pictures, as advertising became more specialized, and as other techniques, some of them extending beyond the boundaries of publicity, evolved to supplement the human voice, pen and ink, and the small town newspaper, which constituted most of the tools needed for effective public relations a century ago.

What does all this signify to society? The question cannot be answered without again referring to the communication system. The mass media are among the principal mechanisms by which complex societies are integrated and kept alive. They

[4] *La Follette Report*, 158.

are indispensable to the dissemination of the miscellaneous general knowledge which is the common currency of social and economic intercourse and without which the individual can neither understand nor participate effectively in social activities beyond his immediate horizon. It is largely through them that society adjusts to changes in ideas, economic conditions, and the distribution of political power. What they mean to democracy was summed up in 1948 by the Committee on Communication of the University of Chicago:

"Today, more people spend more time in reading, seeing, and listening to more formal communications—print, radio, film—than ever before in human history. As much as one-fourth of the waking day of the average American adult is filled by attention to the public or mass media of communication. With increasing leisure time, the extension of literacy and education, and further technological development in the next years, the extent of communication exposure is certain to grow. But the importance of communication for a democracy does not rest upon the sheer magnitude of the communication process. In all its phases, communication exerts a crucial effect upon public and private information and insight, upon the capacity for rational decision and action, upon public taste and aesthetic standards, upon moral judgment, upon group loyalty and group disintegration, upon personality development, upon initiation and adaptation to social changes. There is hardly an area of human life in which the media of communication do not represent an important influence. If we are to construct a theory of society which will be scientifically valid as well as relevant to our most crucial problems, we must allow a large place in it for propositions about the significance of communication." [5]

The public relations practitioner fits into this picture as one of the technicians who feed the flow of communication. His position is ambiguous. On the one hand he helps the organs of communication by supplying material which is valuable to them and which it would be difficult for them to collect for

[5] Memorandum dated February 1948, obtained at University of Chicago.

238

themselves. On the other, his purpose is to manipulate the communication channels in the interest of his employer. This is true even where the manipulation does not extend beyond the attractive presentation of the material in order to facilitate its publication. Hence also the ambiguity in the attitude of the newspapers and other media, as witnessed by the suspicion of press releases and other forms of "publicity," despite the saving in expense and inconvenience which they effect.

The object of manipulating the channels of communication and, where necessary, supplementing them, is either to inform the public or to persuade or otherwise influence it. Often it is both. Most attention has focused on the persuasive aspect. The informational activities—in the strict sense and not as the term is used for propagandist purposes—are also, as we have seen, of great importance. They contribute to the smooth ordering of society by helping to disseminate that minimum of information without which the individual will be unable to play his part as a citizen, an economic unit, a neighbor. They tell him how and when to pay his taxes, what he must do to avoid fires, how he can feed his family to the best advantage, how to conduct himself on the roads, what a labor union stands for, the elementary economics of business, the facilities at the local university, the books he can get from the public library.

In this respect public relations is a valuable ancillary to the educational system, and, as long as a genuine attempt is made to tell the facts with the minimum of adulteration, many "informational" and "educational" programs in which information is a means to other ends may also have an educational value. Examples are the American Heritage and World Trade programs of the Advertising Council; many of the government campaigns which have been mentioned in Part II; and much that is done by business enterprises in the way of institutional advertising, plant tours, employee magazines, stockholder reports, motion pictures, and so on. It may be none the less effective because the educational motive is subordinate. The more highly valued the result, the stronger the incentive to develop techniques of popularization in order to attract attention and to ram the information home.

Here indeed is one of the greatest opportunities for public relations practitioners as a group. Few problems are more serious for American democracy than the gulf which, despite advances in education and communication, exists between "we" —the millions of plain men and women—and "they"—the thousands in business, government, the churches, organized labor, the universities, and elsewhere, who constitute the effective ruling class. Stating the point differently, few problems are more difficult than those presented by the ignorance and apathy of the mass of the people on most public issues which are more serious than the death of a baseball hero or the heavyweight championship of the world; and by the emotional and other psychological factors which marry nearly everybody to prejudices and suspicions and blindly irrational resistances to change.

What has this to do with public relations practitioners? Firstly, as we have seen, one of the reasons for their existence is the gulf between "big" institutions and their "publics." Secondly, the measure of their success is their ability to communicate effectively with popular audiences. Like everybody else, they are in the shotgun stage, but in a more limited sphere their advertising colleagues have shown what can be done to refine a communication technique as a tool of mass information and persuasion. Thirdly, public relations is being used by those who deliberately set out to raise the level of information and interest in serious subjects. There have been campaigns to persuade people to read more, to eat sensibly, to understand their American heritage, to study how the economic system works, to learn about the United Nations, to participate in government, and many more besides.

This is a challenge as well as an opportunity. The problems which are presented by apathy and ignorance will not be solved by public relations techniques. They go much too deep to be susceptible to such simple treatment. At the same time they will not be solved until substantial further advances have been made in the arts of popularization in which public relations practitioners are specialists.

The social significance of the public relations group arises, however, less from its contribution to public information and education than from its persuasive aspect. The line between information and persuasion is shadowy, and to distinguish satisfactorily between the different kinds of persuasive activity is seemingly impossible. Many unsuccessful attempts have been made. Fortunately, there is no need in this book to penetrate the morass.

It is chiefly because public relations specialists are paid propagandists that society has to take cognizance of them. They are propagandists on any view of the term.

Broadly, there are two schools of thought about propaganda. One equates it with what we have called persuasive activities. The other—which corresponds with the popular interpretation—confines it to persuasive activities on controversial issues. On the first view, all public relations practitioners are propagandists. On the second, many are sometimes propagandists. It is mainly because they may be propagandists in the second sense that they are potentially dangerous as well as useful to society. Their nearest counterparts are advertising agents and paid lobbyists. They differ from advertising agents in that they usually operate over a wider field and that their repertoire of media and techniques is broader. They differ from lobbyists in being concerned with the public and "publics" at large instead of primarily with legislators. All three, however, belong to the same family, and they are not easily distinguishable.

Advertising men resent the encroachment of their public relations kinsmen upon provinces they regard as their own; public relations men look with disfavor upon the public relations departments which advertising agencies are increasingly setting up. The rivalry is particularly acute in organizations which place advertising under public relations or vice versa. Similarly with the lobbyists. "Legislative public relations" finds its place in the textbooks, and the public relations counsel or director is expected if occasion arises to know his way around Washington and the state capital. Some of the lobbyists use the public relations title (and because they do so sometimes claim exemption from registration as lobbyists), and it is no accident that the density of public relations firms is higher in Washington, D.C., than in New York or Chicago. For similar reasons to those which have led to the rise of public relations, modern lobbying seeks to influence opinion in the country at large as well as in the ante-chambers and corridors of the Capitol.

Much has been written about propaganda; much still remains to be discovered. It has been shown that in either sense it is coterminous with, and indispensable to, organized society. It has grown and on the whole become more skillful with the development of democracy and with the abrogation of violence as a method of settling disputes inside a national group. It is often unrecognized as propaganda either by the propagandist or the "propagandee."

Propaganda, said Harold D. Lasswell, "refers solely to the control of opinion by significant symbols, or, to speak more concretely and less accurately, by stories, rumors, reports, pictures and other forms of social communication. Propaganda is concerned with the management of opinions and attitudes by the direct manipulation of social suggestion rather than by altering other conditions in the environment or in the organism." [6]

This point is of great importance. Propaganda is an alternative to other changes "in the environment or in the organism" —to the use of policemen, bribes, lockouts, strikes, violence, as a method of settling industrial disputes; to legislation as a method of resisting inflation or securing public compliance with health measures; to changes of policy in response to changing circumstances as a method of maintaining power.

Professor Lasswell concluded:

"Propaganda is a reflex to the immensity, the rationality and wilfulness of the modern world. It is the new dynamic of society, for power is subdivided and diffused, and more can be won by illusion than by coercion. It has all the prestige of the new and provokes all the animosity of the baffled. To illuminate the mechanisms of propaganda is to reveal the secret springs of social action, and to expose to the most searching

[6] Harold D. Lasswell, *Propaganda Technique in the World War* (London, Kegan, Paul, 1927), 9.

criticism our prevailing dogmas of sovereignty, of democracy, of honesty, and of the sanctity of individual opinion." [7]

This pregnant and prophetic statement has weathered twenty years of subsequent experience and study extremely well. Substitute "public relations" for "propaganda," and public relations leaders who are groping for a rationale of their activity could do worse than take it as a text.

Public relations is thus one of the methods by which society adjusts to changing circumstances, and resolves clashes between conflicting attitudes, ideas, institutions, and personalities. How it does so may be seen in practice every day. It is exemplified by the postwar campaigns of business and labor, the battle over socialized medicine, and the perennial struggle between "drys" and "wets." The farm groups use public relations to reinforce their pressure on the federal government. One reason why the federal government has to promote savings is to counteract the publicity of interests which are anxious to stimulate expenditure. Transportation companies appeal to the public for support when applications to increase fares are pending. The consumer organizations try to protect housewives from exploitation by educating them in wise spending. Libraries publicize their services in order to secure a larger share of the municipal budget. Universities compete with social welfare agencies for charitable contributions, political parties compete for votes, states for tourist trade, hospitals with other employers for nurses, churches for congregations, business corporations for customers and workpeople. Minority groups have made use of public relations to eradicate prejudice.

In all these cases public relations is one of the tools of policy; in none of them is it used exclusively. Its use reflects the belief that the attitude of the "publics" who are being addressed is important, not on any ideal view, but because it can influence action—political decisions, elections, consumer preferences, church attendance, racial discrimination. It is, as Professor Lasswell called propaganda, a "dynamic" of society—inevitable, indispensable, socially advantageous as well as potentially dangerous.

[7] *ibid.*, 222.

It may be asked what should be the attitude of the organized community to this force for possible evil. There is earnest discussion in public relations circles about the possibility of public control. Other propagandists have been regulated. Lobbyists are subject to regulation federally and in certain states; doubts about the adequacy of the federal Act of 1946 led to the appointment of the Buchanan Committee in 1949. Advertising is to some extent controlled through the Federal Trade Commission. An attempt was made before the first World War to curb press agentry by legislation. The La Follette Committee condemned the "information" program of the National Association of Manufacturers as contrary to public policy. Various proposals have been put forward for the regulation of public opinion polls, and one of the advocates has been Edward L. Bernays. "The government must protect the public against malpractices in polling. We license doctors, lawyers, accountants and architects to protect the public. We set up standards of character and education which they must meet, and everyone favors this. By the same token, we should license polltakers." [8] Why not, by the same token, public relations practitioners? Writing in *Public Relations Journal*, Thomas W. Parry was looking forward in 1949 to the attainment of professional status within five to ten years—with examining, licensing, and a "practicable, effective means of self-enforcement of a meaningful code of ethics." [9]

The likelihood of public relations—as distinct from particular aspects—being regulated seems so remote that the anxiety on the subject is singular. It may reflect an exaggerated sense of importance on the part of the public relations group. It may be due to qualms of conscience. It may be that it is a useful stick with which to beat those who have most cause to fear regulation.

For several reasons governmental regulation of a general

[8] *Talks* (Columbia Broadcasting System), 12 (2), April 1947. See also Edward L. Bernays, "Should Pollsters be Licensed?" *International Journal of Attitude and Opinion Research*, 3 (1), Spring 1949, 6–12.

[9] Thomas W. Parry, *Public Relations Journal*, 5 (7), July 1949, 10.

character is improbable. There are no signs that the federal or state governments will be pressed to act or that they would want to do so. Most of the discussion has taken place within the public relations group itself. But the chief reason is the difficulty of seeing how regulation could be effective. It would be illogical and impracticable to differentiate between propaganda conducted under the name of public relations and propaganda in other forms. It would be wasteful to attempt to control the general run of public relations activities, including the strictly expository functions. A satisfactory line could not be drawn between those institutions which organize public relations under specialist departments and those in which it is undifferentiated. There would be little sense in regulating public relations counsel in private practice and leaving untouched the public relations executives. No case can be made out for the opposite approach—that of closing public relations practice by law to those who come up to prescribed standards—for some of the above reasons and a number of others which will be discussed later. The whole question is clouded by the lack of any precise definition of public relations work. It is possible that certain aspects of public relations practice might be regulated, but nobody need lose any sleep for fear of more general controls.

That the problem should be discussed is interesting as evidence that public relations practitioners recognize that there is an argument for public control; and the supposed danger of government intervention is used as a reason for self-regulation through the public relations associations. Effective self-regulation would be a major step toward professional status, and one of the first tasks which the Public Relations Society of America set itself was the preparation of a code of professional practice. For much the same reasons that make it hard to imagine a satisfactory scheme of public regulation, the Society will not find the task easy. We saw in the last chapter that it would tax even a moral philosopher who was not restrained by practical considerations. Something of the difficulty was illustrated by the extracts which were then given from the code of the National

Association of Public Relations Counsel. Here—for variety—are a few sentences from the code of the American Public Relations Association:

"Members shall keep faith with the individuals or activities they represent, with the means of communication with the public, and with the public; they shall not accept assignments that are antagonistic to each other or those that are anti-social and they shall shun activities that deviate from the highest ethical standards. . . . Members shall not perform, or cause to be performed, any act which would tend to reflect on or bring into disrepute any part of the practice of public relations."

And, lest it be thought that the difficulty of avoiding vague platitudes in such a context is peculiar to public relations, here are two similar examples from journalism:

"A journalist (said the Code of the American Society of Newspaper Editors) who uses his power for any selfish or otherwise unworthy purpose is faithless to a high trust."

"We condemn (said the American Newspaper Guild) the current practice of requiring the procuring or writing of stories which newspapers know are false or misleading and which work oppression or wrong to persons or to groups."

If it is not self-evident that generalities will not cure the evils against which these provisions were presumably directed, sufficient evidence should be provided by the failure of both the newspaper codes. Generalizations flow easily from the pen, but the trouble is deeper than any lack of drafting skill. It is due to the lack of precise answers to the ethical questions of everyday practice, and still more to the difficulty of framing rules that will be enforceable. A code that is vague and general may have the advantage of being a manifesto of good intentions. One that is more realistic but cannot be enforced may be worse than useless.

Nor does the difficulty end there. The associations are also in another dilemma. They have little enough control over their members. They have none over non-members. Some of the leading men have not joined—they have been criticized for irresponsibility on that account; and no practitioner is seriously

handicapped because he is without the hallmark of membership. As it is, the Public Relations Society of America thinks
that the standards of admission to the American Public Relations Association are too low. It is not easy for an association
to enforce a code of conduct which may handicap its members
in competition with colleagues who are bound by no code at all
or by one which is less exacting.

This situation will tend to correct itself if the associations become stronger and more comprehensive, and membership a
privilege which once obtained will not be lightly imperilled.
There are some who dream of the day when it may be possible
to close the profession. That would certainly simplify the problem of self-regulation, but it is hardly likely to be practicable
with a group whose main sources of recruitment will continue
to be the newspapers and advertising, and whose skills are so
generalized. It would imply that a newspaperman should be
forbidden to set up as a public relations counsel or to take a
post as public relations director of a municipality unless he
satisfied standards of experience and training prescribed by a
professional body. Carried to an absurd extreme, it would imply that the mayor of the municipality could not depute a
trusted associate to act as his public relations adviser, or a university president do the job himself.

The most, therefore, that the associations can reasonably
hope is that in the course of time membership will become so
valuable that all reputable practitioners will seek to qualify
for it, and that clients and employers will demand that they
should do so. When this stage has been reached, internal discipline will be greatly eased, and it may be possible without
undue difficulty to enforce what can be called the mechanics of
a profession—rules such as prohibitions against canvassing,
gross misconduct, and acting for two parties to the same argument.

There remains the most difficult problem of all—the protection of society against the dangers of distortion and deception from which, more than from any others, it needs to be
safeguarded. It is hard to see what can be done about these.
Each may sometimes be innocent; each is often unconscious;

each is endemic. To prove that either was deliberate would ordinarily be impossible.

The laissez-faire school of thought, as we may call it, argues that nothing need be done, because the play of free competition will ensure that both sides of every important question are fully presented, and the public will be able to judge between them. It is naturally attractive to public relations exponents. Its merit is that it involves no interference with the free flow of public discussion, even where the methods used are outrageous. It has few others. It does not justify deliberate deception. The "court of public opinion," as we have seen, is not analogous to a court of law under a trained judge who is competent to discount irrelevancies, and to sift the true from the false. It by no means follows that both sides to the argument will be presented with equal weight. The labor unions complain that public relations advertising works to their disadvantage because of the greater purchasing power of the employers, and there are many subjects on which it is nobody's business to put the other side.

Suggestions have been made for the specific control of particular phases of public relations.

Public relations advertising might be forbidden on the ground that it unduly favors those with most money. "We would also bar institutional advertising," said the Nieman Fellows, "unless it carried some useful information for the consumer. Such advertising often has the specious purpose of either tax evasion or of selfish propaganda. It clearly gives wealth and property an advantage in access to the public. During 1946 the National Association of Manufacturers spent hundreds of thousands of dollars in a national advertising campaign against the price control program. Consumer groups had no such money to spend for counter advertisements to defend price control. In labor disputes, also, managements often spend large amounts on advertising, using slick copywriters to plead their side of the case. Labor union members cannot match such expenditure for advertising nor can they be reimbursed for them in tax refunds or charge them off on income tax returns. The American Federation of Labor's big advertising campaign against the Taft-Hartley Bill in 1947 was a luxury which unions cannot afford." [10]

Other suggestions are that, as they have done with product advertising, newspapers might agree among themselves to insist upon minimum standards of accuracy and taste, and that it should be obligatory to publish full particulars of the advertiser. Such measures would prevent advertisements like a series described by A. J. Liebling, in which a "Conference of American Small Business Organizations" implied that it had a membership of over seven million and made the uncorroborated statement that one of America's top labor leaders had threatened a general strike.[11] The Nieman Fellows gave other examples. The Tool Owners Union, which the New York State Department of Labor described as "fascist," conducted an expensive national advertising campaign; its authors were not disclosed. The Sound National Policy Association—a "people's movement" against strikes and for "sound money"—ran a similar campaign; none of its officers or supporters were named.[12] The La Follette Committee criticized the National Association of Manufacturers for failing to disclose the authorship of some of its prewar advertising.

Whatever may be said about the individual merits of these proposals, their most obvious feature is that they merely tinker with the problem. However, it may be asked what can be learned from the experience of the federal government, where, on the showing of this book, prolonged attention has been given to the protection of society against the misuse of public relations.

Too much will not be expected, because the circumstances of government are unique. It is right to prohibit the use of tax-supported public relations services for purposes which would otherwise be legitimate. It is right to ask in government for higher standards of accuracy, relevance and taste than it is necessary to insist upon elsewhere. There are, however, a few

[10] The Nieman Fellows, *Your Newspaper. Blueprint for a Better Press*, ed. Leon Svirsky (New York, Macmillan, 1947), 158.

[11] A. J. Liebling, *The Wayward Pressman* (Garden City, N.Y., Doubleday, 1947), 159.

[12] Nieman Fellows, 158–9.

lessons of general application which may be learned from federal experience.

Negatively, it has been shown that the most effective sanction against abuses is to demonstrate that they do not pay. The methods of Congress have often been clumsy, but it has left no doubt in the minds either of agency heads or of their information directors that if they are caught in transgression they can expect no mercy. The newspapers have energetically seconded the efforts of Congress, often for partisan reasons, but also effectively.

On the other hand, Congressional experiments over many years have shown the inadequacy of specific prohibitions and restrictions, such as the ban on publicity agents and the elaborate control of government publications. Congress has been driven to the extreme of hampering the Executive in the proper use of an essential administrative tool, and has forced agencies to take evasive action, which has in turn increased the difficulty of control. It has succeeded in virtually eliminating "propaganda"—as defined, for example, by the Harness Subcommittee—from the information divisions, but has driven it —or thinks that it has driven it—underground where it is less easy to expose.

Positively, there seem to be two reasons why the standards of federal public relations are relatively high in such respects as the absence of distortion, and temperance in the use of the emotional approach. The first is that most of the information staffs are civil servants and reasonably, if not absolutely, secure in their status. They differ in their political views. Most of them hope to live with administrations of differing complexions. They have a strong *esprit de corps*—to which the suspicion of Congress has contributed. They have a high professional sense as public servants, if not as information specialists.

The second reason is that, taken as a whole, federal public relations activities are uncontroversial. Motives of personal or agency advantage may not be absent, but the purpose which is uppermost is public service. A change of administration would make no essential difference in most instances. It is unlikely, for example, that it would substantially affect the information programs of the Department of Agriculture or the Customs Bureau. In other words, the motive colors the product. "What," asked Naomi D. White of the National Foundation for Infantile Paralysis, "are the essential differences between a public relations program for a business or an industry, and a public relations program for a social service agency? Probably the answer is: 'There is no difference in techniques. There is only a difference in motivation.' The business or industry exists to show a profit. The social service agency exists to serve human need." [13]

The distinction is sound. So with public administration. Some may question whether federal public relations is as disinterested as this would suggest. That is not the point. The fact is that federal information offices know that any excesses may call them to account before an unfriendly Congress, a critical press, and an unsympathetic public opinion.

To what conclusions are we led? Professionalization will help by increasing the sense of public responsibility of public relations practitioners themselves. Specific controls are likely to be evaded and to drive underground the evils against which they are directed. The most valuable measures will be those which teach clients and employers as well as practitioners that lapses from high standards are unprofitable. Further Congressional investigations like those into the power companies and the employers' associations might do good. The newspapers could help by transferring some of the energy which they devote to attacks upon government "propaganda" to attacking the misuse of public relations by private interests. The universities and agencies like the now deceased Institute for Propaganda Analysis could lend a hand.

The claim is sometimes made that the mere fact of engaging in a public relations program tends to raise the sense of social responsibility of those concerned. It is natural to suspect an argument which is so obviously convenient to those who put it forward. The claim cannot, however, be lightly dismissed. The growth of specialist public relations owes much to the

[13] Press release of speech to American Public Relations Association, Washington, D.C., May 26, 1948.

need to pay more regard to the views of the public. Earnest intentions to do so have long been part of the platform stock in trade of the spokesmen of private interests. It would be as mistaken to discount such statements as necessarily hypocritical and disingenuous as to take them at their face value. As it was expressed by Gary of United States Steel in 1915, many of the spokesmen feel that, "We had become more or less careless in management, indifferent to the rights and interests of others, regardless of our responsibilities towards those for whom we had become trustees, as directors, officials or otherwise, and unmindful of the general public welfare. We did not sufficiently realize our duty toward one another, towards rivals in business and to employees whose welfare we were in duty bound to protect and promote." [14]

Often, no doubt, the authors of the statements delude themselves into equating the general welfare with their personal interests. Even repetition may, however, do some good, and public relations exponents may well be right when they argue that it is in the public interest that there should be at the elbow of management somebody whose specialty is pleasing the public. To this extent there is something in the "public conscience" theory of public relations, but not in the sense taken by most proponents of the theory. The public relations practitioner tends to be a spokesman of the public because it will be easier for him to interpret successfully a policy which the public is predisposed to accept. This is not the same as saying that management looks to him to tell it where the public interest lies.

We saw in the last chapter how the development of public relations had helped to raise the standard of factual accuracy in public discussion. Here it may be given credit for a share in increasing the level of responsibility to the public. "People," said Earl Newsom, "will give us their favorable attention to the extent that the information we want them to have is expressed or pointed up in terms of what it means to *people*—in terms of progress toward solutions of *their* problems, *their* hopes, *their* desires. And people will give us more and more of their respect and confidence if our public actions, the posi-

[14] Quoted by Gras, 24.

tions our companies take in public, leave the impression that *"This is my kind of company, going my way, taking leadership in the steady progress toward a better world for all of us."* [15]

That is an excellent and unusually well-considered statement of the modern conception of public relations from one of the younger leaders. It represents the sincerely held belief of the more thoughtful practitioners. It is realistic because it is couched in terms of the impact upon people and not of abstractions like the "public interest."

What has been said so far in this chapter has been almost entirely confined to eliminating distortion and deception at the source. There are two other points at which the problem might be tackled—at the point of reception, by improving the critical capacity of the "publics" which are the objects of attention, and at the point of channeling through the media of mass communications.

These may also be the points at which it can be tackled most effectively. This does not relieve public relations practitioners of their responsibility for putting their own house in order as far as they can, but a weakness in any approach which starts with reforms in public relations practice is that it involves an illogical and unreal distinction between public relations and other propaganda activities. Public relations practitioners are easy targets for criticism because they are open propagandists, but it is foolish and unfair to single them out for criticisms which are at least as applicable to others.

It is not proposed to deal at length here with the vast questions which are presented to American democracy by the apathy and ignorance of the masses, and by the inadequacy of the mass media as democratic instruments. It is, however, relevant to draw attention to the significance for American public relations of the research which is being undertaken on these closely connected subjects.

Disillusionment with the mass media and anxiety about

[15] Earl Newsom, *Elements of a Good Public Relations Program.* Address to a public relations conference of Standard Oil Co. (N.J.) and affiliated companies, December 3, 1946 (privately printed, n.d.), 14.

ignorance and apathy are among the reasons for the growing interest in the study of mass communications. Hence, for example, the Commission of Freedom of the Press, which made a preliminary survey of the territory largely in institutional and practical terms. Hence the recommendation of the Commission that there should be created "academic-professional centers of advanced study, research, and publication in the field of communications," [16] and the projects which are in progress or in contemplation at different universities. The opinion research organizations—commercial as well as academic—are contributing valuable raw material, the lack of which has hampered public opinion studies in the past. Several universities have set up centers for the study and teaching of communications. Many give courses in public opinion and related subjects, and schools of journalism have tended to develop into centers of training for specialists in the use of all the mass media. The School of Public Relations at Boston University could equally well be described as a School of Communications.

The problem may be illustrated by two research projects which were being undertaken in 1948. One was a study of public apathy at Yale as part of the research project on mass communications sponsored by the Committee on National Policy. It started from the paradoxical hypothesis that the high proportion of responses to public opinion polls was due to "a deep-seated apathy, which is simply one phase of the general problem of 'alienation' or 'apathy' among the great masses in modern industrial society." [17] People understand and feel strongly about so few subjects that they are ready to express opinions on all. This approach starts from the individual. The long-term "Program of Research on the Fundamental Problems of Organizing Human Behavior" of the Institute for Social Research at the University of Michigan set out to explore the "dynamics of group behavior." It proposed using "the theoretical concepts of social psychology, psychiatry, sociology, social anthropology, political science and public and business admin-

[16] Commission on Freedom of the Press, 99.
[17] Information obtained from the Project.

istration" to study "the behavior of man in his relation to others." [18]

The issues may be dramatized by some concrete examples. In his book *Mandate from the People,* Jerome S. Bruner told of a South Carolina sharecropper who, when he was interviewed, consistently used the expression "the Government, he. . . ." "The pronoun was no semantic accident." To this simple man the Government was still the Great White Father.[19]

Paul H. Appleby made a similar point in *Big Democracy* with the anecdote of a letter which was addressed to "U.S. Germint, Washington, D.C.," and began "Dear Mr. Germint." It came from a colored tenant farmer in the South and told a tale of woe. "Personifying the government was the only way he knew of asking for help from the big democracy we have become." [20] These letters were exceptional but not unusual. People often write to the Department of Agriculture as they would to an actual person, "confiding the most wanton and personal details of their lives." [21]

These plain folk are thinking in the personal terms in which through the ages most people have regarded their rulers and still regard them over large areas of the world. Those who have advanced beyond this primitive stage often find themselves baffled by the immensity and complexity of modern society, frustrated by its apparent inhumanity, adrift from old loyalties and at a loss to find new ones. The powers that make it work seem remote, abstract, mechanical, and above all inaccessible and unresponsive to the wishes of the little man. Government is "Washington," "bureaucracy," "they." Business is too "big." "Big" labor has grown up in the wake of big business and is sharing some of its bad public relations.

That is one side. Large sections of the population are unso-

[18] Information obtained from the Institute.

[19] Jerome S. Bruner, *Mandate from the People* (New York, Duell, Sloan, and Pearce, 1944), 194.

[20] Paul Appleby, *Big Democracy* (New York, Alfred A. Knopf, 1945), v.

[21] T. Swann Harding, 235.

phisticated as well as ignorant. No less disturbing is the state of affairs illustrated by the following incident; some sections combine ignorance with pseudo-sophistication. Investigators asked this question of a sample of the population:

Which of the following statements most closely coincides with your opinion of the Metallic Metals Act?

It would be a good move on the part of the U.S.	(21.4%)
It would be a good thing but should be left to individual states	(58.6%)
It is all right for foreign countries but should not be required here	(15.7%)
It is of no value at all	(4.3%)

Seventy per cent had opinions distributed as shown—and the Metallic Metals Act had been invented for the purpose of the experiment! [22] This was a population of which 63.5% could recognize "Elsie," the Borden cow, and 51% had not heard of the Marshall Plan in 1947.[23] It was also a population which, on the average, read more newspaper and magazine pages, listened to more broadcasts, and saw more motion pictures, than any in history. According to the Committee of Communication of the University of Chicago, attention to the public or mass media of communication occupied a quarter of the waking day of the average American adult.[24]

Here, as it has become a commonplace to point out, are ingredients of a crisis for democracy, and a serious challenge to contemporary social science. The solution extends beyond the area of communication research, but at the same time depends upon answers to the many unresolved questions which the various research projects are exploring—from the apathetic individual at one end to the "dynamics of group behavior" at the other, from the refinement of communication techniques to the reform of the mass media.

[22] *Tide*, 21 (12), March 14, 1947.
[23] Thomas Whiteside, "Holy Cow," *New Republic*, January 13, 1947: and *Washington Post*, October 8, 1947.
[24] supra, p. 238.

As craftsmen in the use of communication methods and as agents of groups and individuals who wish to inform and influence the ordinary man and woman, public relations practitioners will be closely affected by the progress of communication research. The most obvious impact will be upon their technical equipment. They may hope to learn how to use their tools with greater precision and to gain a better understanding of their "publics." The Commission on Freedom of the Press was opposed to the establishment of new professional or technical schools in the field of communications—as distinct from centers of research; but there is every sign that the trend in that direction will gather speed. If it is accepted—the point is highly arguable—that the universities are the proper place for training specialists in journalism, radio, and other communication media, it is logical that they should provide for public relations specialists. The Schools of Communications can feed the group with recruits who are trained in a broad social science approach as well as in actual communication techniques, and serve as the channel through which the results of research are transmitted to practitioners.

The long-term effect of communication research upon the future of public relations practitioners is likely, however, to be more fundamental. Their chief significance for society is, as we have seen, twofold. They are experts in popularizing information. They play an essential part in "group dynamics." The roles overlap. Both are important. The better the job of popularization, the more smoothly will society function, but also the greater the understanding which the plain citizen will have of his own place in relation to the "big" and seemingly inhuman groups whose interplay is important for the "dynamics of group behavior." The more that is understood about group dynamics and the working of the mass media, the clearer will be the role of the public relations group itself. And the easier will be the problem—though it will never be easy—of adapting the mass media to the needs of American democracy and of curbing the excesses of propaganda.

These developments will bring nearer the day when public relations practitioners can properly claim that they are applying the social sciences, and when they will have solved the biggest public relations problem of their own—persuading the public to accept them as a new profession. As they tell their clients, the prerequisite of good public relations is to "deserve" it. They have moved some way toward "deserving" professional status. Their biggest handicaps—which they cannot do much to remove—are the deep-seated suspicion of "fixers," and "propagandists," and "ghost-thinkers," and the lack of a clearly demarcated area of expert knowledge which is special to themselves. There are also some respects in which further progress toward professional recognition is largely in their own hands. Their techniques are still rudimentary, and, with the aid of the social sciences, can be much improved. The public relations associations are too weak, and need to broaden their membership and strengthen their discipline.

The public relations group is still young. One of its assets is that, as we have seen, it has the vitality, the enthusiasm, and the self-confidence of youth. It also has some of the faults, and it will take time to grow out of them. The confusion of thought about the scope of public relations activities reflects the half-finished differentiation of a management function which is becoming increasingly important. There is every reason to expect that it will continue to grow in importance. Only the surface has been uncovered of the many and complex problems which are presented by the management of large-scale organizations, but it seems clear that better methods of communication will be one of the ways in which they will be solved.

Like other tools, public relations can be misused. It is most likely to be misused when the stakes are highest; and the danger to society may be grave. The remedy does not, however, lie in doctoring the symptoms—though this may be desirable—, and the fact that public relations may be abused should not be allowed to obscure the essential and constructive contribution which it has to make. This contribution should not be exaggerated—as is commonly done by public relations advocates. Neither should it be belittled.

INDEX

INDEX

Mallon, Paul, 140
March of Time films, 174, 179, 202
Marine Corps, 71, 172
Maritime Commission, 228
Markel, Lester, 12
market research, 136
Marshall, Sec. George C., 81, 145
Massachusetts, 180
mass media of communication, 80-81, 97-100, 108, 163, 237-238, 253, 257
Matthews, Doris, 192
Maverick, Rep. Maury, 158
Mayer, Raymond C., 49n.
Mayo, Elton, 227
Mead, Senator James, 41
Mediation and Conciliation Service, Federal, 120
Merritt, Leroy Charles, 154
Merton, Robert K., 12, 37, 38n., 84, 215
Meyer, Eugene, 190
Michelson, Charles, 74, 152
Michigan, University of, Institute for Social Research, 136, 254
Miller, Raymond W., 221
Miller, Rep. William J., 87, 88
Mines, Bureau of, 123, 181, 183
Minneapolis Star-Tribune, 25
Missouri, 180
Mortimer, Charles G., Jr., 188n., 190, 195
motion pictures, 60, 88; responsibilities of the industry, 97-98, 178-179, 184-185; in government public relations, 105, 111, 113, 117, 176-185
Murphy, Mr. Justice, 98
Murray, Philip, 39
music in government public relations, 163
Mutual Broadcasting Company, 173

National Association of Accredited Publicity Directors, 9; *see also* Public Relations Society of America
National Association of Broadcasters, 191
National Association of Manufac-

turers, 15, 42, 184, 207, 210, 211, 223, 227, 230, 237, 244, 248, 249
National Association of Public Relations Counsel, 9, 15, 208, 209, 246; *see also*, Public Relations Society of America
National Broadcasting Company, 170, 172, 173
National Consumer Finance Association, 29
National Dunking Association, 27
National Emergency Council, 118
National Ice Public Relations, 28
National Opinion Research Center, 136
National Park Service, 117, 120
National Policy, Committee on, 254
National Press Club, 114
National Publicity Council for Health and Welfare Services, 16, 18
National Recovery Administration, 74, 146
Navy Day, 124, 175
Navy Department, 74, 104, 124, 171
Nejelski, Leo, 222
Nelson, Donald, 188
Nelson, Representative, 71
Nevins, Bert, 27
New Republic, 206
New Rochelle, 40
Newsom, Earl, 21, 252-253
newspapers, *see* press
New York Central System, 53
New York City Health Department, 36-37
New York Times, 13, 141
New York University, 40-41
Niebuhr, Reinhold, 190
Nieman Fellows, 248, 249

Obermeyer, Henry, 55
O'Dwyer, Mayor, 36
Office of Public Affairs, 137-138
Office of War Information, 111, 113, 118, 134, 148, 171, 186, 189, 219-220
open house, 166; *see also* plant tours
Operation Palette, 163

263